T0266897

Financial Modelling in Python

For other titles in the Wiley Finance Series
please see www.wiley.com/finance

Financial
Modelling in
Python

"Python is extensively used in quantitative finance applications, and yet there is a surprising scarcity of material covering this area. This book helps fill that gap, by showing how to unlock the power of the Python language for financial modeling, and providing an excellent insight into the programming techniques needed if it is to be used for practical pricing applications in the industry. Key language capabilities are described in parallel with the development of a comprehensive framework for the pricing of derivatives in a powerful and generic way. The authors also share their mathematical expertise, giving us a tour of an array of advanced numerical and quantitative techniques."

Peter Broadhurst, Complex Foreign-Exchange Option Analytics, Bank of America Merrill Lynch

About the authors

S. FLETCHER has a BSc. from the University of Sydney, Australia. He has had more than 10 years experience working for major investment banks in London, The Netherlands and Japan. In 2009 he founded QuantSoft (http://www.quantsoft.co.jp) providing technical consulting services to meet the financial engineering programming needs of its clients.

C. GARDNER has a PhD in Applied Mathematics from King's College, London. He began his career working for UKAEA Fusion at Culham Laboratory before moving to the City of London. He has 10 years experience working as a quantitative analyst. He is currently working on the pricing of Life derivatives for the Asset Management Pricing Desk at Swiss Re.

Financial Modelling in Python

S. Fletcher & C. Gardner

A John Wiley and Sons, Ltd., Publication

This edition first published 2009
© 2009 John Wiley & Sons Ltd

Registered office
John Wiley & Sons Ltd, The Atrium, Southern Gate, Chichester, West Sussex, PO19 8SQ, United Kingdom

For details of our global editorial offices, for customer services and for information about how to apply for permission to reuse the copyright material in this book please see our website at www.wiley.com.

The right of the author to be identified as the author of this work has been asserted in accordance with the Copyright, Designs and Patents Act 1988.

All rights reserved. No part of this publication may be reproduced, stored in a retrieval system, or transmitted, in any form or by any means, electronic, mechanical, photocopying, recording or otherwise, except as permitted by the UK Copyright, Designs and Patents Act 1988, without the prior permission of the publisher.

Wiley also publishes its books in a variety of electronic formats. Some content that appears in print may not be available in electronic books.

Designations used by companies to distinguish their products are often claimed as trademarks. All brand names and product names used in this book are trade names, service marks, trademarks or registered trademarks of their respective owners. The publisher is not associated with any product or vendor mentioned in this book. This publication is designed to provide accurate and authoritative information in regard to the subject matter covered. It is sold on the understanding that the publisher is not engaged in rendering professional services. If professional advice or other expert assistance is required, the services of a competent professional should be sought.

Library of Congress Cataloging-in-Publication Data
Fletcher, Shayne.
   Financial modeling in Python / Shayne Fletcher and Christopher Gardner.
     p. cm. — (Wiley finance series)
   Includes bibliographical references and index.
   ISBN 978-0-470-98784-1 (cloth : alk. paper)   1. Finance—Mathematical models—Computer programs.
2. Python (Computer program language)   I. Gardner, Christopher.   II. Title.
   HG106.F59 2009
   332.0285′5133—dc22

                                           2009019336

ISBN 978-0-470-98784-1

A catalogue record for this book is available from the British Library.

Typeset in 10/12pt Times by Aptara Inc., New Delhi, India

Contents

Note to reader – CD content can be downloaded from http://booksupport.wiley.com

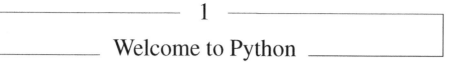

1
Welcome to Python

In this introductory chapter, we welcome the reader to Python and make some arguments that we hope will serve to motivate Python programming in finance.

1.1 WHY PYTHON?

We contend that the Python programming language is particularly suited to quantitative analysts/programmers working in the field of financial engineering. This assertion centres on two axes: the first, Python's expressiveness and high-level nature; the second, Python's extensibility and interoperability with other programming languages. Other (arguably not so,) minor arguments to be made for Python programming in general, are the benefits to be had from the use of Python's wealth of standard libraries ('Python comes with batteries included') and Python's support for functional programming idioms.

We certainly do not wish to assert that Python is 'better' in any way than other programming languages (we rejoice in the diversity of programming languages!), but instead wish to emphasise how Python can interoperate with and complement other languages to be found in financial institutions.

1.1.1 Python is a General-Purpose High-Level Programming Language

Python's high-level nature and its rich collection of built-in data types serve to allow the analyst/programmer to focus more on the problems they are solving and less on low-level mechanical constructs relating to such things as memory management in contrast to other programming languages in common use in this domain. Taken together with the simplicity and renowned expressiveness of the Python programming language syntax, this goes some way to explaining the often reported large productivity pickups that result from choosing Python over other languages. As another consequence of these features, programs in Python can be expected to be much shorter and more concise than their representations in other programming languages.

For quantitative analysts, and indeed computational scientists in general, very useful Python packages exist to make the task of numerical analysis programs much easier (SciPy).[1] In addition, quantitative analysts 'in the field' well know that writing programs for finance will often typically involve much more than numerical code alone, as many of these programs are concerned with acquiring and organising data on which the numerical aspects of the program are applied. We have often found that these tasks can be achieved in less lines of code and with significantly less effort in Python than other programming languages.

---

[1] SciPy is open-source (Python) software for mathematics, science and engineering. See http://www.scipy.org for details for example.

1.1.2   Python Integrates Well with Data Analysis, Visualisation and GUI Toolkits

Another compelling argument for the use of Python by quantitative analysts is the ease with which Python integrates with visualisation software such as GNUPlot[2] making it possible for the analyst to construct personalised 'Matlab-like'[3] enivronments. Furthermore, quantitative analysts generally have neither the interest or time to invest in producing graphical user interfaces (GUIs). They can be nonetheless important. Python provides Tk-based[4] GUI tools making it straightforward to wrap programs into GUIs. Readers interested in learning more about how Python can be integrated with GUI building, data analysis and visualisation software are particularly recommended to consult Hans Peter Langtangen's *Python Scripting for Computational Science* [14].

1.1.3   Python 'Plays Well with Others'

A variety of techniques exist to extend Python from the C and C++ programming languages. Conversely, a Python interpreter is easily embedded in C and C++ programs. In the world of financial engineering, C/C++ prevails and large bodies of this code exist in most financial institutions. The ability for new programs to be written in Python that can interoperate with these code investments is a huge victory for the analyst and the institutions considering its use.

1.2   COMMON MISCONCEPTIONS ABOUT PYTHON

There are a number of ill-informed arguments oft encountered that, when made, impede the propogation or acceptance of Python programming in finance. The most common include 'it is not fast enough', 'it does not engender a clear structure to your code' and (the most incorrect proposition) 'it has no type checking'. In fact, for most applications Python is 'fast enough' and those parts of the application that are computationally intensive can be implemented in fast 'traditional' programming languages like C or C++, bringing the best of both worlds. As for the argument that Python does not engender a clear structure to code, this is hard to understand. Python supports encapsulation at the function, class and namespace levels as well as any of the modern object-oriented or multiparadigm programming languages. Now, what about Python having no type checking? This is simply wrong. Python is dynamically typed, that is to say, type checking is performed at run-time but type checking does happen! Furthermore, the absence of explicit type declarations in the code is one of the keys to why a Python program can be so much more succinct and faster to produce than languages with static type checking. Staying with the topic of Python's type system, it is interesting to note that Python's dynamic type system implicitly supports generic programming. Consider an example taken from the ppf.math[5] module

```
def solve_tridiagonal_system(N, a, b, c, r):
    ...
    return result
```

---

[2] GNUPlot is a cross platform function plotting utility. See http://www.gnuplot.info for details.

[3] Matlab is a numerical computing environment and programming language popular in both industry and academia. See http://www.mathworks.com/ for details.

[4] Tk is an open-source, cross-platform graphical user interface toolkit. See http://www.tcl.tk for details.

[5] Look ahead to the section 'Roadmap for this book' for an explanation of PPF.

Here N is the dimension of an $N \times N$ linear system, a, b, c are the subdiagonal, diagonal, and superdiagonal of the system respectively, and r the right hand side. The point to be made is that the function will work with any types that are consistent with being *Indexable* (i.e. satisfy an *Indexable* concept in the C++0x[6] sense of the word). This admits the use of the function with Python lists, NumPy[7] arrays or some other user-defined array type ... generic programming!

1.3   ROADMAP FOR THIS BOOK

Chapter-by-chapter this book gradually presents a practical body of working code referred to as PPF or the ppf package, that implements a minimal but extensible Python-based financial engineering system.

Chapter 2 looks at the overall topology of the ppf package, its dependencies and how to build, install and test it (newcomers to Python may be served by looking ahead to Appendix A where a quick tutorial on Python basics is offered).

Chapter 3 considers the topic of implementing Python extension modules in C++ with an emphasis on fostering interoperability with existing C++ financial engineering systems and, in particular, how certain functionality present in ppf in fact is underlied by C++ in this fashion.

Chapter 4 lays the groundwork for later chapters (concerned with pricing using techniques from numerical analysis) in that it presents those mathematical algorithms and tools that arise over and over again in computational quantitative analysis, including:

(1) (pseudo) random number generation;
(2) estimation of the standard normal cumulative distribution function;
(3) a variety of interpolation schemes;
(4) root-finding algorithms;
(5) various operations for linear algebra;
(6) generalised linear least-squares data fitting;
(7) stable calculation techniques for computing quadratic and cubic roots; and
(8) calculation of the expectation of a function of a random variable.

Chapter 5 looks at how the ppf represents common market information such as discount-factor functions and volatility surfaces.

Chapter 6 is entirely concerned with looking at the data structures used in the ppf for representing financial structures: 'flows', 'legs', 'exercise opportunities', 'trades' and the like.

Chapter 7 details the concepts and classes that govern the interactions between the trade representations and pricing models in the ppf package.

Chapter 8 offers an implementation of a fully functional Hull–White model in Python, where the characteristic features of the model are assembled from (in as much as is possible) functionally orthogonal components.

Chapter 9 present two general numerical pricing frameworks invariant over pricing models: one lattice based, the other Monte-Carlo based.

---

[6] The next version of the C++ standard, expected to be completed in 2009.

[7] The fundamental package for scientific computing with Python. SciPy (as indeed PPF) depends on NumPy. See http://numpy.scipy.org for details.

Chapter 10 applies the pricing frameworks and the Hull–White model developed in the preceding chapters to pricing financial structures, specifically, Bermudan swaptions and target redemption notes.

Chapter 11, while keeping things tractable, introduces the idea of and practical techniques for C++/Python 'Hybrid Systems' against the backdrop of existing derivative security pricing and risk management systems in C++.

Chapter 12 gives concrete examples of implementing COM servers in Python and utilising the functionality so exposed in the context of Microsoft Excel.

In the appendices section, Appendix A offers newcomers to Python a brief tutorial. Appendix B provides a primer for the use of the C++ Boost.Python library for fostering interoperability between C++ and Python. Appendix C covers the mathematics of the Hull–White model and Appendix D the mathematics of a simple regression scheme for determining the early exercise premium of a callable structure when pricing using Monte-Carlo techniques.

2

The PPF Package

The source code accompanying this book implements a minimal library, ppf, for exploring financial modelling in Python. The sections ahead outline the structure and ideas of the package.

The following is a first example of a financial program expressed in Python – the 'Hello World' of Quantitative Analysis programs, that is, the Black–Scholes formula for a European option on a single asset:

```python
from math import log, sqrt, exp
from ppf.math import N

def black_scholes(S, K, r, sig, T, CP, *arguments, **keywords):
    """The classic Black and Scholes formula.

    >>> print black_scholes(S=42., K=40., r=0.1, sig= 0.2, T=0.5,
    CP=CALL) 4.75942193531

    >>> print black_scholes(S=42., K=40., r=0.1, sig= 0.2, T=0.5,
    CP=PUT) 0.808598915338

    """
    d1 = (log(S/K) + (r + 0.5*(sig*sig))*T)/(sig*sqrt(T))
    d2 = d1 - sig*sqrt(T)

    return CP*S*N(CP*d1) - CP*K*exp(-r*T)*N(CP*d2)

CALL, PUT = (1, -1)

def _test():
    import doctest
    doctest.testmod()

if __name__ == '__main__': _test()
```

2.1 PPF TOPOLOGY

The ppf library is a Python package containing a family of sub-packages. The black_scholes function listed above is housed in the ppf.core subpackage. The topology of ppf is as follows:

```
ppf/
   com/
   core/
   date_time/
```

```
market/
math/
model/
   hull_white/
      lattice/
      monte_carlo/
pricer/
   payoffs/
test/
utility/
```

Here is a brief summary of the nature and main roles of each of the ppf sub-packages:

com   COM servers wrapping ppf market, trade and pricing functionality (see Chapter 12).

core   Types and functions relating to the representation of financial quantities such as flows and LIBOR rates.

date_time   Date and time manipulation and computations.

market   Types and functions for the representation of common curves and surfaces that arise in financial programming such as discount factor curves and volatility surfaces.

math   General mathematical algorithms.

model   Code specific to implementing numerical pricing models.

pricer   Types and functions for the purpose of valuing financial structures.

text   The ppf unit test suite.

utility   Utilities of a less numerical, general nature such as algorithms for searching and sorting.

2.2   UNIT TESTING

Code in the ppf library employs two approaches to testing: interactive Python session testing using the doctest module and formalised unit testing using the PyUnit module. Both of these testing frameworks are part of the Python standard libraries.

2.2.1   doctest

The way that the doctest module works is to search a module for pieces of text that look like interactive Python sessions, and then to execute those sessions to verify that they work as expected. In this way ppf modules come with a form of tutorial-like executable documentation:

```
C:\Python25\lib\site-packages\ppf\core>python black_scholes.py -v
python black_scholes.py -v
Trying:
    print black_scholes(S=42., K=40., r=0.1, sig= 0.2, T=0.5, CP=CALL)
Expecting:
    4.75942193531
ok
```

```
Trying:
    print black_scholes(S=42., K=40., r=0.1, sig= 0.2, T=0.5, CP=PUT)
Expecting:
    0.808598915338
ok
2 items had no tests:
    __main__
    __main__._test
1 items passed all tests:
    2 tests in __main__.black_scholes
2 tests in 3 items.
2 passed and 0 failed.
Test passed.
```

2.2.2 PyUnit

A full suite of unit tests for all modules in the `ppf` package is provided in the `ppf.test` sub-package. The tests can be run module-by-module or, to execute all tests in one go, a driver 'test_all.py' is provided:

```
C:\Python25\Lib\site-packages\ppf\test>python test_all.py --verbose
python test_all.py --verbose
test_call (test_core.black_scholes_tests) ... ok
test_put (test_core.black_scholes_tests) ... ok
test (test_core.libor_rate_tests) ... ok
    .
    .
    .
test_upper_bound (test_utility.bound_tests) ... ok
test_equal_range (test_utility.bound_tests) ... ok
test_bound (test_utility.bound_tests) ... ok
test_bound_ci (test_utility.bound_tests) ... ok

------------------------------------------------------------------
Ran 51 tests in 25.375s

OK
```

2.3   BUILDING AND INSTALLING PPF

In this section we look at what it takes to build and install the `ppf` package.

2.3.1   Prerequisites and Dependencies

`ppf` is composed of a mixture of pure Python modules underlied by some supporting extension modules implemented in standard C++. Accordingly, to build and install `ppf` requires a modern C++ compiler. The C++ extension modules have some library dependencies of their own, notably the Boost C++ libraries and the Blitz++ C++ library. Instructions for downloading and installing the Boost C++ libraries can be found at http://www.boost.org and instructions for Blitz++ can be found at http://www.oonumerics.org. Naturally, an installation of Python is also required. On Windows, the authors favour the freely available ActiveState Python distribution, see http://www.activestate.com for download and installation details. Also required on the Python side for ppf is an installation of the NumPy package, see http://www.scipy.org for download and installation details.

2.3.2   Building the C++ Extension Modules

The ppf C++ extension modules are most conveniently built using the Boost.Build system[1] a copy of which is included with the ppf sources. Also provided with the ppf sources for the convenience of Windows users is a pre-built executable 'bjam.exe'. Although these notes will become a little Windows-centric at this point, the basic principles will hold for *NIX users also. On Windows, the ppf package has been successfully built and tested with the Microsoft Visual Studio C++ compiler versions 7.1, 8.0 (express edition), 9.0 (express edition), mingw/gcc-3.4.5,[2] mingw/gcc-4.3.0 with Python versions 2.4 and 2.5, Boost versions 1.33.1, 1.34.0, 1.35, 1.36, 1.37 and Blitz++ version 0.9. The ppf package has also been built and tested on the popular Linux-based operating system, Ubuntu-8.04.1 with Boost version 1.36.0, Blitz++ version 0.9 and gcc-4.2.3.

In the remainder of this section, without loss of generality, we will assume a Windows operating system, Blitz++ version 0.9, the ActiveState distribution of Python version 2.5 and Boost version 1.36.

Build Instructions

- Prerequisites
  - Copy c:/path/to/ppf/ext/bjam.exe to somewhere in your %PATH%
  - Install
    o Blitz++-0.9
    o Boost-1.36
    o ActiveState Python 2.5
    o NumPy for Python 2.5 (version 1.0.4 or 1.1.0)
  - Edit as appropriate for your site
    o c:/path/to/ppf/ext/build/user-config.jam
    o c:/path/to/ppf/ext/build/site-config.jam
- Build
  - c:/path/to/ppf>cd ext&&bjam [debug|release]
    This will create:
    o c:/path/to/ppf/ppf/math/ppf_math.pyd and
    o c:/path/to/ppf/ppf/date_time/ppf_date_time.pyd

---

[1] See http://www.boost.org/doc/tools/build/index.html.
[2] Minimalist GNU for Windows – see http://www.mingw.org.

2.3.3   Installing the PPF Package

Assuming the steps of the previous section have been performed, installation of the ppf package which relies on the standard Python Distutils package is very simple.

- Install
  - c:/path/to/ppf>python setup.py install

which will copy the ppf package to the standard Python installation location (c:/python25/lib/site-packages/ppf).

2.3.4   Testing a PPF Installation

The easiest way to verify a ppf installation is to run the ppf unit test suite.

- Test
  - c:/python25/lib/site-packages/ppf/test>python test_all.py --
    verbose

3

Extending Python from C++

It is usual in financial institutions that make use of quantitative analysis programs to have a considerable investment in C++. Thus it can be important to foster interoperability between C++ and Python. This chapter studies how Python modules can be implemented in C++ by means of the Boost.Python[1] library (see also Appendix B for a primer on the Boost.Python library).

3.1 BOOST.DATE_TIME TYPES

It is common in quantitative analysis programming to require manipulation of and computations involving dates. The 'Python Library' contains excellent functionality for such activities. Pricing systems written in C++, however, will be implemented using C++ datatypes for the representation of dates and times. For pricing frameworks implemented in a hybrid of Python and C++, it would be convenient to settle on a common representation of these fundamental types. Accordingly, in this section we demonstrate the 'reflection' of functionality from the C++ Boost.Date_Time library to Python.

Our reflection of the C++ date types into Python will be housed in the Python module 'ppf_date_time.pyd', implemented in C++. We declare this intention in the entry point to our Python module in the file 'module.cpp':

```cpp
#include <boost/python/module.hpp>

namespace ppf
{
  namespace date_time
  {
    void register_date();
    void register_date_more();

  } // namespace date_time

} // namespace ppf

BOOST_PYTHON_MODULE(ppf_date_time)
{
  using namespace ppf::date_time;

  register_date();
  register_date_more();
}
```

---

[1] Boost provides free peer-reviewed portable C++ source libraries. See http://www.boost.org for details.

In 'register_date.cpp' we instantiate Boost.Python `class_` objects describing the C++ types and functions we intend to use from Python:

```
void register_date()
{
  using namespace boost::python;
  namespace bg = boost::gregorian;
  namespace bd = boost::date_time;

  // types and functions ...

  class_<bg::date>(
      "date"
     ,"A date type based on the gregorian calendar"
     , init<>("Default construct not_a_date_time"))
    .def(init<bg::date const&>())
    .def(init
         <
           bg::greg_year
         , bg::greg_month
         , bg::greg_day
         >((arg("y"), arg("m"), arg("d"))
         , "Main constructor with year, month, day "))
    .def("year", &bg::date::year)
    .def("month", &bg::date::month)
    .def("day", &bg::date::day)

    // ...

    ;

  class_<std::vector<bg::date> >(
      "date_vec"
    , "vector (C++ std::vector<date> ) of date")
    .def(vector_indexing_suite<std::vector<bg::date> >())
    ;

  // more types and functions ...
}
```

Once exposed in this fashion, the types so defined in the `ppf_date_time` module are imported into the `ppf` subpackage `ppf.date_time` by means of import statements in the module's '_init_.py':

```
from ppf_date_time import *
```

3.1.1 Examples

IMM Dates

As an example of what we have achieved, let's see how, in Python, we can compute so-called IMM (international money market) dates for a given year, i.e. the 3rd Wednesday of March, June, September, and December in the year. The `ppf.date_time` package provides the module `nth_imm_of_year` in which is defined `class nth_imm_of_year`. The workhorse of the class implementation is the Boost.Date_Time function `nth_kday_of_month`:

```
from ppf_date_time import    \
      weekdays               \
    , months_of_year         \
    , nth_kday_of_month      \
    , year_based_generator

class nth_imm_of_year(year_based_generator):
    '''Calculate the nth IMM date for a given year

    '''
    first = months_of_year.Mar
    second = months_of_year.Jun
    third = months_of_year.Sep
    fourth = months_of_year.Dec

    def __init__(self, which):
      year_based_generator.__init__(self)
      self._month = which

    def get_date(self, year):
      return nth_kday_of_month(
            nth_kday_of_month.third
          , weekdays.Wednesday
          , self._month).get_date(year)

    def to_string(self):
      pass
```

Exercising the `class nth_imm_of_year` functionality in an interactive Python session goes like this:

```
>>> from ppf.date_time import *
>>> imm = nth_imm_of_year
>>> imm_dates = []
>>> imm_dates.append(imm(imm.first).get_date(2005))
>>> imm_dates.append(imm(imm.second).get_date(2005))
>>> imm_dates.append(imm(imm.third).get_date(2005))
>>> imm_dates.append(imm(imm.fourth).get_date(2005))
>>> for t in imm_dates:
...    print t
2005-Mar-16
2005-Jun-15
2005-Sep-21
2005-Dec-21
```

With `class nth_imm_of_year` some useful questions regarding IMM dates can now be answered elegantly and easily. For example, what is the IMM date immediately preceding a given date? This is answered in the `ppf.date_time.first_imm_before` module:

```
from ppf_date_time import    \
      weekdays               \
```

```
    , months_of_year           \
    , nth_kday_of_month         \
    , year_based_generator
from nth_imm_of_year import *

def first_imm_before(start):
    '''Find the IMM date immediately preceding the given date.
    '''
    imm = nth_imm_of_year
    first_imm_of_year = imm(imm.first).get_date(start.year())
    imm_date = None
    if start <= first_imm_of_year:
      imm_date = imm(imm.fourth).get_date(start.year() - 1)
    else:
      for imm_no in reversed([imm.first, imm.second, imm.third,
                              imm.fourth]):
        imm_date = imm(imm_no).get_date(start.year())
        if imm_date < start:
          break

    return imm_date
```

In an interactive Python session:

```
>>> from ppf.date_time import *
>>> print first_imm_before(date(2007, Jun, 27))
2007-Jun-20
```

The ppf.date_time package also contains the symmetric first_imm_after function.

Holidays, Rolls and Year Fractions

Other common activities in financial modelling include determining if a date is a business day, 'rolling' a date to a business day and the computation of elapsed time between two dates according to common market conventions.

The ppf.date_time.shift_convention module shows an easy way to emulate C++ enum types:

```
class shift_convention:
    none                    \
    , following             \
    , modified_following    \
    , preceding             \
    , modified_preceding = range(5)
```

This idiom is employed again in the ppf.date_time.day_count_basis module:

```
class day_count_basis:
    basis_30360     \
    , basis_act_360 \
    , basis_act_365 \
    , basis_act_act = range(4)
```

The ppf.date_time.is_business_day module provides the means to answer the question of whether or not a given date is a business day:

```
from ppf_date_time import weekdays

def is_business_day(t, financial_centres=None):
    ''' Test whether the given date is a business day.
        In this version, only weekends are considered
        holidays.
    '''
    Saturday, Sunday = weekdays.Saturday, weekdays.Sunday
    return t.day_of_week().as_number() != Saturday \
        and t.day_of_week().as_number() != Sunday
```

The ppf.date_time.shift module provides functionality to 'shift' a date according to the common market shift conventions:

```
from ppf_date_time import *
from is_business_day import *
from shift_convention import *

def shift(t, method, holiday_centres=None):
    d = date(t)
    if not is_business_day(d):
        if method == shift_convention.following:
            while not is_business_day(d, holiday_centres):
                d = d + days(1)
        elif method == shift_convention.modified_following:
            while not is_business_day(d, holiday_centres):
                d = d + days(1)
            if d.month().as_number() != t.month().as_number():
                d = date(t)
                while not is_business_day(d, holiday_centres):
                    d = d - days(1)
        elif method == shift_convention.preceding:
            while not is_business_day(d, holiday_centres):
                d = d - days(1)
        elif method == shift_convention.modified_preceding:
            while not is_business_day(d, holiday_centres):
                d = d - days(1)
            if d.month().as_number() != t.month().as_number():
                while not is_business_day(d, holiday_centres):
                    d = d + days(1)
        else: raise RuntimeError, "Unsupported method"

    return d
```

The ppf.date_time.year_fraction module provides functionality to compute year fractions:

```
from ppf_date_time \
    import date, gregorian_calendar_base
from day_count_basis import *
```

```
is_leap_year = gregorian_calendar_base.is_leap_year

def year_fraction(start, until, basis):
  '''Compute accruals
  '''
  result = 0
  if basis == day_count_basis.basis_act_360:
    result = (until - start).days()/360.0
  elif basis == day_count_basis.basis_act_365:
    result = (until - start).days()/365.0
  elif basis == day_count_basis.basis_act_act:
    if start.year() != until.year():
      start_of_to_year = date(until.year(), 1, 1)
      end_of_start_year = date(start.year(), 12, 31)
      result = (end_of_start_year - start).days()/ \
          (365.0, 366.0)[is_leap_year(start.year())] \
        + (int(until.year()) - int(start.year()) - 1) + \
          (until - start_of_to_year).days()/ \
              (365.0, 366.0)[is_leap_year(until.year())]
    else:
      result = (until - start).days()/ \
              (365.0, 366.0)[is_leap_year(util.year())]
  elif basis == day_count_basis.basis_30360:
    d1, d2 = start.day(), until.day()
    if d1 == 31:
        d1 -= 1
    if d2 == 31:
        d2 -= 1
    result = (int(d2) - int(d1)) + \
            30.0*(int(until.month()) - int(start.month())) + \
                  360.0*(int(until.year()) - int(start.year()))
    result = result / 360.0
  else:
    raise RuntimeError, "Unsupported basis"

  return result
```

In the following interactive session, the year fraction between two dates is computed under a variety of different day count basis conventions:

```
>>> from ppf.date_time import *
>>> add_months = month_functor
>>> Nov = months_of_year.Nov
>>> begin = date(2004, Nov, 21)
>>> until = begin + add_months(6).get_offset(begin)
>>> year_fraction(begin, until, day_count_basis.basis_30360)
0.5
>>> year_fraction(begin, until, day_count_basis.basis_act_365)
0.49589041095890413
>>> year_fraction(begin, until, day_count_basis.basis_act_act)
0.49285126132195523
```

3.2   BOOST.MULTIARRAY AND SPECIAL FUNCTIONS

The use of multidimensional arrays in quantitative analysis programs is ubiquitous. Python, or rather the Python libraries provide a variety of types that serve for their representation. Like the date types of the previous section, however, we prefer to emphasise interoperability with C++ and so, to this end, might favour reflection of C++ array types into Python. The ppf package exposes the Boost.MultiArray multidimensional array types `boost::multi_array<double,N>` for $N = 1, 2, 3$ to Python. To achieve this, advantage was taken of a C++ template meta-program that facilitates reflection of the arrays, the code for which is present in the source code accompanying this book (see 'ext/boost/multi_array/multi_array.hpp').

The array types are housed in the `ppf_math` module implemented in the C++ Python extension 'ppf_math.pyd' and imported into the namespace of the `ppf.math` subpackage. Usage of the array types is natural and intuitive. Here is an example taken from the `ppf.math` unit tests:

```
class solve_upper_diagonal_system_tests(unittest.TestCase):
  def test(self):

    # Solve upper diagonal system of linear equations ax = b
    # where
    #
    # a = 3x3
    #     [  1.75    1.5     -2.5
    #        0      -0.5      0.65
    #        0       0        0.25 ]
    #
    # and b = [0.5, -1.0, 3.5].

    a = ppf.math.array2d([3,3])
    a[0, 0], a[0, 1], a[0, 2] = (1.75, 1.5, -2.5)
    a[1, 0], a[1, 1], a[1, 2] = (0.0, -0.5,  0.65)
    a[2, 0], a[2, 1], a[2, 2] = (0.0,  0.0,  0.25)
    b = ppf.math.array1d([3])
    b[0] =   0.5
    b[1] = -1.0
    b[2] =   3.5

    # Expected solution vector is x = [2.97142857  20.2   14.0].

    x = ppf.math.solve_upper_diagonal_system(a, b)
    assert len(x) == 3 and math.fabs(x[0] - 2.971428571) < 1.0e-6 \
        and math.fabs(x[1] - 20.2) < 1.0e-6 and math.fabs(x[2] -
        14.0) < 1.0e-6
```

In addition to the multi-array types, the module `ppf_math` also exposes some useful utility functions implemented in C++. In the file 'ppf/math/limits.hpp' are the following template function definitions:

```
#if !defined(LIMITS_5DDE828B_9989_44F5_9728_47AA72323D96_INCLUDED)
#   define LIMITS_5DDE828B_9989_44F5_9728_47AA72323D96_INCLUDED
```

```
#   if defined(_MSC_VER) && (_MSC_VER >= 1020)
#     pragma once
#   endif // defined(_MSC_VER) && (_MSC_VER >= 1020)

#   include <boost/config.hpp>

#   include <limits>

namespace ppf { namespace math {

template <class T>
T epsilon()
{
  return std::numeric_limits<T>::epsilon();
}

template <class T>
T min BOOST_PREVENT_MACRO_SUBSTITUTION ()
{
  return (std::numeric_limits<T>::min)();
}

template <class T>
T max BOOST_PREVENT_MACRO_SUBSTITUTION ()
{
  return (std::numeric_limits<T>::max)();
}

}} // namespace ppf::math

#endif//!defined(LIMITS_5DDE828B_9989_44F5_9728_47AA72323D96_INCLUDED)
```

In 'ext/lib/math/src/register_special_functions.cpp', instantiations of these templates are exposed to Python:

```
#include <boost/python/def.hpp>

#include <ppf/math/limits.hpp>

namespace ppf { namespace math {

void register_special_functions()
{
  using namespace boost::python;

  def("epsilon", epsilon<double>);
  def("min_flt", min BOOST_PREVENT_MACRO_SUBSTITUTION <double>);
  def("max_flt", max BOOST_PREVENT_MACRO_SUBSTITUTION <double>);
}

}} // namespace ppf::math
```

An example of the use of the `epsilon` function is again provided by a `ppf.math` unit test:

```
class bisect_tests(unittest.TestCase):
  def test1(self):
    tol = 5*ppf.math.epsilon()
    left, right, num_its = \
          ppf.math.bisect(lambda x: x*x + 2.0*x - 1.0
                          , -3, -2
                          , lambda x, y: math.fabs(x-y) < tol, 100)
```

Further examples of the use of these special functions can be found in the next chapter.

3.3 NUMPY ARRAYS

Despite the efforts of the preceding section regarding reflection of C++ Boost.MultiArray types into Python, in practice, when working in Python, the authors have found the facilities of NumPy arrays to be far more convenient (NumPy was mentioned briefly in section 1.2). Specifically, their notational conveniences and the large body of functionality provided by the NumPy library motivates their use in Python beyond the argument of C++ interoperability. Indeed, when working in C++, a library dedicated to scientific manipulation of arrays such as Blitz++[2] wins the authors' favour for such work over 'lower-level' container types like native C arrays or Boost.MultiArray types. But now to the crux of the matter. If we haven't made this point earlier then we'll make it for the first time now. One of the great strengths of Python is the ability to drop into C or C++ code 'when performance counts'. That is, the ability to factor out that characteristic operation that must be done as efficiently as possible and pull it down into a compiled component is essential. Now, in the field of numerical programming, doesn't that characteristic operation almost always involve operating on arrays of data?

So, can we have it all? Can we have the convenience of NumPy in Python combined with the convenience and efficiency of Blitz++ in C++ where the data is shared between these array types? The short answer is 'yes we can', as we will demonstrate in the next subsection.

3.3.1 Accessing Array Data in C++

This subsection is concerned with the topic of accessing a NumPy array's data in C++. To do this, we need to work with the Python C API and we'll also take advantage of Boost.Python where we can. The approach is fairly idiomatic and can be more or less wrapped up in a set of reasonably small utility functions. Let's begin with this most simple of functions from 'ppf/util/python/detail/decref.hpp':

```
#if !defined(DECREF_4A1F1D9D_CE18_4CA1_AF52_DA1C51847FB4_INCLUDED)
#   define DECREF_4A1F1D9D_CE18_4CA1_AF52_DA1C51847FB4_INCLUDED

#   if defined(_MSC_VER) && (_MSC_VER >= 1020)
#       pragma once
#   endif // defined(_MSC_VER) && (_MSC_VER >= 1020)
```

---

[2] Blitz++ is a C++ class library for scientific computing which provides performance on par with Fortran 77/90. See http://www.oonumerics.org/blitz for details.

```
#   include <boost/python/detail/wrap_python.hpp>

namespace ppf { namespace util { namespace python {

namespace detail
{
  //Py_DECREF() is a macro which makes it unsuitable
  //for use with bind constructs in scope guards.
  template <class T>
  inline void decref(T* obj)
  {
    Py_DECREF(obj);
  }
}

}}} // namespace ppf::util::python

#endif // !defined(DECREF_4A1F1D9D_CE18_4CA1_AF52_DA1C51847FB4_INCLUDED)
```

The motivation for this function will become apparent in a moment but, briefly, Python objects in the Python C – API are reference counted, and the manipulation of the reference counts (although automatic in Python) must be carried out manually in C++. As the comment in the code above indicates, the facility for decrementing the reference count of a Python object is actually a macro and so we need a wrapper for it should we wish to take advantage of 'scope guard'[3] techniques.

Here is the code from 'ppf/util/python/detail/object_as_array.hpp' that wraps up the business of getting us from a Python C API `PyObject*` to a NumPy `PyArrayObject*`:

```
#if !defined(OBJECT_AS_ARRAY_0067910E_F5F1_4BD6_9565_3BF98B4A12C1_
              INCLUDED)
#   define OBJECT_AS_ARRAY_0067910E_F5F1_4BD6_9565_3BF98B4A12C1_INCLUDED

#   if defined(_MSC_VER) && (_MSC_VER >= 1020)
#     pragma once
#   endif // defined(_MSC_VER) && (_MSC_VER >= 1020)

#include <ppf/util/python/detail/decref.hpp>

#include <boost/python/errors.hpp>
#include <boost/shared_ptr.hpp>
#include <boost/bind.hpp>

namespace ppf { namespace util { namespace python {

namespace detail
{

template <int = 0>
```

---

[3] See "Generic: Change the way you write exception-safe code – forever" by Andrei Alexandrescu and Petru Marginean, available online at http://www.ddj.com/cpp/184403758.

```
struct object_as_array_impl_
{
  static boost::shared_ptr<PyArrayObject> get(
    PyObject* input, int type, int min_dim, int max_dim)
  {
    if(PyArray_Check(input))
    {
      if(!PyArray_ISCARRAY(reinterpret_cast<PyArrayObject*>(input)))
      {
        PyErr_SetString(PyExc_TypeError, "not a C array");

        boost::python::throw_error_already_set();
      }

      return boost::shared_ptr<PyArrayObject>(
              reinterpret_cast<PyArrayObject*>(
                    boost::python::expect_non_null(
                        PyArray_ContiguousFromObject(
                              input, type, min_dim, max_dim))
              )
            , boost::bind(
                ::ppf::util::python::detail::decref<PyArrayObject>, _1)
          );
    }
    else
    {
      PyErr_SetString(PyExc_TypeError, "not an array");

      boost::python::throw_error_already_set();
    }

    return boost::shared_ptr<PyArrayObject>();
  }
};

typedef object_as_array_impl_<> object_as_array_impl;

inline boost::shared_ptr<PyArrayObject>
object_as_array(
  PyObject* input, int type, int min_dim, int max_dim)
{
  return object_as_array_impl::get(input, type, min_dim, max_dim);
}

}}}} // namespace ppf::util::python::detail

#endif // !defined(OBJECT_AS_ARRAY_0067910E_F5F1_4BD6_9565_3BF98B4A12C1_
                  INCLUDED)
```

Note that this code lives in the ppf::util::python::detail namespace and is not tied to any particular ppf C++ Python extension module.

To explain this code, let's work top-down rather than bottom-up and look to the last function of the file first.

```
inline boost::shared_ptr<PyArrayObject>
object_as_array(
   PyObject* input, int type, int min_dim, int max_dim)
{
   return object_as_array_impl::get(input, type, min_dim, max_dim);
}
```

The first thing to note is the return type, that is a boost::shared_ptr <PyArrayObject>. The reason to return one of these over a raw PyArrayObject* is to do with the use of Py_DECREF as alluded to above. The long and the short of it is that should the attempt to get an array from a PyObject* succeed, by the time the resultant array is going out of scope it must have Py_DECREF called on it to avoid a resource leak. This should happen even in the event of a C++ exception. As we will see, the wrapping of the array up in the shared_ptr means that this will be automated for us.

We can give a quick explanation of the arguments: input is the incoming PyObject* which we hope is an array; the type is the expected element type, for ppf purposes this is always the constant PyArray_DOUBLE; the arguments min_dim and max_dim are the expected minimum dimension (guarantee no smaller than) and maximum dimension of the array (guarantee no larger than). If max_dim is set to zero, the check on the array will have no upper bound with respect to dimensions.

The body of this inline function delegates to a static function get of class type object_as_array_impl. The type object_as_array_impl is in fact a typedef for a specific instantiation of a template class template <int> class object_as_array_impl_. That is really nothing to stop and concern ourselves with too much; it's a fairly often observed C++ 'trick' that enables us to present this functionality from a C++ header file without the need to provide clients of the functionality compiled library code as well.

So, with the interface function covered, let's have a quick review of the implementation details of the get function:

```
static boost::shared_ptr<PyArrayObject> get(
   PyObject* input, int type, int min_dim, int max_dim)
{
  if(PyArray_Check(input))
  {
    if(!PyArray_ISCARRAY(reinterpret_cast<PyArrayObject*>(input)))
    {
      PyErr_SetString(PyExc_TypeError, "not a C array");

      boost::python::throw_error_already_set();
    }

    return boost::shared_ptr<PyArrayObject>(
            reinterpret_cast<PyArrayObject*>(
                    boost::python::expect_non_null(
                        PyArray_ContiguousFromObject(
                                input, type, min_dim, max_dim))
      )
```

```
           , boost::bind(
               ::ppf::util::python::detail::decref<PyArrayObject>, _1)
        );
   }
   else
   {
      PyErr_SetString(PyExc_TypeError, "not an array");

      boost::python::throw_error_already_set();
   }

   return boost::shared_ptr<PyArrayObject>();
}
```

Well, it's fairly easy to see that – bar a few wrinkles, we'll discuss in a moment – it's for the most part fairly standard Python C API style programming. In short, the incoming input is checked to ensure that it's an array and, if it is, then it is a standard C style array (row major). In the event that it fails to meet these conditions, the error is indicated to Python and a quick exit is made by calling the Boost.Python function throw_error_already_set(). If the object has been determined to be an array, the crucial call is made to the NumPy API function PyArray_ContiguousFromObject which, for our purpose, checks that the array has the requested element data type and dimensionality. The use of the Boost.Python expect_non_null is the means by which, we detect if those conditions have been met (the result of PyArray_ContiguousFromObject will be non-null or 0 if they have not); the Python error indicator is set and an implicit call to boost::python::throw_error_already_set() will occur on failure. The non-null array object is cast to the required type and installed into a boost shared pointer with a custom deleter built from a boost::bind to the ppf::util::python::detail::decref function.

3.3.2 Examples

The 'ppf_math.pyd' C++ Python extension module exports some (trivial) examples of manipulating NumPy arrays from C++. The code for these examples can be found in the source file 'lib/math/src/register_numpy.cpp'. The examples all live in the C++ namespace ppf::math::numpy::examples. They are available through the ppf.math.numpy_examples module by the names sum_array, trace, assign_zero and make_array. The code to register the functions in the 'ppf_math.py' module reads:

```
void register_numpy()
{
  using namespace boost::python;

  def("numpy_sum_array", numpy::examples::sum_array);
  def("numpy_trace", numpy::examples::trace);
  def("numpy_assign_zero", numpy::examples::assign_zero);
  def("numpy_make_array", numpy::examples::make_array);

  import_array();//this is a required NumPy API function call
}
```

Sum the Elements of an Array

The first example simply sums the elements of the incoming array.

```
double sum_array(PyObject* input)
{
  boost::shared_ptr<PyArrayObject> obj = ::ppf::util::python
        ::detail::object_as_array(input, PyArray_DOUBLE, 0, 0);

  // compute size of array
  int n = 1;
  if(obj->nd > 0)
    for(int i = 0; i < obj->nd; ++i)
      n *= obj->dimensions[i];

  double* array = reinterpret_cast<double*>(obj->data);

  return std::accumulate(array, array + n, 0.);
}
```

In Python:

```
>>> import numpy
>>> from ppf.math.numpy_examples import *
>>> a = numpy.array([1., 2., 3., 4.])
>>> print sum_array(a)
10.0
```

Compute the Trace of an Array

The next function computes the trace of a two-dimensional array sum (of the main diagonal elements).

```
double trace(PyObject* input)
{
  boost::shared_ptr<PyArrayObject> obj = ::ppf::util::python
        ::detail::object_as_array(input, PyArray_DOUBLE, 2, 2);

  int n = obj->dimensions[0];
  if(n > obj->dimensions[1]) n = obj->dimensions[1];

  double sum = 0.;
  for(int i = 0; i < n; ++i)
    sum += *reinterpret_cast<double*>(
      obj->data + i*obj->strides[0] + i*obj->strides[1]);

  return sum;
}
```

Continuing the above example interpreter session:

```
>>> a = numpy.zeros((3, 4))
>>> for i in range(3):
```

```
...      a[i, i] = 1
...
>>> a[2, 3] = 1
>>> print a
[[ 1.   0.   0.   0.]
 [ 0.   1.   0.   0.]
 [ 0.   0.   1.   1.]]
>>> print trace(a)
3.0
```

Assign an Array's Contents to Zero

This function does more than just compute something from an array defined in Python. It shares the underlying data with a Blitz++ array in C++ and affects the source array by setting all of its elements to zero.

```
void assign_zero(PyObject* input)
{
   boost::shared_ptr<PyArrayObject> obj = ::ppf::util::python
         ::detail::object_as_array(input, PyArray_DOUBLE, 2, 2);

   blitz::Array<double, 2> array(
       reinterpret_cast<double*>(obj->data)
     , blitz::shape(obj->dimensions[0], obj->dimensions[1])
     , blitz::neverDeleteData);

   array = 0;
}
```

Continuing in the interpreter:

```
>>> print a
[[ 1.   0.   0.   0.]
 [ 0.   1.   0.   0.]
 [ 0.   0.   1.   1.]]
>>> assign_zero(a)
>>> print a
[[ 0.   0.   0.   0.]
 [ 0.   0.   0.   0.]
 [ 0.   0.   0.   0.]]
```

Create a New NumPy Array in C++ and Return it to Python

This code creates a new one-dimensional array of extent n, where n is provided by the caller and assigns it the values $0, \ldots, n-1$.

```
PyObject* make_array(int n)
{
   int dimensions[1]; dimensions[0] = n;
   PyArrayObject* result =
```

```
    reinterpret_cast<PyArrayObject*>(
        boost::python::expect_non_null(
            PyArray_FromDims(1, dimensions, PyArray_DOUBLE)));
  double* buffer = reinterpret_cast<double*>(result->data);
  for(int i = 1; i < n; ++i) buffer[i] = i;

  return PyArray_Return(result);
}
```

Back to the interpreter for one last time:

```
>>> a = make_array(6)
>>> print a
[ 0.  1.  2.  3.  4.  5.]
```

4

Basic Mathematical Tools

There are some basic mathematical tools and algorithms that are used constantly in computational quantitative analysis. Reviewing the implementation of these in Python gives us a good workout in Python programming and the implementations provide us with needed tools to construct more advanced programs in later chapters.

4.1 RANDOM NUMBER GENERATION

A module for pseudo-random number generators is provided in the Python libraries. It uses the *Mersenne Twister*[1] algorithm as the core generator, one of the most extensively tested random number generation schemes of all time. The following is a program demonstrating how the module can be used. The program prints, firstly, 100 samples from a Gaussian distribution with mean $\mu = 0$ and standard deviation $\sigma = 1$, and then 100 samples from a lognormal distribution with the same μ and σ.

```python
import random, sys, getopt

def _print_gauss():
  g = random.Random(1234)
  print [g.gauss(mu = 0, sigma = 1) for i in range(100)]

def _print_lognormal_variate():
  g = random.Random(1234)
  print [g.lognormvariate(mu = 0, sigma = 1) for i in range(100)]

def _usage():
  print "usage: %s" % sys.argv[0]
  print "Try 'python %s -h' for more information." % sys.argv[0]

def _help():
  print "usage: %s" % sys.argv[0]
  print "-h (--help)          : print this help message and exit"
  print "-v (--version)       : print the version number and exit"

if __name__ == '__main__':
  try:
   opts, args, = getopt.getopt(sys.argv[1:], "vh",
             ["version", "help", ])
  except getopt.GetoptError:
    _usage()
    sys.exit(2)
```

---

[1] The Mersenne Twister 19939 (often referred to as just 'MT19939') is a psuedo-random generator developed in 1977 by Makoto Matsumoto and Takuji Nishimura.

```
for o, a in opts:
  if o in ("-h", "--help"):
    _help()
    sys.exit()
  if o in ("-v", "--version"):
    print "'%s', Version 0.0.0" % sys.argv[0]
    sys.exit()
_print_gauss()
_print_lognormal_variate()
```

4.2   N(.)

In the ppf.math.special_functions module, N is a function that approximates the standard normal cumulative distribution function, $N(.)$, as used in the celebrated Black–Scholes option-pricing equation.

```
import math

def N(x):
  a   =   0.3535533905933
  b1  = -1.2655122300000
  b2  =   1.0000236800000
  b3  =   0.3740919600000
  b4  =   0.0967841800000
  b5  = -0.1862880600000
  b6  =   0.2788680700000
  b7  = -1.1352039800000
  b8  =   1.4885158700000
  b9  = -0.8221522300000
  b10 =   0.1708727700000

  t, term, result = 0, 0, 0

  if(x > 0):
    if (x > 10): result = 1.0
    else:
      t = 1/(1 + a*x)
      term = b9 + t*b10
      term = b8 + t*term
      term = b7 + t*term
      term = b6 + t*term
      term = b5 + t*term
      term = b4 + t*term
      term = b3 + t*term
      term = b2 + t*term
      term = b1 + t*term
      term = term + -0.5*(x*x)

      result = 1.0 - 0.5*t*math.exp(term)
  else:
```

```
if(x < -10): result = 0.0
else:
    t = 1/(1 - a*x)
    term = b9 + t*b10
    term = b8 + t*term
    term = b7 + t*term
    term = b6 + t*term
    term = b5 + t*term
    term = b4 + t*term
    term = b3 + t*term
    term = b2 + t*term
    term = b1 + t*term
    term = term + -0.5*(x*x)

    result = 0.5*t*math.exp(term)

return result
```

4.3   INTERPOLATION

Interpolation is the process of estimating the values of a function $y(x)$ for arguments between $x_0, \ldots, x_n$ at which the values $y_0, \ldots, y_n$ are known. To elegantly implement interpolation schemes in a single dimension, it is helpful to first define some utility functions for searching an ordered sequence of numbers. The ppf.utility.bound module defines a family of such functions in the spirit of the C++ STL[2] functions of the same names.

```
import operator

def lower_bound(x, values, cmp=operator.lt):
    """Find the first position in values
    where x could be inserted without violating
    the ordering.
    """
    first, count = 0, len(values)
    while count > 0:
        half = count/2
        middle = first + half
        if cmp(values[middle], x):
            first = middle + 1
            count = count - half - 1
        else: count = half

    return first

def upper_bound(x, values, cmp=operator.lt):
    """Find the last position in values
    where x could be inserted without changing
    the ordering.
```

---

[2] The C++ STL (Standard Template Library) is a generic library of class templates and algorithms.

```
    """
    first, count = 0, len(values)
    while count > 0:
        half = count/2
        middle = first + half
        if cmp(x, values[middle]):
            count = half
        else:
            first = middle + 1
            count = count - half - 1

    return first

def equal_range(x, values, cmp=operator.lt):
    """Find the largest subrange in which
        x could be inserted in any place without
        changing the ordering.
    """
    return (lower_bound(x, values, cmp), upper_bound(x, values, cmp))

def bound(x, values, cmp=operator.lt):
    """Raise if x is outside of the domain
        else find indices, i, j such that values[i] <= x <= values[j].

    """
    count = len(values)
    left, right = equal_range(x, values, cmp)
    if left == count:
        raise RuntimeError, "%f lies right of the domain" % x
    elif right == 0:
        raise RuntimeError, "%f lies left of the domain" % x

    if right == count: right -= 1
    if left == right:   left -= 1

    return (left, right)
```

The classic user case for the bound function in the context of interpolation is to find an index j such that, given an ordered sequence of real numbers, $x_1, \ldots, x_N, x_{j-1} \le x \le x_j$:

```
    def test_bound(self):
        bound = ppf.utility.bound
        values = [1, 2, 3]
        i, j = bound(1.5, values)
        assert i == j -1 and values[i] <= 1.5 <= values[j]
        i, j = bound(2.0, [1, 2, 3])
        assert i == j -1 and values[i] <= 2.0 <= values[j]
        self.assertRaises(RuntimeError, bound, 4, values)
```

The parameterisation of the bound algorithm by the user provided less-than predicate admits other interesting uses. The following unit test shows bound in conjunction with case-insensitive string comparison:

```
def test_bound_ci(self):
  bound = ppf.utility.bound
  values = ['ape', 'Apple', 'caNada']
  i, j = bound('bananana', values
                , lambda x, y: x.lower() < y.lower())
  assert i == j -1 and values[i].lower() <= 'banana' <=
  values[j].lower()
```

With the function bound at our disposal, implementing a variety of interpolation schemes becomes easy. First, the ppf.math.interpolation module defines a base class for interpolators:

```
import math
import ppf.utility
import linear_algebra


class interpolation_base:
  def __init__(self, abscissae, ordinates):
    if not sorted(abscissae) or \
        len(abscissae) != len(ordinates):
      raise RuntimeError, \
            'abscissae/ordinates length mismatch'
    self.N = len(abscissae)
    self.abscissae, self.ordinates = abscissae, ordinates

  def locate(self, x):
    i, j = ppf.utility.bound(x, self.abscissae)
    x_lo, x_hi = self.abscissae[i], self.abscissae[j]
    y_lo, y_hi = self.ordinates[i], self.ordinates[j]

    return (i, j, x_lo, x_hi, y_lo, y_hi)
```

This base class essentially wraps up the business of locating the points in a sequence that will participate in the interpolation by virtue of the bound function. With this utility in hand, we move on to a variety of interpolation schemes.

4.3.1 Linear Interpolation

In this scheme, if $x_{i-1} \le x < x_i$ we estimate $y(x)$ by

$$y = \left(\frac{x - x_{i-1}}{x_i - x_{i-1}} \right) (y_i - y_{i-1}) + y_{i-1}. \tag{4.1}$$

If we define the quantity R by $R = \frac{x - x_{i-1}}{x_i - x_{i-1}}$, then in terms of R we find

$$y = R (y_i - y_{i-1}) + y_{i-1}. \tag{4.2}$$

So, saying this in Python code yields

```
class linear(interpolation_base):
  def __init__(self, abscissae, ordinates):
    interpolation_base.__init__(self, abscissae, ordinates)
```

```
def __call__(self, x):
  i, j, x_lo, x_hi, y_lo, y_hi = \
    interpolation_base.locate(self, x)
  R = 1.0 - (x_hi - x)/(x_hi - x_lo)

  return R*(y_hi - y_lo) + y_lo
```

4.3.2 Loglinear Interpolation

In this scheme, we estimate $y(x)$ by

$$y = e^{\ln(y_{i-1})+(\ln(y_i)-\ln(y_{i-1}))R}.$$

(4.3)

In Python:

```
class loglinear(interpolation_base):
  def __init__(self, abscissae, ordinates):
    interpolation_base.__init__(self, abscissae, ordinates)

  def __call__(self, x):
    i, j, x_lo, x_hi, y_lo, y_hi = \
      interpolation_base.locate(self, x)
    ln_ylo, ln_yhi = math.log(y_lo), math.log(y_hi)
    R = 1.0 - (x_hi - x)/(x_hi - x_lo)

    return math.exp(ln_ylo+(ln_yhi - ln_ylo)*R)
```

4.3.3 Linear on Zero Interpolation

In this scheme, we estimate $y(x)$ in the following way. First, if $i - 1 = 0$ then

$$y = y_i^{\left(\frac{x-x_0}{x_i-x_{i-1}}\right)}$$

(4.4)

otherwise

$$y = e^{-(z_{i-1}+R(z_i-z_{i-1}))(x-x_0)}$$

(4.5)

with

$$z_i = \frac{-\ln(y_i)}{x_i - x_0}.$$

(4.6)

Putting the above into Python code we get

```
class linear_on_zero(interpolation_base):
  def __init__(self, abscissae, ordinates):
    interpolation_base.__init__(self, abscissae, ordinates)

  def __call__(self, x):
    x_0 = self.abscissae[0]
    i, j, x_lo, x_hi, y_lo, y_hi = \
      interpolation_base.locate(self, x)
    dx = (x_hi - x_lo)
```

```
R, R_ = (1.0 - ((x_hi - x)/dx)), (x - x_0)/dx
y = 0
if i == 0:
  y = math.pow(y_hi, R_)
else:
  r, r_lo, r_hi = x - x_0, x_lo - x_0, x_hi - x_0
  z_lo, z_hi = -math.log(y_lo)/r_lo, -math.log(y_hi)/r_hi
  y = math.exp(-(z_lo + R*(z_hi - z_lo))*r)

return y
```

4.3.4 Cubic Spline Interpolation

Another popular interpolation method, popular because the curves it produces are particularly smooth, is to let the fitting function be a piecewise union of cubic polynomials. That is, we define a polynomial P_i on each interval $[a_{i-1}, a_i]$ such that the endpoints of the polynomial pass through the ordinates y_i and that the first and second derivatives of the cubic match with the next cubic along, i.e.:

$$P_i(x_i) = y_i$$
$$P_{i-1}(x_i) = y_i$$
$$\frac{d}{dx}P_i(x_{i-1}) = \frac{d}{dx}P_{i-1}(x_i)$$
$$\frac{d^2}{dx^2}P_i(x_{i-1}) = \frac{d^2}{dx^2}P_{i-1}(x_i)$$

for all i. By imposing conditions on the values of the derivative at the very endpoints of the function x_0 and x_{N-1} there are sufficiently many conditions for the coefficients of all the cubics to be determined uniquely by solving a linear system of equations. The exact form of this linear system varies from one source to another. We use the form found in [20].

Given x, let i be such that $a_{i-1} < x < a_i$. Then our formulation says that our cubic for this i-th segment is

$$p(x) = \frac{c_{i-1} * (a_i - x)^3}{6h_i}$$
$$+ \frac{c_i(x - a_{i-1})^3}{6h_i(a_i - a_{i-1})}$$
$$+ \left(y_{i-1} - \frac{c_{i-1}h_i^2}{6}\right)\left(\frac{a_i - x}{h_i}\right)$$
$$+ \left(y_i - \frac{c_i h_i^2}{6}\right)\left(\frac{x - a_{i-1}}{h_i}\right) \tag{4.7}$$

where c is a set of vectors linearly dependent on the ordinates y_i that we will determine and h_i is the width of the segment ($= a_i - a_{i-1}$). c is determined by the linear system of equations $Ac = b$ where A is square tridiagonal matrix whose values are dependent only on the segment widths h_i and each b is a linear combination of the y_i. More specifically

$$b_0 = d_{left}$$

$$b_i = \frac{6}{h_i + h_{i+1}} \left(\frac{y_{i+1} - y_i}{h_{i+1}} - \frac{y_i - y_{i-1}}{h_i} \right)$$

$$b_n = d_{right} \tag{4.8}$$

where d_{left} and d_{right} are constants dependent only on the choice of the value of the derivatives at the endpoints of the curve.[3] Implementation of this scheme in Python requires a little more effort than the earlier cases:

```
class cubic_spline(interpolation_base):
  def __init__(self, abscissae, ordinates, a_0 = 0.5, d_0=0, b_n=0.5,
                                    d_n=0):
    interpolation_base.__init__(self, abscissae, ordinates)
    xs, ys, N = self.abscissae, self.ordinates, self.N
    b = [d_0]+(N - 1)*[0]
    A_sub, A_dia, A_sup = N*[0], [2.0] + (N - 1)*[0], [a_0] +
                          (N - 1)*[0]
    for i in range(1, N - 1):
      H, h = xs[i + 1]- xs[i], xs[i] -  xs[i - 1]
      b[i] = (6./(h + H))*(((ys[i + 1] - ys[i])/H) -
             ((ys[i] - ys[i - 1])/h))
      a_i = H/(h + H)
      b_i = 1.0 - a_i
      A_dia[i], A_sup[i], A_sub[i] = 2., a_i, b_i
    A_sub[N - 1], A_dia[N - 1], b[N - 1] = b_n, 2.0, d_n
    self.C = linear_algebra.solve_tridiagonal_system(N, A_sub, A_dia,
             A_sup, b)

  def __call__(self, x):
    xs, ys, C = self.abscissae, self.ordinates, self.C
    i, j, _, _, _, _ = interpolation_base.locate(self, x)
    h_i = xs[j] - xs[i]
    x_low = xs[j] - x
    x_low3 = math.pow(x_low, 3)
    x_high = x - xs[i]
    x_high3 = math.pow(x_high, 3)
    hi_sqrd_6 = h_i*h_i/6.0

    return  C[i]*x_low3/(6.0*h_i)+C[j]*x_high3/(6.0*h_i)+\
            (ys[i]-C[i]*hi_sqrd_6)*x_low/h_i+(ys[j]-
            C[j]*hi_sqrd_6)*x_high/h_i
```

---

[3] In the case of the so-called *natural spline*, we set the derivatives at the endpoints to be zero, and have $d_{left} = d_{right} = 0.0$.

4.4   ROOT FINDING

We will present two schemes in this section for finding the roots of a function $y = f(x)$ with $f : \mathbb{R} \mapsto \mathbb{R}$.

4.4.1   Bisection Method

The bisection method is a classiscal root-finding routine that does not require derivative information. The `ppf.math.root_finding` module provides the following implementation derived from the Boost.Math_Toolkit library:

```
import math
from special_functions import sign, max_flt

def bisect(f, min, max, tol, max_its):
  """Bisection method
  """

  fmin, fmax = f(min), f(max)
  if fmin == 0: return (min, min, 0)
  if fmax == 0: return (max, max, 0)
  if min >= max: raise RuntimeError, "Arguments in wrong order"
  if fmin*fmax >= 0: raise RuntimeError,  "Root not bracketed"

  count = max_its
  if count < 3:
    count = 0
  else: count -= 3

  while count and tol(min, max) == 0:
    mid = (min + max)/2.
    fmid = f(mid)
    if mid == max or mid ==min:
        break
    if fmid == 0:
      min = max = mid
      break
    elif sign(fmid)*sign(fmin) < 0:
      max, fmax = mid, fmid
    else:
      min, fmin = mid, fmid
    --count

  max_its -= count

  return (min, max, max_its)
```

The quadratic $y(x) = x^2 + 2x - 1$ has roots

$$-1 - \sqrt{2} = -2.4142135623730950488016887242097$$
$$-1 + \sqrt{2} = +0.4142135623730950488016887242097.$$

In the example interactive session, we find those roots by bisection:

```
>>> bisect(lambda x: x*x + 2*x - 1, -3, -2,
... lambda x, y: math.fabs(x-y) < 0.000001, 10)
(-2.4142141342163086, -2.4142131805419922, 3)

>>> bisect(lambda x: x*x + 2*x - 1, 0, 1,
... lambda x, y: math.fabs(x-y) < 0.000001, 10)
(0.41421318054199219, 0.41421413421630859, 3)
```

4.4.2   Newton–Raphson Method

Newton–Raphson is a root-finding routine using derivatives with a faster rate of convergence than bisection. The `ppf.math.root_finding` module offers an implementation again derived from a `Boost.Math_Toolkit` implementation:

```
def newton_raphson(f, guess, min, max, digits, max_its):
  """Newton-Raphson method

  """

  def _handle_zero_derivative(f, last_f0, f0, delta,
                              result, guess, min, max):
    if last_f0 == 0:
      # must be first iteration
      if result == min: guess = max
      else: guess = min
      last_f0, _ = f(guess)
      delta = guess - result
    if sign(last_f0)*sign(f0) < 0:
      # we've crossed over so move in opposite
      # direction to last step
      if delta < 0:
        delta = (result - min)/2.0
      else:
        delta = (result - max)/2.0
    else:
      # move in same direction of last step
      if delta < 0:
        delta = (result - max)/2.0
      else:
        delta = (result - min)/2.0
    return (last_f0, delta, result, guess)

  f0, f1, last_f0, result = 0.0, 0.0, 0.0, guess
  factor = math.ldexp(1.0, 1 - digits)
  delta, delta1, delta2 = 1.0, max_flt(), max_flt()
  count = max_its
```

```
while True:
    last_f0 = f0
    delta2 = delta1
    delta1 = delta
    f0, f1 = f(result)
    if f0 == 0:
        break
    if f1 == 0:
        last_f0, delta, result, guess = \
                 _handle_zero_derivative( \
                     f, last_f0, f0, delta, result, guess, min, max)
    else:
        delta = f0/f1

    if math.fabs(delta*2.0) > math.fabs(delta2):
        # last two steps haven't converged, try bisection
        delta = ((result - max)/2.0, (result - min)/2.0)[delta > 0]
    guess = result
    result -= delta
    if result <= min:
        delta = 0.5*(guess - min)
        result = guess - delta
        if result == min or result == max:
            break
    elif result >= max:
        delta = 0.5*(guess - max)
        result = guess - delta
        if result == min or result == max: break

    # update brackets
    if delta > 0:
        max = guess
    else:
        min = guess

    count -= 1

    if count != 0 and \
            math.fabs(result*factor) < math.fabs(delta):
        continue
    else:
        break

max_its -= count

return (result, max_its)
```

We apply it in the following interactive session to once again compute a root of the polynomial from the preceding section:

```
>>> newton_raphson(lambda x: (x*x+2*x-1,2*x+2),-3,-3,-2,22,100)
(-2.414213562373094, 5)
```

4.5   LINEAR ALGEBRA

The Python NumPy package contains a module that covers most of what is required from linear algebra from a financial engineering perspective. For the most part, this section provides some examples of its use for problems common in financial engineering. This section just touches on the capabilities of NumPy for linear algebra. The interested reader is referred to the NumPy documentation for further detail. Readers with an interest in the development of linear algebra routines in Python are encouraged to consult Jaan Kiusalaas's *Numerical Methods in Engineering with Python* [12].

4.5.1   Matrix Multiplication

The ordinary matrix product.

```
>>> from numpy import *
>>> from numpy.linalg import inv
>>> A = array([ [1, 3, 2], [1, 0, 0], [2, 1, 1]])
>>> M = matrix(A)
>>> print M*M
[[8 5 4]
 [1 3 2]
 [5 7 5]]
```

Note the use of the matrix construction function in the example above. It is this that gives the interpretation of the operation as a matrix product. Multiplying two arrays, on the other hand, gives the product element-wise, e.g.

```
>>> print A*A
[[1 9 4]
 [1 0 0]
 [4 1 1]]
```

Matrix multiplication can be performed on arrays by use of the dot function, as illustrated below.

```
>>> print dot(A, A)
[[8 5 4]
 [1 3 2]
 [5 7 5]]
```

4.5.2   Matrix Inversion

Find the inverse of a square non-singular matrix.

```
>>> from numpy import *
>>> from numpy.linalg import inv
>>> A = array([ [1, 3, 2], [1, 0, 0], [2, 1, 1]])
```

```
>>> print A
[[1 3 2]
 [1 0 0]
 [2 1 1]]
>>> A_inv = inv(A)
>>> print A_inv
[[ 0.  1.  0.]
 [ 1.  3. -2.]
 [-1. -5.  3.]]
>>> print dot(A_inv, A)
[[ 1.  0.  0.]
 [ 0.  1.  0.]
 [ 0.  0.  1.]]
```

4.5.3 Matrix Pseudo-Inverse

Find the pseudo-inverse of a matrix.

```
>>> from numpy import *
>>> from numpy.linalg import inv
>>> A = array([ [1, 3, 2], [1, 0, 0 ] ])
>>> b = array([1, 3])
>>> x = dot(pinv(A), b)
>>> print x
[ 3.          -0.46153846 -0.30769231]
```

4.5.4 Solving Linear Systems

Solve the linear system $\mathbf{Ax} = \mathbf{B}$.

```
>>> from numpy import *
>>> from numpy.linalg import solve
>>> A = array([ [1, 3, 2], [1, 0, 0], [2, 1, 1]])
>>> b = array([4, 5, 6])
>>> print solve(A, b)
[ 5.   7. -11.]
```

4.5.5 Solving Tridiagonal Systems

Efficiently solve the linear system $\mathbf{Ax} = \mathbf{b}$ where $\mathbf{A}$ is tridiagonal. This implementation is from the ppf.math.linear_algebra module.

```
def solve_tridiagonal_system(N, a, b, c, r):
    """Efficiently solve a tridiagonal system.

    For example if,

        x +  y = 3
        y +  z = 5
        y + 2z = 8
```

```
then,

A = 3x3
    [   1    1    0
        0    1    1
        0    1    2 ]

and r = [ 3, 5, 8 ] for which the expected
result is x = [1, 2, 3].

>>> a, b, c = [None, 0, 1], [1, 1, 2], [1, 1, None]
>>> r =[3, 5, 8]
>>> print solve_tridiagonal_system(3, a, b, c, r)
[ 1.   2.   3.]


"""
u, gam = numpy.zeros(N), numpy.zeros(N)
bet = b[0]
if bet == 0.0:
  raise RuntimeError, "Solve diagonal system error"
u[0] = r[0]/bet
for j in range(1, N):
  gam[j] = c[j - 1]/bet
  bet = b[j]- a[j]*gam[j]
  if bet == 0.0:
    raise RuntimeError, "Solve diagonal system error"
  u[j] = (r[j] - a[j]*u[j - 1])/bet
for j in range(N - 2, -1, -1):
  u[j] -= gam[j + 1]*u[j + 1]

return u
```

4.5.6 Solving Upper Diagonal Systems

Efficiently solve the linear system $Ax = b$ where A is upper diagonal. The implementation shown below is from the ppf.math.linear_algebra module.

```
def solve_upper_diagonal_system(a, b):
  """Efficiently solve an upper diagonal system.

  For example, if

    A = 3 x 3
        [   1.75    1.5    -2.5
            0      -0.5     0.65
            0       0       0.25 ]
  and

    b = [   0.5    -1       3.5],
```

```
the expected result is x = [2.97142857  20.2  14].

>>> from numpy import *
>>> A = matrix(array(
... [[1.75, 1.5, -2.5],
... [0.0, -0.5, 0.65],
... [0.0, 0.0, 0.25]], float))
>>> A
matrix([[ 1.75,   1.5 , -2.5 ],
        [ 0.  ,  -0.5 ,  0.65],
        [ 0.  ,   0.  ,  0.25]])
>>> b = array([0.5, -1.0, 3.5])
>>> b
array([ 0.5, -1. ,   3.5])
>>> x = solve_upper_diagonal_system(A, b)
>>> x = matrix(x).transpose() # column vector
>>> x
matrix([[  2.97142857],
        [ 20.2       ],
        [ 14.        ]])
>>> A*x   #matrix vector product
matrix([[ 0.5],
        [-1. ],
        [ 3.5]])

"""
if len(a.shape) <> 2:
  raise RuntimeError, "Expected 'a' to be a matrix"
if a.shape[0] <> a.shape[1]:
  raise RuntimeError, "Expected 'a' to be a square matrix"
if len(b.shape) <> 1:
  raise RuntimeError, "Expected 'b' to be a column vector"
if b.shape[0] <> a.shape[0]:
  raise RuntimeError, "Expected 'b' to be a column vector"
N = a.shape[0]
for i in range(N):
  if a[i, i] == 0.0:
    raise RuntimeError, "Singular upper diagonal matrix"
  for j in range(0, i):
    if a[i, j] <> 0.0: raise RuntimeError, "Matrix not upper"
    "diagonal"

x = numpy.zeros(N)
for i in range(N-1, -1, -1):
  tmp = 0.0
  for j in range(i+1, N):
    tmp += a[i, j]*x[j]
  x[i] = (b[i]-tmp)/a[i, i]

return x
```

4.5.7   Singular Value Decomposition

We show how to calculate the singular value decomposition of an $M \times N$ matrix **A**, with $M \geq N$, into the product of a $M \times N$ orthogonal matrix **U**, an $N \times N$ diagonal matrix **W** with positive or zero elements (the singular values), and the transpose of an $N \times N$ orthogonal matrix **V**. The actual implementation of the singular value decomposition algorithm is from numpy.linalg.svd and the following code snippet illustrates a sample call to svd.

```
>>> from numpy import *
>>> from numpy.linalg import svd
>>> A = transpose(array([[1., 3., 5.],[2., 4., 6.]]))
>>> print A
[[ 1.  2.]
 [ 3.  4.]
 [ 5.  6.]]
>>> U, sig, V = svd(A)
>>> print U
[[-0.2298477   0.88346102  0.40824829]
 [-0.52474482  0.24078249 -0.81649658]
 [-0.81964194 -0.40189603  0.40824829]]
>>> print sig
[ 9.52551809  0.51430058]
>>> print V
[[-0.61962948 -0.78489445]
 [-0.78489445  0.61962948]]
>>> n = 2
>>> W=numpy.zeros((n+1,n))
>>> W[:n, :n] = diag(sig)
>>> print W
[[ 9.52551809  0.        ]
 [ 0.          0.51430058]
 [ 0.          0.        ]]
>>> dot(U, dot(W, V))
array([[ 1.,  2.],
       [ 3.,  4.],
       [ 5.,  6.]])
```

Given a singular value decomposition of a matrix $\mathbf{A} = \mathbf{UWV}$, we can easily solve the matrix equation $\mathbf{Ax} = \mathbf{b}$ using back substitution. The following implementation is from the ppf.math.linear_algebra module.

```
def singular_value_decomposition_back_substitution(u, w, v, b):
    """Solve an upper diagonal system using svd.

    For example, if

        A = 3 x 3
            [  1.75    1.5    -2.5
               0      -0.5     0.65
               0       0       0.25 ]
    and

        b = [  0.5    -1       3.5],
```

```
the expected result is x = [2.97142857   20.2    14].
>>> from numpy import *
>>> from numpy.linalg import svd
>>> A = matrix(array(
... [[1.75, 1.5, -2.5],
... [0.0, -0.5, 0.65],
... [0.0, 0.0, 0.25]], float))
>>> A
matrix([[ 1.75,   1.5 ,  -2.5 ],
        [ 0.  ,  -0.5 ,   0.65],
        [ 0.  ,   0.  ,   0.25]])
>>> b = array([0.5, -1.0, 3.5])
>>> b
array([ 0.5, -1. ,   3.5])
>>> u, w, v = svd(A)
>>> x = singular_value_decomposition_back_substitution(u, w, v, b)
>>> x = matrix(x).transpose() # column vector
>>> x
matrix([[  2.97142857],
        [ 20.2       ],
        [ 14.        ]])
"""

if len(u.shape) <> 2:
  raise RuntimeError, "Expected 'u' to be a matrix"
if len(w.shape) <> 1:
  raise RuntimeError, "Expected 'w' to be a column vector"
if len(v.shape) <> 2:
  raise RuntimeError, "Expected 'v' to be a matrix"
if len(b.shape) <> 1:
  raise RuntimeError, "Expected 'b' to be a column vector"

m = u.shape[0]
n = u.shape[1]

if w.shape[0] <> n:
  raise RuntimeError, "'w' column vector has incorrect size"
if b.shape[0] <> m:
  raise RuntimeError, "'b' column vector has incorrect size"
if v.shape[0] <> n or v.shape[1] <> n:
  raise RuntimeError, "'v' matrix has incorrect size"

tmp = numpy.zeros(n)
for j in range(n):
  s = 0.0
  if w[j] <> 0:
    for i in range(m):
      s += u[i, j]*b[i]
    s /= w[j]
  tmp[j] = s
x = numpy.zeros(n)
```

```
for j in range(n):
    s = 0.0
    for jj in range(n):
        s += v[jj, j]*tmp[jj]
    x[j] = s
return x
```

4.6   GENERALISED LINEAR LEAST SQUARES

Generalised linear least squares is a method for fitting a set of data points $(x_i, y_i)_{i = 1,...,N}$ to a linear combination of basis functions. The general form of this kind of model is

$$y(x) = \sum_{k=1}^{M} a_k f_k(x) \tag{4.9}$$

where $f_1(x), \ldots, f_M(x)$ are the basis functions. The central idea behind the method is to find the fitting coefficients $a_1, \ldots, a_M$ by minimising the merit function

$$\chi^2 = \sum_{i=1}^{N} \left[\frac{y_i - \sum_{k=1}^{M} a_k f_k(x_i)}{\sigma_i} \right]^2. \tag{4.10}$$

The σ_i represent the measurement error, or equivalently the standard deviation, of the ith data point. In [5] it is shown that the solution of the above equation can be calculated by solving the normal equations

$$\sum_{j=1}^{M} \alpha_{kj} a_j = \beta_k \tag{4.11}$$

where

$$\alpha_{kj} = \sum_{i=1}^{N} \frac{f_j(x_i) f_k(x_i)}{\sigma_i^2} \tag{4.12}$$

and

$$\beta_k = \sum_{i=1}^{N} \frac{y_i f_k(x_i)}{\sigma_i^2}. \tag{4.13}$$

The normal equations can be solved using LU decomposition and backsubstitution but the solution is susceptible to roundoff error. It is common practice to use singular value decomposition to solve this problem, and this is the route we have taken.

The implementation of the generalised linear least squares algorithm can be found in the ppf.math.generalised_least_squares module and the details of the implementation are shown below.

```
def generalised_least_squares_fit(y, x, sig, fit_fos):
    tol = 1.0e-13

    if len(y.shape) <> 1:
        raise RuntimeError, "Expected 'y' to be a column vector"
```

```
if len(x.shape) <> 2:
  raise RuntimeError, "Expected 'x' to be a matrix"
if len(sig.shape) <> 1:
  raise RuntimeError, "Expected 'sig' to be a column vector"

ndata = x.shape[0]
ma = len(fit_fos)

if sig.shape[0] <> ndata:
  raise RuntimeError, "'sig' column vector has incorrect size"
if y.shape[0] <> ndata:
  raise RuntimeError, "'y' column vector has incorrect size"


a = numpy.zeros(ma)

if ndata == 0:
 return a
else:
 b = numpy.zeros(ndata)
 cu = numpy.zeros([ndata, ma])

 for i in range(ndata):
   xi = x[i, :]
   tmp = 1.0/sig[i]
   for j in range(ma):
     cu[i, j] = fit_fos[j](xi)*tmp
   b[i] = y[i]*tmp

 u, w, v = numpy.linalg.svd(cu, 0)
 wmax = numpy.max(w)
 threshold = tol*wmax
 for j in range(ma):
   if w[j] < threshold:
     w[j] = 0.0
 a = singular_value_decomposition_back_substitution(u, w, v, b)
 return a
```

In an interpreter session, the generalised least squares algorithm can be invoked as follows.

```
>>> class linear_fo:
...     def __call__(self, x):
...         return x[0]
>>> class quadratic_fo:
...     def __call__(self, x):
...         return x[0]*x[0]
>>> generator = random.Random(1234)
>>> ndata = 100
>>> sig = numpy.zeros(ndata)
>>> sig.fill(1.0)
>>> y = numpy.zeros(ndata)
```

```
>>> x = numpy.zeros([ndata, 1])
>>> a = 0.25
>>> b = -0.1
>>> for i in range(ndata):
...     v = generator.gauss(0, 1.0)
...     x[i, 0] = v
...     y[i] = a*v+b*v*v
>>> fit_fos = []
>>> fit_fos.append(linear_fo())
>>> fit_fos.append(quadratic_fo())
>>> coeffs = generalised_least_squares_fit(y, x, sig, fit_fos)
>>> coeffs
array([ 0.25, -0.1 ])
```

4.7 QUADRATIC AND CUBIC ROOTS

It is not uncommon in finance to want to find the real roots of either a quadratic or cubic equation. The module ppf.math.quadratic_roots provides an implementation for finding the real roots of a quadratic. The real roots of the quadratic equation

$$ax^2 + bx + c = 0, \qquad a, b, c \in \mathbb{R} \tag{4.14}$$

exist provided $b^2 - 4ac \geq 0$ and are given by the expression

$$r_\pm = -\frac{b}{2a} \pm \frac{\sqrt{b^2 - 4ac}}{2a}. \tag{4.15}$$

For numerical stability reasons one shouldn't use the above equation to determine the real roots. Instead it is better to calculate the roots via the relations below

$$q = -\frac{1}{2}\left(b + \text{sgn}(b)\sqrt{b^2 - 4ac}\right) \tag{4.16}$$

$$r_+ = \frac{q}{a} \tag{4.17}$$

$$r_- = \frac{c}{q} \tag{4.18}$$

and this is precisely the way the real roots are calculated in the ppf.math.quadratic_roots module, as can been seen below.

```
import math
def quadratic_roots(a, b, c, xl, xh):
  # find roots
  roots = []
  d = b*b-4*a*c
  if d > 0:
    r1 = 0
    r2 = 0
    if a <> 0:
      sgn = 1
      if b < 0: sgn = -1
      q = -0.5*(b+sgn*math.sqrt(d))
```

```
    r1 = q/a
    r2 = r1
    if q <> 0: r2 = c/q
  else:
    r1 = -c/b
    r2 = r1
  # order roots
  if r1 > r2:
    tmp = r1
    r1 = r2
    r2 = tmp
  if r1 >= xl and r1 <= xh:
    roots.append(r1)
  if r2 <> r1 and r2 >= xl and r2 <= xh:
    roots.append(r2)
else:
  if a <> 0:
    r1 = -b/(2*a)
    if r1 >= xl and r1 <= xh:
      roots.append(r1)

return roots
```

The real roots of the cubic equation

$$ax^3 + bx^2 + cx + d = 0, \qquad a, b, c, d \in \mathbb{R} \tag{4.19}$$

are marginally more difficult to compute. The module `ppf.math.cubic_roots` contains an implementation of the cubic roots algorithm. If $a \neq 0$ we proceed as follows. First we set b, c and d to $\frac{b}{a}$, $\frac{c}{a}$ and $\frac{d}{a}$ respectively. Then we compute the variables q and r defined below

$$q := \frac{a^2 - 3b}{9} \tag{4.20}$$

$$r := \frac{2a^3 - 9ab + 27}{54} \tag{4.21}$$

For the case when $r^2 \leq q^3$ the three real roots are given by

$$r_1 = -2\sqrt{q}\cos\left(\frac{\theta}{3}\right) - \frac{a}{3} \tag{4.22}$$

$$r_2 = -2\sqrt{q}\cos\left(\frac{\theta + 2\pi}{3}\right) - \frac{a}{3} \tag{4.23}$$

$$r_3 = -2\sqrt{q}\cos\left(\frac{\theta - 2\pi}{3}\right) - \frac{a}{3} \tag{4.24}$$

with

$$\theta := \arccos\left(\frac{r}{\sqrt{q}}\right) \tag{4.25}$$

Otherwise there is only one real root, given by

$$r = \frac{A + B}{3} \tag{4.26}$$

with

$$A = -\text{sgn}(r)\left(\text{sgn}(r)r + \sqrt{r^2 - q^3}\right)^{\frac{1}{3}} \tag{4.27}$$

$$B = \frac{q}{A} \tag{4.28}$$

Naturally, if a is zero, then we fall back on the quadratic roots algorithm already described. The implementation is summarised below.

```
import math
from quadratic_roots import *

def cubic_roots(a, b, c, d, xl, xh):
    if a <> 0:
        roots = []
        aa = a
        a = b/aa
        b = c/aa
        c = d/aa
        q = (a*a-3*b)/9.0
        r = (2*a*a*a-9.0*a*b+27.0*c)/54.0
        q3 = q*q*q
        diff = r*r-q3
        if diff <= 0:
            ratio = r/math.sqrt(q3)
            theta = math.acos(ratio)
            qr = -2.0*math.sqrt(q)
            a_over_3 = a/3.0
            r1 = qr*math.cos(theta/3.0)-a_over_3
            r2 = qr*math.cos((theta+2.0*math.pi)/3.0)-a_over_3
            r3 = qr*math.cos((theta-2.0*math.pi)/3.0)-a_over_3
            rs = [r1, r2, r3]
            rs.sort()
            [r1, r2, r3] = rs
            if r1 >= xl and r1 <= xh:
                roots.append(r1)
            if r2 <> r1 and r2 >= xl and r2 <= xh:
                roots.append(r2)
            if r3 <> r1 and r3 <> r2 and r3 >= xl and r3 <= xh:
                roots.append(r3)
        else:
            biga = 0
            if r > 0:
                biga = -math.pow(r+math.sqrt(diff), 1.0/3.0)
            else:
                biga = math.pow(-r+math.sqrt(diff), 1.0/3.0)
            bigb = 0.0
```

```
    if biga <> 0: bigb = q/biga
    r1 = (biga+bigb)-a/3.0
    if r1 >= xl and r1 <= xh:
        roots.append(r1)
    return roots
  else:
    return quadratic_roots(b, c, d, xl, xh)
```

Finally, note that in the actual implementations we only return the real roots, quadratic or cubic, if they lie in the range $[x_l, x_h]$. Moreover we always sort the real roots. The reason for doing this will become clear in the next section when we apply the above algorithms in the context of integrating a polynomial.

4.8 INTEGRATION

In finance we often need to calculate the expectation of some function $f : \mathbb{R}^n \mapsto \mathbb{R}$ of a number of random variables $X : \Omega \mapsto \mathbb{R}^n$. Throughout this section we will only consider financial payoffs that can be written in terms of a single random variable $X : \Omega \mapsto \mathbb{R}$ and belong to the space $C^3(\mathbb{R})$, that is the space of continuous three-times differentiable functions on $\mathbb{R}$. But the following can be extended to higher dimensions with more effort.

4.8.1 Piecewise Constant Polynomial Fitting

Let X denote a random variable on $\mathbb{R}$ which we sample on a uniform lattice $\{x_1, x_2, \ldots, x_N\}$ with spacing Δ. The corresponding values of the function f on the uniform lattice are denoted by $\{f_1, f_2, \ldots, f_N\}$. Similarly the first, second and third derivatives of f at any node of the lattice x_i are denoted by f_i', f_i'' and f_i''' respectively. Our aim is to fit the function f piecewise on each interval $[x_i, x_{i+1}]$ to the following cubic polynomial

$$f(x) = a_i + b_i x + c_i x^2 + d_i x^3, \qquad \text{for } x \in [x_i, x_{i+1}] \tag{4.29}$$

Taking the derivatives of the cubic polynomial we derive the following upper diagonal matrix equation

$$\begin{pmatrix} 1 & x_i & x_i^2 & x_i^3 \\ 0 & 1 & 2x_i & 3x_i^2 \\ 0 & 0 & 2 & 6x_i \\ 0 & 0 & 0 & 6 \end{pmatrix} \begin{pmatrix} a_i \\ b_i \\ c_i \\ d_i \end{pmatrix} = \begin{pmatrix} f_i \\ f_i' \\ f_i'' \\ f_i''' \end{pmatrix} \tag{4.30}$$

It remains to derive expressions for the derivatives. If we wish the fitted polynomial to be exact when the function f happens to be a cubic, then we have to be careful how we calculate the derivatives numerically. One choice is given as

$$f_i' = \frac{\frac{1}{6}(f_{i-2} - f_{i+2}) + \frac{4}{3}(f_{i+1} - f_{i-1})}{2\Delta} \tag{4.31}$$

$$f_i'' = \frac{(f_{i+1} - 2f_i + f_{i-1})}{\Delta^2} \tag{4.32}$$

$$f_i''' = \frac{(f_{i+2} - 2f_{i+1} + 2f_{i-1} - f_{i-2})}{2\Delta^3} \tag{4.33}$$

Note that the form of the derivatives means that we either have to introduce ghost grids points at $\{x_{-1}, x_0\}$ and $\{x_{N+1}, x_{N+2}\}$, or we only perform the fit on the sublattice $\{x_2, x_3, \ldots, x_{N-3}, x_{N-2}\}$. The following implementation from the ppf.math.piecewise_polynomial_fitting module performs the fitting on the sublattice and the solution of the upper diagonal system of linear equations is carried out by the solve_upper_diagonal_system function to be found in the ppf.math.linear_algebra module.

```python
def piecewise_cubic_fit(x, y):

    if len(x.shape) <> len(y.shape) and len(x.shape) <> 1:
        raise RuntimeError, "Mismatching 'x' and 'y' vectors"
    if x.shape[0] <> y.shape[0]:
        raise RuntimeError, "Mismatching 'x' and 'y' vectors"
    N = x.shape[0]
    if N < 4:
        raise RuntimeError, "Need at least 4 points"

    # assume uniform spacing
    one_sixth = 1.0/6.0
    four_thirds = 4.0/3.0
    dx_inv = 1.0/(x[1]-x[0])
    dx_inv2 = dx_inv*dx_inv
    dx_inv3 = dx_inv2*dx_inv
    coeffs = numpy.zeros((4, N - 4))

    a = numpy.zeros((4, 4))
    b = numpy.zeros(4)

    for i in range(2, N-2):
        # value
        b[0] = y[i]
        # first derivative
        b[1] = (one_sixth*(-y[i+2]+y[i-2])+four_thirds*(y[i+1]-y
                [i-1]))*0.5*dx_inv
        # second derivative
        b[2] = (y[i+1]-2.0*y[i]+y[i-1])*dx_inv2
        # third derivative
        b[3] = (y[i+2]-2.0*(y[i+1]-y[i-1])-y[i-2])*0.5*dx_inv3

        # fit matrix
        xi = x[i]
        xi2 = xi*xi
        xi3 = xi2*xi
        a[0][0] = 1.0
        a[0][1] = xi
        a[0][2] = xi2
        a[0][3] = xi3
        a[1][1] = 1.0
        a[1][2] = 2.0*xi
        a[1][3] = 3.0*xi2
        a[2][2] = 2.0
```

```
a[2][3] = 6.0*xi
a[3][3] = 6.0

tmp = solve_upper_diagonal_system(a, b)
for j in range(0, 4):
  coeffs[j, i-2] = tmp[j]

return coeffs
```

4.8.2 Piecewise Polynomial Integration

Every random variable induces a distribution on $\mathbb{R}^n$. In this section we assume that the distribution induced by the random variable X is normal. In the case of the normal distribution, the distribution is fully specified by two parameters: the mean μ and the volatility σ. Suppose we have a polynomial representation of our function f on the interval $[x_l, x_h]$, then the expectation of f restricted to this interval is given by

$$\int_{x_l}^{x_h} f(x)n(x)dx = \sum_{j=0}^{m} c_j \int_{x_l}^{x_h} x^j n(x)dx \tag{4.34}$$

$$= \sum_{j=0}^{m} c_j \left(\int_{-\infty}^{x_r} x^j n(x)dx - \int_{-\infty}^{x_l} x^j n(x)dx \right) \tag{4.35}$$

$$= \sum_{j=0}^{m} c_j \left(M_j(x_r) - M_j(x_l) \right) \tag{4.36}$$

with $M_j(y) := \int_{-\infty}^{y} x^j n(x)dx$ and $n(x)$ denotes the normal probability distribution function. The partial moments can be easily computed via the following recursion relationship:

$$M_0(y) =: N(y) \tag{4.37}$$
$$M_1(y) = -\sigma^2 n(y) + \mu M_0(y) \tag{4.38}$$
$$M_m(y) = \sigma^2 \left(-y^{m-1}n(y) + (m-1)M_{m-2} \right) + \mu M_{m-1} \tag{4.39}$$

with

$$n(y) = \frac{1}{\sqrt{2\pi}\sigma} \exp\left(-\frac{1}{2}\left(\frac{x-\mu}{\sigma}\right)^2 \right) \tag{4.40}$$

$$N(y) = \frac{1}{\sqrt{2\pi}\sigma} \int_0^y \exp\left(-\frac{1}{2}\left(\frac{x-\mu}{\sigma}\right)^2 \right)dx \tag{4.41}$$

The ppf.math.normal_distribution module contains an implementation of the integration of a piecewise polynomial function in a random variable with normal distribution. The method integral on the normal_distribution class carries out the integration.

```
class normal_distribution:
  def __init__(self, mean=0.0, vol=1.0):
    self.mean = mean
    self.vol = vol
    if vol < 0.0:
```

```
      raise RuntimeError, 'negative volatility'
    if vol <> 0.0:
      self.vol_inv = 1.0/vol
    else:
      self.vol_inv = 1.0;
    self.unit_norm = 1.0/math.sqrt(2.0*math.pi)

  def unit_pdf(self, x):
    return math.exp(-0.5*x*x)*self.unit_norm

  def pdf(self, x):
    y = x*self.vol_inv
    return self.unit_pdf(y)*self.vol_inv

  def unit_cdf(self, x):
    return N(x)

  def cdf(self, x):
    y = (x-self.mean)*self.vol_inv
    return self.unit_cdf(y)

  def moments(self, n, x):
    ys = (n)*[0.0]
    ys[0] = self.cdf(x)
    if n > 1:
      vol2 = self.vol*self.vol
      pdfx = self.pdf(x)
      ys[1] = -vol2*pdfx+self.mean*ys[0]
      xn = x
      for i in range(2, n):
        ys[i] = vol2*(-xn*pdfx+(i-1)*ys[i-2])+self.mean*ys[i-1]
        xn = xn*x
    return ys

  def integral(self, cs, xl, xh, yls = None, yhs = None):
    if xl > xh:
      raise RuntimeError, \
            "lower bound greater than upper bound of integration" \
            "domain"
    n = len(cs)
    if yls == None:
      yls = self.moments(n, xl)
    else:
      if len(yls) <> n:
        raise RuntimeError, \
              "number of moments doesn't match number of" \
              "coefficients"
    if yhs == None:
      yhs = self.moments(n, xh)
    else:
      if len(yhs) <> n:
```

```
        raise RuntimeError, \
            "number of moments doesn't match number of" \
            "coefficients"
    sum = 0.0
    for i in range(n):
      sum += cs[i]*(yhs[i]-yls[i])
    return sum

  def state(self, stddev, n):
    if n < 2:
      raise RuntimeError, 'number of points must be greater than one'
    s = numpy.zeros(n)
    dx = 2*stddev/(n-1)
    for i in range(n):
      s[i] = self.mean+self.vol*(-stddev+i*dx)
    return s
```

Now suppose we wish to calculate $\int_{x_l}^{x_h} \max(f(x), 0)n(x)dx$. We can rewrite this integral as $\int_{x_l}^{x_h} f(x)\mathbb{1}_{f(x)>0}n(x)dx$. In other words the original integral is a specialisation of the more general integral $\int_{x_l}^{x_h} f(x)\mathbb{1}_{g(x)>0}n(x)dx$. To calculate the more general integral we need to find the critical point x^* at which $g(x^*) = 0$. Assuming we have a piecewise polynomial representation of g, then the algorithm for finding the critical root is trivial. All we need to do is delegate to the cubic_roots function in the module ppf.math.cubic_roots to see if there are any real roots in the interval. The method __bounds_ on the normal_distribution class determines the corresponding subintervals from the roots.

```
class normal_distribution:
  def __bounds_(self, cs, xl, xh):
    # cubic coefficients
    n = len(cs)
    a = 0
    b = 0
    c = 0
    d = 0
    if n >= 1:
      d = cs[0]
    if n >= 2:
      c = cs[1]
    if n >= 3:
      b = cs[2]
    if n == 4:
      a = cs[3]
    if n > 4:
      raise RuntimeError, 'can only handle up to cubics'
    # roots
    roots = cubic_roots(a, b, c, d, xl, xh)
    bounds = []
    # calculate bounds
    xprev = xl
    for root in roots:
```

```
    xcurr = root
    xmid = 0.5*(xprev+xcurr)
    if d+xmid*(c+xmid*(b+xmid*a)) > 0:
      bounds.append([xprev, xcurr])
    xprev = xcurr
  xcurr = xh
  xmid = 0.5*(xprev+xcurr)
  if d+xmid*(c+xmid*(b+xmid*a)) > 0:
    bounds.append([xprev, xcurr])
  return bounds
```

Note that if there are real roots, then we loop through each of the roots and only add a subinterval if the function at the mid-point is positive. The actual integration then reduces to a loop over the bounds and is implemented in the method `integral_indicator`.

```
class normal_distribution:
  def integral_indicator(self, cs, indicator, xl, xh, yls = None,
                          yhs = None):
    '''
    >>> mean = 0.05
    >>> vol = 0.1
    >>> f = normal_distribution(mean, vol)
    >>> yls = f.moments(4, -1)
    >>> yhs = f.moments(4, 10000)
    >>> cs = [0.0,0.0,1.0,1.0]
    >>> print f.integral_indicator(cs, cs, -10000, 10000)
    0.014125
    >>> print cs[2]*(yhs[2]-yls[2])+cs[3]*(yhs[3]-yls[3])
    0.014125
    '''
    if xl > xh:
      raise RuntimeError, \
          "lower bound greater than upper bound of integration" \
          "domain"

    bounds = self.__bounds_(indicator, xl, xh)
    sum = 0
    for bound in bounds:
      xll = bound[0]
      xrr = bound[1]
      yll = None
      yrr = None
      if xll == xl:
        yll = yls
      if xrr == xh:
        yrr = yhs
      sum += self.integral(cs, xll, xrr, yll, yrr)
    return sum
```

We will discover later that it is often useful to regrid a piecewise polynomial representation onto another grid. The regridding algorithm is simple. Suppose we have a piecewise polynomial representation of f on the grid $\{x_2, x_3, \ldots, x_{N-3}, x_{N-2}\}$ and wish to regrid the function onto the grid $\{y_1, y_2, \ldots, y_{N-1}, y_N\}$. Then all we have to do is loop through each of the y_i's and determine the closest interval $[x_j, x_{j+1}]$ using the equal_range function from the ppf.utility.bound module. Once we have the closest interval we reconstruct the function at y_i by using the polynomial representation corresponding to the closest interval. The regrid method on the normal_distribution class is an implementation of the regridding algorithm.

```
class normal_distribution:
  def regrid(self, xs, cs, regrid_xs):
    m = len(xs)
    n = len(regrid_xs)
    # regrid function
    regrid_fs = numpy.zeros(n)
    for i in range(n):
      x = regrid_xs[i]
      # bound
      left, right = ppf.utility.equal_range(x, xs)
      if right == m: right -= 1
      if left == right: left -= 1
      idx = left
      # saturate
      if idx < 2: idx = 2
      if idx > m-3: idx = m-3
      csi = cs[:, idx-2]
      regrid_fs[i] = csi[0]+x*(csi[1]+x*(csi[2]+x*csi[3]))
    return regrid_fs
```

For completeness we also provide the method integral_max on the normal_distribution class. As expected, the calculation of the integral is performed by the integral_indicator.

```
class normal_distribution:
  def integral_max(self, cs, xl, xh, yls = None, yhs = None):
    '''
    >>> mean = 0.05
    >>> vol = 0.1
    >>> f = normal_distribution(mean, vol)
    >>> yls = f.moments(4, -1)
    >>> yhs = f.moments(4, 10000)
    >>> cs = [0.0,0.0,1.0,1.0]
    >>> print f.integral_max(cs, -10000, 10000)
    0.014125
    >>> print cs[2]*(yhs[2]-yls[2])+cs[3]*(yhs[3]-yls[3])
    0.014125
    '''
    if xl > xh:
    raise RuntimeError, \
          'lower bound greater than upper bound of integration domain'

    return self.integral_indicator(cs, cs, xl, xh, yls, yhs)
```

For reasons of optimum speed, we allow the client of the `normal_distribution` to supply precomputed moments at the integral bounds. By default, if the moments are not supplied, then the moments get calculated on the fly.

We conclude the section with a few sample calls onto the methods of the normal distribution class. First, we check that if the initial grid used in the fitting is identical to the regridding grid, then the regridded function should be the same as the original function. The following code snippet confirms this.

```
>>> mean = 0.05
>>> vol = 0.1
>>> f = normal_distribution(mean, vol)
>>> xs = f.state(4.5, 10)
>>> cs = numpy.zeros((4,6))
>>> for i in range(6): cs[:, i] = 1.0, 0.0, 1.0, 0.0
>>> regrid_fs = f.regrid(xs, cs, xs)
>>> for i in range(2, 8): print "%f, %f" % (regrid_fs[i]\
      , cs[0,i-2]+xs[i]*(cs[1,i-2]+xs[i]*(cs[2,i-2]+xs[i]*
                       cs[3,i-2])))
1.040000, 1.040000
1.010000, 1.010000
1.000000, 1.000000
1.010000, 1.010000
1.040000, 1.040000
1.090000, 1.090000
```

The next code snippet checks various limits of the `integral` method. First we check that the expectation of 1 is also 1. Second we check that the expectation of a normal variable X with mean 0.05 is equal to the mean. Finally we check the expectation of the square of the normal variable with mean 0.05 and volatility 0.1 is equal to the sum of the mean and the volatility squared.

```
>>> mean = 0.05
>>> vol = 0.1
>>> f = normal_distribution(mean, vol)
>>> cs = [1.0]
>>> print f.integral(cs, -10000, 10000)
1.0
>>> cs = [0.0,1.0]
>>> print f.integral(cs, -10000, 10000)
0.05
>>> cs = [0.0,0.0,1.0]
>>> print f.integral(cs, -10000, 10000)
0.0125
```

The final code snippet verifies that the expectation of $\max(X^2 + X^3, 0)$ is equivalent to $\int_{-1}^{\infty} (x^2 + x^3)n(x)dx$.

```
>>> mean = 0.05
>>> vol = 0.1
>>> f = normal_distribution(mean, vol)
>>> yls = f.moments(4, -1)
>>> yhs = f.moments(4, 10000)
```

```
>>> cs = [0.0,0.0,1.0,1.0]
>>> print f.integral_max(cs, -10000, 10000)
0.014125
>>> print cs[2]*(yhs[2]-yls[2])+cs[3]*(yhs[3]-yls[3])
0.014125
```

4.8.3   Semi-analytic Conditional Expectations

In the previous subsection we discussed how we can calculate the integral of a function of a normally distributed random variable by fitting the function piecewise to a polynomial. In this subsection we discuss how to use this integration scheme to compute conditional expectations. Throughout this section we denote the function of the one-dimensional Brownian motion[4] X_T by $y_T := f(X_T)$ and the filtration at time t by $\mathcal{F}_t$. A full mathematical definition of Brownian motion can be found in [16] but for the purposes of what follows all we need to know is that $X_T - X_t$ is independent of X_t for $t < T$ and is normally distributed with zero mean and variance $T - t$. The aim of this subsection is to explain how to compute the following conditional expectations:

$$y_t := \mathbb{E}[y_T|\mathcal{F}_t] \tag{4.42}$$

$$y_t^+ := \mathbb{E}[\max(y_T, 0)|\mathcal{F}_t] \tag{4.43}$$

Because the increments of a Brownian motion are independent of each other, the above conditional expectations can be written as

$$y_t(x) = \mathbb{E}[f(x + X_T - X_t)|x_t = x] \tag{4.44}$$

$$y_t^+(x) = \mathbb{E}[\max(f(x + X_T - X_t), 0)|x_t = x] \tag{4.45}$$

We donote the discrete grid of states for the Brownian motion increment $X_T - X_t$ by x_{tT}. If we fit the function f on the discrete grid of X_T, denoted by x_T, then $x + x_{tT}$ for $X_t = x$ will generally lie outside the domain of the discrete grid x_T. Therefore we are forced to regrid the function f. Fortunately we already know how to do this if the function f is fitted piecewise to a polynomial. In summary, the conditional expectations at $X_t = x$ are calculated in three steps: (a) given the piecewise polynomial fit of f on X_T regrid the function onto the grid $x + x_{tT}$; (b) fit the regridded f to a piecewise polynomial on the grid x_{tT}; and (c) use the integration schemes of the previous subsection to calculate the integrals. Obviously in a standard application of the algorithm, the steps are repeated for a discrete grid of X_t, denoted x_t.

The code for computing the conditional expectations can be found in the module `ppf.math.semi_analytic_domain_integrator` and is detailed below. The actual implementation of the conditional integrals is done by the private method `_rollback_`. To make this possible we are forced to pass through the regridder and integrator functions. In the case of the `rollback` method the integrator is simply the `integral` member function of the distribution class represented by `ftT`, and in the case of the `rollback_max` method the integrator is the `integral_max` member function of `ftT`.

```
class semi_analytic_domain_integrator:

    def __create_cached_moments(self, x, f):
```

---

[4] In 1828 the Scottish botanist Robert Brown observed that pollen grains suspended in liquid performed an irregular motion – Brownian motion.

```
    n = x.shape[0]
    self._ys = numpy.zeros([n, 4])
    self._ys[2] = f.moments(4, x[2]) # cubic
    for j in range(2, n-2):
      self._ys[j+1] = f.moments(4, x[j+1]) # cubic

def _rollback_(self, t, T, xt, xT, xtT, yT, regridder, integrator):
  if len(xt.shape) <> len(xT.shape) or \
     len(xT.shape) <> len(yT.shape) or \
     len(xt.shape) <> 1 or len(xtT.shape) <> 1:
    raise RuntimeError, 'expected one dimensional arrays'

  nt = xt.shape[0]
  nT = xT.shape[0]
  ntT = xtT.shape[0]

  if nt <> nT or ntT <> nT:
    raise RuntimeError, 'expected array to be of same size'

  if yT.shape[0] <> nT:
    raise RuntimeError, \
        'array yT has different number of points to xT'

  yt = numpy.zeros(nt)
  cT = piecewise_cubic_fit(xT, yT)
  for i in range(nt):
    # regrid
    regrid_xT = numpy.zeros(nT)
    xti = xt[i]
    for j in range(nT):
      regrid_xT[j] = xti+xtT[j]
    regrid_yT = regridder(xT, cT, regrid_xT)
    # polynomial fit
    cs = piecewise_cubic_fit(xtT, regrid_yT)
    # perform expectation
    sum = 0
    xl = xtT[2]
    for j in range(2, nT-2): # somehow this should be
                             enscapsulated
      xh = xtT[j+1]
      sum = sum + integrator(cs[:, j-2], xl, xh, self._ys[j],
          self._ys[j+1])
      xl = xh
    yt[i] = sum
    if t == 0.0:
      for j in range(1, nt):
        yt[j] = yt[0]
      break

  return yt
```

```
def rollback(self, t, T, xt, xT, xtT, ftT, yT):
  # create cache of moments
  self.__create_cached_moments(xtT, ftT)

  return self.__rollback_(t, T, xt, xT, xtT, yT, ftT.regrid,
                ftT.integral)
def rollback_max(self, t, T, xt, xT, xtT, ftT, yT):
  # create cache of moments
  self.__create_cached_moments(xtT, ftT)

  return self.__rollback_(t, T, xt, xT, xtT, yT, ftT.regrid,
                ftT.integral_max)
```

Note that we precompute the moments in the function __create_cached_moments() prior to performing the rollback. Doing this improves the efficiency of the algorithm dramatically because otherwise we keep computing (unnecessarily) the moments nt times. Typically nt ≈ 41, so you can see why we make such a huge computational saving by precomputing the moments.

A number of tests have been written for the semi-analytic domain integrator. The tests can be found in the module ppf.test.test_math with each separate test represented by a method of the class integrator_tests. The first test checks that we can perform the conditional expectation of the following classical exponential martingale correctly[5]:

$$y_T = \exp\left(\sigma X_T - \frac{1}{2}\sigma^2 T\right) \tag{4.46}$$

with $\sigma \in \mathbb{R}^+$. Because we know y_T is a martingale the following identity must hold.

$$\mathbb{E}[y_T|\mathcal{F}_t] = \exp\left(\sigma X_t - \frac{1}{2}\sigma^2 t\right) \tag{4.47}$$

The snippet of code below gives the details of the test just described.

```
def lognormal_martingale_test(self):
  integrator = ppf.math.semi_analytic_domain_integrator()
  nt = 31
  nT = 31
  ntT = 31
  t = 0.5
  T = 1.0
  mut = 0.0
  muT = 0.0
  vol = 0.2
  volt = vol*math.sqrt(t)
  volT = vol*math.sqrt(T)
  ft = ppf.math.normal_distribution(mut, volt)
  fT = ppf.math.normal_distribution(muT, volT)
  xt = ft.state(5.5, nt)
  xT = fT.state(5.5, nT)
```

---

[5] A martingale M_t is a random variable satisfying the properties: $\mathbb{E}[|M_t|] > \infty$ for all t and $\mathbb{E}[M_t|\mathcal{F}_t] = M_s$ for $s \le t$.

```
    meantT = muT-mut
    voltT = math.sqrt(volT*volT-volt*volt)
    ftT = ppf.math.normal_distribution(meantT, voltT)
    xtT = ftT.state(5.5, ntT)
    yT = numpy.zeros(nT)
    for i in range(nT):
      yT[i] = math.exp(xT[i]-0.5*volT*volT) # lognormal martingale
    yt = integrator.rollback(t, T, xt, xT, xtT, ftT, yT)
    assert math.fabs(yt[15] - 0.990050) < 1.0e-6
```

The second test verifies that the tower law holds, i.e.

$$\mathbb{E}[y_T|\mathcal{F}_s] = \mathbb{E}[\mathbb{E}[y_T|\mathcal{F}_t]\mathcal{F}_s] \text{ for } s \leq t \leq T. \tag{4.48}$$

The following code snippet provides the details of the tower law test.

```
def tower_law_test(self):
    integrator = ppf.math.semi_analytic_domain_integrator()
    nt = 31
    nT = 31
    ntT = 31
    t = 0.5
    T = 1.0
    mut = 0.0
    muT = 0.0
    vol = 0.2
    volt = vol*math.sqrt(t)
    volT = vol*math.sqrt(T)
    ft = ppf.math.normal_distribution(mut, volt)
    fT = ppf.math.normal_distribution(muT, volT)
    xt = ft.state(5.5, nt)
    xT = fT.state(5.5, nT)
    meantT = muT-mut
    voltT = math.sqrt(volT*volT-volt*volt)
    ftT = ppf.math.normal_distribution(meantT, voltT)
    xtT = ftT.state(5.5, ntT)
    yT = numpy.zeros(nT)
    for i in range(nT):
      yT[i] = math.exp(xT[i]-0.5*volT*volT) # lognormal martingale
    yt = integrator.rollback(t, T, xt, xT, xtT, ftT, yT)
    ns = 31
    s = 0
    mus = 0.0
    vols = 0.0
    fs = ppf.math.normal_distribution(mus, vols)
    xs = fs.state(5.5, ns)
    meansT = muT-mus
    volsT = math.sqrt(volT*volT-vols*vols)
    fsT = ppf.math.normal_distribution(meansT, volsT)
    xsT = fsT.state(5.5, ntT)
    ys = integrator.rollback(s, T, xs, xT, xsT, fsT, yT)
    meanst = mut-mus
```

```
volst = math.sqrt(volt*volt-vols*vols)
fst = ppf.math.normal_distribution(meanst, volst)
xst = fst.state(5.5, ntT)
ys1 = integrator.rollback(s, t, xs, xt, xst, fst, yt)
for i in range(ns):
  assert math.fabs(ys[i]-ys1[i]) < 1.0e-6
```

Lastly, the third test verifies that the value of the at-the-money option price satisfies the relation

$$\mathbb{E}[\max(y_T - 1, 0)] = 2N(d_1) - 1 \qquad (4.49)$$

with $N(x)$ the cumulative distribution function of the normal distribution with zero mean and volatility σ and

$$d_1 = \frac{\sigma \sqrt{T}}{2} \qquad (4.50)$$

The code snippet below provides the details of the at-the-money option test.

```
def atm_option_test(self):
  integrator = ppf.math.semi_analytic_domain_integrator()
  nT = 31
  t = 0.5
  T = 1.0
  mut = 0.0
  muT = 0.0
  vol = 0.2
  volt = vol*math.sqrt(t)
  volT = vol*math.sqrt(T)
  fT = ppf.math.normal_distribution(muT, volT)
  xT = fT.state(5.5, nT)
  yT = numpy.zeros(nT)
  for i in range(nT):
    yT[i] = math.exp(xT[i]-0.5*volT*volT) # lognormal martingale
  ns = 31
  nsT = 31
  s = 0
  mus = 0.0
  vols = 0.0
  fs = ppf.math.normal_distribution(mus, vols)
  xs = fs.state(5.5, ns)
  meansT = muT-mus
  volsT = math.sqrt(volT*volT-vols*vols)
  fsT = ppf.math.normal_distribution(meansT, volsT)
  xsT = fsT.state(5.5, nsT)
  for i in range(nT):
    yT[i] -= 1.0 # strike 1.0
  ys = integrator.rollback_max(s, T, xs, xT, xsT, fsT, yT)
  d1 = 0.5*volT
  for i in range(ns):
    assert math.fabs(ys[i] - (2.0*fsT.unit_cdf(d1)-1.0)) < 1.0e-4
```

## 5

Market: Curves and Surfaces

A financial market is made up out of lots of pieces of information. For example, foreign exchange rates, equity spot prices, yield curves, volatility surfaces and correlation surfaces, to name a few. In this chapter we discuss simple classes for representing curves and surfaces provided in the ppf.market subpackage. The chapter is concluded with a discussion of the market environment which is designed to represent a financial market.

5.1 CURVES

Fundamentally, without regard to the specific market variable being modelled (e.g. discount factors, forward rates, volatilities at a fixed strike and expiry for a range of tenors), a curve is the association between a set of points at which the function is known (abscissae), the known function values at those points (ordinates) and an interpolation algorithm for estimating the value of the function between the known abscissae. Utilisation of the interpolation algorithms presented in section 4.3 deals with the 'heavy lifting' of curve representation. From the ppf.market.curve module we have the simple curve

```
class curve:
  def __init__(self, times, factors, interp):
    self.__impl = interp(times, factors)
  def __call__(self, t): return self.__impl(t)
```

The following interpreter transcript (simulating a discount factor curve) shows how easily a curve can be modelled by these components:

```
>>> import math
>>> from ppf.math.interpolation import loglinear
>>> times = range(0, 22)
>>> factors = [math.exp(-0.05*T) for T in times]
>>> P = curve(times, factors, loglinear)
>>> for t in times: print P(t)
1.0
0.951229424501
0.904837418036
0.860707976425
0.818730753078
0.778800783071
0.740818220682
0.704688089719
0.670320046036
0.637628151622
0.606530659713
0.57694981038
0.548811636094
```

```
0.522045776761
0.496585303791
0.472366552741
0.449328964117
0.427414931949
0.406569659741
0.386741023455
0.367879441171
0.349937749111
```

5.2 SURFACES

A surface is the common name ascribed to a model of a multivariabled function. In the interest of brevity, we restrict our attention to modelling functions in just two variables $f = f(x, y)$. The ppf.market.surface module offers the class surface for their representation, which is associated with the commonly encountered bilinear–interpolation scheme that relies on the ppf.utility.bound function (refer to section 4.3):

```python
import ppf.utility

class surface:
  def __init__(self, first_axis, second_axis, values):
    self.__first_axis = first_axis
    self.__second_axis = second_axis
    self.__values = values

  def __call__(self, x, y):
    i1, i2 = ppf.utility.bound(x, self.__first_axis)
    j1, j2 = ppf.utility.bound(y, self.__second_axis)
    f = self.__values
    x1 = self.__first_axis[i1]
    x2 = self.__first_axis[i2]
    y1 = self.__second_axis[j1]
    y2 = self.__second_axis[j2]
    r = (x2 - x1)*(y2 - y1)
    return (f[i1, j1]/r)*(x2 - x)*(y2 - y) + \
           (f[i2, j1]/r)*(x - x1)*(y2 - y) + \
           (f[i1, j2]/r)*(x2 - x)*(y - y1) + \
           (f[i2, j2]/r)*(x - x1)*(y - y1)
```

The ppf.test.test_market module provides us with an example of using instances of this type for surface representation, in this case an expiry-tenor volatility surface:

```python
class surface_tests(unittest.TestCase):
  def test(self):
    from ppf.date_time import date
    from ppf.date_time import months
    from ppf.date_time import Feb, Apr, Jul, Oct, Jan
    from numpy import zeros

    expiries = [
      date(2006, Feb, 11)
```

```
    , date(2006, Apr, 11)
    , date(2006, Jul, 11)
    , date(2006, Oct, 11)
    , date(2007, Jan, 11)
    , date(2008, Jan, 11)
    , date(2009, Jan, 11)
    , date(2010, Jan, 11)
    , date(2011, Jan, 11)
    , date(2012, Jan, 11)
    , date(2013, Jan, 11) ]

tenors = [ months(12), months(24), months(36) ]

vols = zeros((len(expiries), len(tenors)))
# expiry, tenor surface                        1y      2y     3y
vols[ 0, 0], vols[ 0, 1], vols[ 0, 2] = 200.00, 76.25, 64.00 # 1m
vols[ 1, 0], vols[ 1, 1], vols[ 1, 2] =  98.50, 84.75, 69.00 # 3m
vols[ 2, 0], vols[ 2, 1], vols[ 2, 2] =  98.00, 81.75, 68.00 # 6m
vols[ 3, 0], vols[ 3, 1], vols[ 3, 2] = 101.25, 82.25, 69.25 # 9m
vols[ 4, 0], vols[ 4, 1], vols[ 4, 2] = 106.00, 82.00, 69.25 # 1y
vols[ 5, 0], vols[ 5, 1], vols[ 5, 2] =  78.75, 73.25, 61.25 # 2y
vols[ 6, 0], vols[ 6, 1], vols[ 6, 2] =  66.25, 59.00, 50.00 # 3y
vols[ 7, 0], vols[ 7, 1], vols[ 7, 2] =  55.25, 47.75, 41.75 # 4y
vols[ 8, 0], vols[ 8, 1], vols[ 8, 2] =  44.75, 40.25, 35.50 # 5y
vols[ 9, 0], vols[ 9, 1], vols[ 9, 2] =  32.00, 30.50, 28.25 # 6y
vols[10, 0], vols[10, 1], vols[10, 2] =  26.50, 24.25, 24.25 # 7y

base = date(2006, Jan, 11);
sig = ppf.market.surface(
      [int(t - base)/365.0 for t in expiries]
    , [m.number_of_months().as_number() for m in tenors]
    , vols)

tol=1.0e-8
for i in range(len(expiries)):
  expiry = expiries[i]
  t = int(expiry - base)/365.0
  for j in range(len(tenors)):
    tenor = tenors[j]
    T = tenor.number_of_months().as_number()
    assert math.fabs(sig(t, T) - vols[i, j]) <= tol
```

5.3 ENVIRONMENT

For the purposes of pricing it is often convenient to aggregate all the different pieces of market data (e.g. curves and surfaces) into a single container. The class environment from ppf.market.environment provides us with a simple container for all the bits of market data. In addition, the class is also the single point of access to the market data for the pricing models. As well as containing surfaces and curves, the environment contains constants. An example of a constant could be the speed of mean reversion used in the Hull–White model to control terminal correlation.

An environment is constructed with a pricing date and pieces of market data are added to it using the add methods. Each piece of data is stored against a unique key which is later used to retrieve the data via the retrieve methods. Typically in a fully productionised pricing framework, there would be another level of indirection to insulate clients of the libraries from the internal representation of the market data keys. Or, more specifically, one would write environment factories taking in a dictionary of market data against the physical names and map the physical names to the market data keys.

```python
import ppf.date_time

class environment:
  def __init__(self, pd = ppf.date_time.date(2008, 01, 01)):
    self.pd = pd
    self.curves = {}
    self.surfaces = {}
    self.constants = {}

  def pricing_date(self):
    return self.pd

  def relative_date(self, d):
    ret = ppf.date_time.days.days(d-self.pd)
    if ret < 0:
      raise RuntimeError, 'date before pricing date'
    return ret

  def add_curve(self, key, curve):
    if self.curves.has_key(key):
      del self.curves[key]
    self.curves[key] = curve

  def add_surface(self, key, surface):
    if self.surfaces.has_key(key):
      del self.surfaces[key]
    self.surfaces[key] = surface

  def add_constant(self, key, constant):
    if self.constants.has_key(key):
      del self.constants[key]
    self.constants[key] = constant

  def has_curve(self, key):
    return self.curves.has_key(key)

  def has_surface(self, key):
    return self.surfaces.has_key(key)

  def has_constant(self, key):
    return self.constants.has_key(key)

  def retrieve_curve(self, key):
```

```
      if not self.has_curve(key):
        raise RuntimeError, 'unable to find curve'
      return self.curves[key]

  def retrieve_surface(self, key):
      if not self.has_surface(key):
        raise RuntimeError, 'unable to find surface'
      return self.surfaces[key]

  def retrieve_constant(self, key):
      if not self.has_constant(key):
        raise RuntimeError, 'unable to find constant'
      return self.constants[key]
```

Later chapters will make use of instances of class environment constantly. An example from the ppf.test.test_hull_white module should suffice to give an idea of its usage for now:

```
class fill_tests(unittest.TestCase):
  def test_numeraire_rebased_bond(self):
    env = ppf.market.environment()
    times = numpy.linspace(0, 2, 5)
    factors = numpy.array([math.exp(-0.05*t) for t in times])
    env.add_curve("zc.disc.eur"
      , ppf.market.curve(times, factors, ppf.math.interpolation.
      loglinear))
    expiries, tenors = [0.1, 0.5, 1.0, 1.5, 2.0, 3.0, 4.0, 5.0], [0, 90]
    env.add_surface("ve.term.eur.hw"
                , ppf.market.surface(expiries, tenors, numpy.zeros
                ((8, 2))))
    env.add_constant("cv.mr.eur.hw", 0.0)
    r = ppf.model.hull_white.requestor()
    s = ppf.model.hull_white.lattice.state(11, 3.5)
    sx = s.fill("eur", 0.25, r, env)
    f = ppf.model.hull_white.fill(2.0)
    PtT = f.numeraire_rebased_bond(0.25, 1.5, "eur", env, r, sx)
    exp = \
        [1.02531512052
        ,1.02531512052
        ,1.02531512052
        ,1.02531512052
        ,1.02531512052
        ,1.02531512052
        ,1.02531512052
        ,1.02531512052
        ,1.02531512052
        ,1.02531512052
        ,1.02531512052]

  _assert_seq_close(exp, PtT)
```

## 6

Data Model

As noted in Chapter 1, writing programs for financial modelling involves more than numerical analysis alone. Designing a trade representation is a case in point and the focus of this chapter. From experience, if we get the design of the trade description correct, then the rest of the analytical framework falls naturally into place.

In finance a financial contract is commonly called a trade. Trades are built from legs and exercise schedules. A leg is a collection of cash flows, simply referred to as flows, and each cash flow can depend upon an arbitrary number of market observables. An exercise schedule is a collection of exercise decisions, simply referred to as exercises. Each exercise decision represents the right to either call or cancel the trade on a particular date. In the following sections we will go through each of these building blocks in turn, starting with observables.

6.1 OBSERVABLES

As mentioned already, the cash flows of a financial instrument depend upon the values of market observables. Examples of market observables are (i) the spot price of an asset (e.g. stock, index or commodity), (ii) the fixing of an interest rate (e.g. LIBOR)[1] or (iii) the measured rainfall over a certain period in a given location. Associated with an observable is its time of observation, normally called its reset date. Before the reset date, the observable isn't known and has to be estimated but on the reset date the market publishes a value for the observable. An observable with a reset date in the past is deemed to have been *fixed*. The ppf.core.fixing module encapsulates this simple idea:

```
class fixing:
  def __init__(self, is_fixed=False, value=None):
    self._is_fixed = is_fixed
    self._value = value
  def is_fixed(self): return self._is_fixed
  def value(self): return self._value
```

While the universe of observables is rich and varied, all observables have some properties in common. The class observable from the ppf.core.observable module encodes these common properties:

```
class observable:
  def __init__(self
              , attributes
              , flow_id
              , reset_id
              , reset_ccy
              , reset_date
```

---

[1] LIBOR is discussed in section 6.1.1.

```
                , last_important_date
                , fix
                , spread):
        self.__attributes = attributes
        self.__flow_id = flow_id
        self.__reset_id = reset_id
        self.__reset_ccy = reset_ccy
        self.__reset_date = reset_date
        self.__last_important_date = last_important_date
        self.__fix = fix
        self.__spread = spread
    def flow_id(self): return self.__flow_id
    def reset_id(self): return self.__reset_id
    def reset_currency(self): return self.__reset_ccy
    def reset_date(self): return self.__reset_date
    def last_important_date(self): return self.__last_important_date
    def spread(self): return self.__spread
    def fix(self) : return self.__fix
    def attributes(self) : return self.__attributes
```

Associated with every observable is a flow id, a reset id, a reset currency, a reset date, a last important date, a fixing and a spread. The flow id refers to the index of the flow in a sequence of flows that is associated with the observable. The reset id refers to the index of the observable in the collection of observables associated with the referenced flow. The reset currency can be a traded currency such as USD for an interest rate observable, or a pair of currencies such as GBPUSD for a foreign exchange observable, or the currency associated with an equity index such as EUR for DAX. The reset date represents the date of observation. If the date of observation is in the past, then the observable will require a fixing. In the event that the fixing is missing, a runtime exception will be raised in the ppf pricing framework. The last important date is typically equal to the reset date, but for some observables, such as swap rates, it represents the last important date required to be known in order to calculate its value. It is not uncommon for a financial transaction to be dependent on the value of an observable plus or minus a spread, which explains the presence of the last parameter in the constructor. The first parameter of the constructor, attributes, is for future extension: In section 6.1.2 we will encounter a concrete use case for the attributes parameter.

In the following two subsections we present two examples of market observables.

6.1.1 LIBOR

In the world of interest rate trading, one frequently observed quantity on which a payoff may depend is the LIBOR[2] rate. The class libor in module ppf.core.libor_rate offers an implementation of the LIBOR observable. The libor_rate constructor takes in the properties common to all observables plus the projection start and end date together with the projection basis. The projection period, defined by the difference between the projection end date and start date, determines the period over which the LIBOR rate is to apply. As an example, for GBP LIBOR the projection period is six months. Furthermore, there is usually a

---

[2] London Interbank Offer Rate – a daily reference rate on which banks in the London money market offer to lend each other unsecured funds.

lag between the date on which the rate is set and the beginning of the projection period. Once again, as an example, for GBP LIBOR the lag is two business days.

```
from ppf.date_time import year_fraction
from fixing import *
from observable import *

class libor_rate(observable):
  def __init__(self
                , attributes
                , flow_id
                , reset_id
                , reset_date
                , reset_currency
                , proj_start_date
                , proj_end_date
                , proj_basis
                , fix
                , spread=None):
    observable.__init__(self
                        , attributes
                        , flow_id
                        , reset_id
                        , reset_currency
                        , reset_date
                        , proj_end_date
                        , fix
                        , spread)
    self.__proj_start_date = proj_start_date
    self.__proj_end_date = proj_end_date
    self.__proj_basis = proj_basis

  def proj_start_date(self): return self.__proj_start_date
  def proj_end_date(self): return self.__proj_end_date
  def proj_basis(self): return self.__proj_basis

  def year_fraction(self):
    return year_fraction(self.__proj_start_date
                         , self.__proj_end_date
                         , self.__proj_basis)

  def __str__(self):
      s = "%d, " %  self.flow_id()
      s += "%d, " % self.reset_id()
      s += "%s, " % self.reset_currency()
      s += "[%s, %s], " % (self.__proj_start_date, self.__proj_end_date)
      s += "%s, " % day_count_basis_strings[self.__proj_basis]
      fix = self.fix()
      if fix.is_fixed():
          s += "%f, " % fix.value()
      spread = self.spread()
```

```
      if spread <> None:
         s += "%f, " % spread
      return s
```

For completeness the `libor_rate` class provides a method `forward` for determining the value of the LIBOR rate at a particular point in time.

```
class libor_rate(observable):
  def forward(self, t, curve):
    fix = self.fix()
    if fix.is_fixed():
      return fix.value()

    start = self.__proj_start_date
    until = self.__proj_end_date
    Ts, Te = (int(start - t)/365.0, int(until - t)/365.0)
    Ps, Pe = (curve(Ts), curve(Te))
    dcf = year_fraction(start, until, self.__proj_basis)
    forward = (Ps/Pe-1.0)/dcf

    return forward
```

In practice, it is frequently necessary to generate collections of LIBOR observables. Accordingly the `ppf.core.generate_observables` module offers the function `generate_libor_observables()` for this purpose.

```
def generate_libor_observables(
    start
  , end
  , roll_period = 6
  , roll_duration = ppf.date_time.months
  , reset_period = 6
  , reset_duration = ppf.date_time.months
  , tenor_period = 6
  , tenor_duration = ppf.date_time.months
  , reset_currency = "USD"
  , reset_basis = ppf.date_time.basis_act_360
  , reset_holiday_centres = None
  , reset_shift_method = ppf.date_time.modified_following
  , reset_lag = 0
  , *arguments
  , **keywords):
  from ppf.date_time import days
  shift = ppf.date_time.shift

  if reset_lag > 0:
    raise RuntimeError, "index lag expected less or equal to zero"

  day, flow_id, all_observables = 0, 0, []
  while day < end:
      roll_start = start + roll_duration(flow_id*roll_period)
      roll_end = start + roll_duration((flow_id+1)*roll_period)
```

```
        reset_id = 0
        proj_roll = roll_start
        observables = []
        while proj_roll < roll_end:
                proj_start = shift(
                        proj_roll
                    , reset_shift_method, reset_holiday_centres)
                proj_end = shift(
                        proj_roll+tenor_duration(tenor_period)
                    , reset_shift_method, reset_holiday_centres)
                reset_date = shift(
                        proj_start+days(reset_lag)
                    , reset_shift_method, reset_holiday_centres)
                observables.append(
                        libor_rate(None, flow_id,  reset_id, reset_date
                            , reset_currency, proj_start, proj_end
                            , reset_basis, fixing(False)))
                reset_id += 1
                proj_roll = roll_start+reset_duration(reset_id*reset
                        _period)
        day = roll_end
        all_observables.append(observables)
        flow_id += 1

    return all_observables
```

Here is an example of generate_libor_observables() in use.

```
>>> observables = generate_libor_observables(
...     start = date(2007, Jun, 29)
...     , end = date(2012, Jun, 29)
...     , roll_period = 6
...     , roll_duration = ppf.date_time.months
...     , reset_period = 3
...     , reset_duration = ppf.date_time.months
...     , tenor_period = 3
...     , tenor_duration = ppf.date_time.months
...     , reset_currency = "JPY"
...     , reset_basis = basis_act_360
...     , reset_shift_method = shift_convention.modified_following)
>>> for obs_per_flow in observables:
...   for obs in obs_per_flow:
...     print obs
0, 0, JPY, [2007-Jun-29, 2007-Sep-28], basis_act_360,
0, 1, JPY, [2007-Sep-28, 2007-Dec-31], basis_act_360,
1, 0, JPY, [2007-Dec-31, 2008-Mar-31], basis_act_360,
1, 1, JPY, [2008-Mar-31, 2008-Jun-30], basis_act_360,
2, 0, JPY, [2008-Jun-30, 2008-Sep-29], basis_act_360,
2, 1, JPY, [2008-Sep-29, 2008-Dec-29], basis_act_360,
3, 0, JPY, [2008-Dec-29, 2009-Mar-30], basis_act_360,
3, 1, JPY, [2009-Mar-30, 2009-Jun-29], basis_act_360,
```

```
4, 0, JPY, [2009-Jun-29, 2009-Sep-29], basis_act_360,
4, 1, JPY, [2009-Sep-29, 2009-Dec-29], basis_act_360,
5, 0, JPY, [2009-Dec-29, 2010-Mar-29], basis_act_360,
5, 1, JPY, [2010-Mar-29, 2010-Jun-29], basis_act_360,
6, 0, JPY, [2010-Jun-29, 2010-Sep-29], basis_act_360,
6, 1, JPY, [2010-Sep-29, 2010-Dec-29], basis_act_360,
7, 0, JPY, [2010-Dec-29, 2011-Mar-29], basis_act_360,
7, 1, JPY, [2011-Mar-29, 2011-Jun-29], basis_act_360,
8, 0, JPY, [2011-Jun-29, 2011-Sep-29], basis_act_360,
8, 1, JPY, [2011-Sep-29, 2011-Dec-29], basis_act_360,
9, 0, JPY, [2011-Dec-29, 2012-Mar-29], basis_act_360,
9, 1, JPY, [2012-Mar-29, 2012-Jun-29], basis_act_360,
```

The sample invocation above has generated a sequence of LIBOR rate observables. The sequence has been generated such that there are two observables per flow, each with a projection period of three months and reset date equal to the projection start date.

6.1.2   Swap Rate

Like the LIBOR rate of section 6.1.1, another commonly observed quantity in interest rate structures is the swap rate. To calculate the value of the swap rate we need to have a description of the two legs making up the swap. The fixed leg is simply a collection of flows paying a fixed coupon at regular intervals. Similarly the funding leg is a collection of flows paying LIBOR at regular intervals. We will properly define *flows* in section 6.2 but, for now, we simply assume the existence of a class flow and function generate_flows(). The class swap_rate in module ppf.core.swap_rate provides an implementation of the swap rate. The constructor signature is identical to that of the libor_rate constructor. The attributes constructor parameter is expected to be a Python dictionary and is used to store information relating to the fixed and funding legs making up the swap. The constructor invokes the __generate() method which uses the information contained in that dictionary together with the projection start and end dates to generate the underlying legs of the swap.

```python
from fixing import *
from observable import *
from generate_flows import *
from generate_observables import *

class swap_rate(observable):
  def __init__(self
               , attributes
               , flow_id
               , reset_id
               , reset_date
               , reset_ccy
               , proj_start_date
               , proj_end_date
               , fix
               , spread=None):
    observable.__init__(self
                        , attributes
```

```
                             , flow_id
                             , reset_id
                             , reset_ccy
                             , reset_date
                             , proj_end_date
                             , fix
                             , spread)
         self._proj_start_date = proj_start_date
         self._proj_end_date = proj_end_date
         self._generate()

      def proj_start_date(self): return self._proj_start_date
      def proj_end_date(self): return self._proj_end_date
      def fixed_pay_basis(self) : return self._fixed_pay_basis
      def float_pay_basis(self) : return self._float_pay_basis
      def proj_basis(self): return self._proj_basis
      def fixed_flows(self): return self._fixed_flows
      def float_flows(self): return self._float_flows

      def _generate(self):
         start = self._proj_start_date
         until = self._proj_end_date
         attributes = self.attributes()

         fixed_period = attributes["fixed-pay-period"]
         fixed_period_duration = attributes["fixed-pay-period-duration"]
         fixed_pay_basis = attributes["fixed-pay-basis"]
         fixed_pay_holiday_centres = attributes["fixed-pay-holiday-"
                                 "centres"]
         fixed_shift_convention = attributes["fixed-shift-convention"]
         float_period = attributes["float-pay-period"]
         float_period_duration = attributes["float-pay-period-duration"]
         float_pay_basis = attributes["float-pay-basis"]
         float_pay_holiday_centres = attributes["float-pay-holiday-"
                                 "centres"]
         float_shift_convention = attributes["float-shift-convention"]

         libor_basis = attributes["index-basis"]
         libor_holiday_centres = attributes["index-holiday-centres"]
         libor_shift_convention = attributes["index-shift-convention"]

         self._fixed_flows = \
            generate_flows(start
                      , until
                      , period = fixed_period
                      , duration = fixed_period_duration
                      , pay_shift_method = fixed_shift_convention
                      , pay_currency = self.reset_currency()
                      , pay_basis = fixed_pay_basis
                      , pay_holiday_centres = fixed_pay_holiday_centres
                      , accrual_shift_method = fixed_shift_convention
```

```
                    , accrual_holiday_centres = \
                        fixed_pay_holiday_centres)
    libor_observables = \
        generate_libor_observables(
                        start
                    , until
                    , roll_period = float_period
                    , roll_duration = float_period_duration
                    , reset_period = float_period
                    , reset_duration = float_period_duration
                    , tenor_period = float_period
                    , tenor_duration = float_period_duration
                    , reset_currency = self.reset_currency()
                    , reset_basis = libor_basis
                    , reset_holiday_centres = libor_holiday_centres
                    , reset_shift_method = libor_shift_convention)
    self.__float_flows = \
        generate_flows(start
                    , until
                    , period = float_period
                    , duration = float_period_duration
                    , pay_shift_method = float_shift_convention
                    , pay_currency = self.reset_currency()
                    , pay_basis = float_pay_basis
                    , pay_holiday_centres = float_pay_holiday_centres
                    , accrual_shift_method = float_shift_convention
                    , accrual_holiday_centres = \
                        float_pay_holiday_centres
                    , observables = libor_observables)

  def __str__(self):
    s = "%d, " % self.flow_id()
    s += "%d, " % self.reset_id()
    s += "%s, " % self.reset_currency()
    s += "[%s, %s], " % (self.__proj_start_date, self.__proj_end_date)
    return s
```

Once again for completeness the swap_rate class provides a method forward for determining the value of the swap rate at a particular point in time.

```
class swap_rate(observable):
  def forward(self, t, curve):
    fund_pv = 0
    for f in self.__float_flows:
      obs = f.observables()[0]
      proj_start, proj_end, reset_accrual_dcf = \
          (obs.proj_start_date(), obs.proj_end_date(),
           obs.year_fraction())
      dfs, dfe = \
          curve(int(proj_start - t)/365.0), curve(int(proj_end
          - t)/365.0)
```

```
      libor = (dfs/dfe - 1.0)/reset_accrual_dcf
      pay_date, accrual_dcf = (f.pay_date(), f.year_fraction())
      dfp = curve(int(pay_date - t)/365.0)
      fund_pv += dfp*libor*accrual_dcf

    fixed_pv = 0
    for f in self.__fixed_flows:
      pay_date, accrual_dcf = (f.pay_date(), f.year_fraction())
      dfp = curve(int(pay_date - t)/365.0)
      fixed_pv += dfp*accrual_dcf

    return fund_pv/fixed_pv
```

Like the `generate_libor_observables()` function of section 6.1.1, a function for generating a sequence of swap rate observables, `generate_swap_observables()`, can be found in the `ppf.core.generate_observables` module.

```
def generate_swap_observables(
    start
  , end
  , attributes
  , spread = 0
  , roll_period = 6
  , roll_duration = ppf.date_time.months
  , tenor_period = 10
  , tenor_duration = ppf.date_time.years
  , reset_currency = "USD"
  , reset_basis = ppf.date_time.basis_act_360
  , reset_holiday_centres = None
  , reset_shift_method = ppf.date_time.modified_following
  , reset_lag = 0
  , *arguments
  , **keywords):
  from ppf.date_time import days
  shift = ppf.date_time.shift

  if reset_lag > 0:
    raise RuntimeError, "index lag expected less or equal to zero"

  day, flow_id, all_observables = 0, 0, []
  while day < end:
    roll_start = start + roll_duration(flow_id*roll_period)
    roll_end = start + roll_duration((flow_id+1)*roll_period)
    reset_id = 0
    proj_roll = roll_start
    proj_start = \
      shift(
          proj_roll
        , reset_shift_method
        , reset_holiday_centres
        )
```

```
      proj_end = \
        shift(
              proj_roll+tenor_duration(tenor_period)
            , reset_shift_method, reset_holiday_centres
            )
      reset_date = \
        shift(
              proj_start+days(reset_lag)
            , reset_shift_method, reset_holiday_centres
            )
      all_observables.append(
        swap_rate(
              attributes
            , flow_id
            , reset_id
            , reset_date
            , reset_currency
            , proj_start
            , proj_end
            , fixing(False)
            , spread) )
      flow_id += 1; reset_id += 1; day = roll_end

  return all_observables
```

The following is an example session demonstrating the generation of a sequence of swap rate observables.

```
>>> props = {}
>>> props["fixed-pay-period"] = 1
>>> props["fixed-pay-period-duration"] = years
>>> props["fixed-pay-basis"] = basis_act_360
>>> props["fixed-pay-holiday-centres"] = None
>>> props["fixed-shift-convention"] = modified_following
>>> props["float-pay-period"] = 6
>>> props["float-pay-period-duration"] = months
>>> props["float-pay-basis"] = basis_act_365
>>> props["float-pay-holiday-centres"] = None
>>> props["float-shift-convention"] = modified_following
>>> props["index-basis"] = basis_act_365
>>> props["index-holiday-centres"] = None
>>> props["index-shift-convention"] = modified_following
>>> observables = generate_swap_observables(
...       start = date(2007, Jun, 29)
...     , end = date(2017, Jun, 29)
...     , attributes = props
...     , roll_period = 1
...     , roll_duration = years
...     , tenor_period = 10
...     , tenor_duration = years)
>>> for o in observables: print o
```

```
0, 0, USD, [2007-Jun-29, 2017-Jun-29],
1, 0, USD, [2008-Jun-30, 2018-Jun-29],
2, 0, USD, [2009-Jun-29, 2019-Jun-28],
3, 0, USD, [2010-Jun-29, 2020-Jun-29],
4, 0, USD, [2011-Jun-29, 2021-Jun-29],
5, 0, USD, [2012-Jun-29, 2022-Jun-29],
6, 0, USD, [2013-Jun-28, 2023-Jun-29],
7, 0, USD, [2014-Jun-30, 2024-Jun-28],
8, 0, USD, [2015-Jun-29, 2025-Jun-30],
9, 0, USD, [2016-Jun-29, 2026-Jun-29],
```

6.2 FLOWS

A flow describes a cash flow to be made at some point in time. The actual value of the cash flow will depend on a number of things. Firstly, it will depend on the principal or notional of the financial contract. Secondly, it depends on the currency in which the payment is made. Thirdly, the payment is typically accrued over a period of time determined by the accrual start date and the accrual end date. The actual formula for calculating the accrued amount is controlled by the accrual basis. Fourthly, the date on which the payment is made will affect its overall value. Lastly, the payment will depend in some way on the value of market observables. For simplicity we treat known coupons, such as those on a coupon-bearing bond, as observables. In other words, a flow will always have at least one observable.

The class flow models the characteristics of a flow and can be found in the ppf.core.flow module. As well as accessors to the underlying properties of the flow, a method is also provided for calculating the accrual period as a year fraction.

```
from ppf.date_time import year_fraction

class flow:
  def __init__(self
               , notional
               , pay_currency
               , accrual_start_date
               , accrual_end_date
               , accrual_basis
               , pay_date
               , observables = None):
    self.__notional = notional
    self.__pay_currency = pay_currency
    self.__accrual_start_date = accrual_start_date
    self.__accrual_end_date = accrual_end_date
    self.__accrual_basis = accrual_basis
    self.__pay_date = pay_date
    self.__observables = observables

  def notional(self): return self.__notional
  def pay_currency(self): return self.__pay_currency
  def accrual_start_date(self): return self.__accrual_start_date
  def accrual_end_date(self): return self.__accrual_end_date
```

```
def pay_date(self): return self.__pay_date
def observables(self): return self.__observables
def set_observables(self, observables): self.__observables = \
observables

def year_fraction(self):
  return year_fraction(
      self.__accrual_start_date
    , self.__accrual_end_date
    , self.__accrual_basis)

def __str__(self):
  s = "%f, " % self.__notional
  s += "%s, " % self.__pay_currency
  s += "[%s, %s], " % (self.__accrual_start_date
                       ,self.__accrual_end_date)
  s += "%s, " % day_count_basis_strings[self.__accrual_basis]
  s += "%s, " %  self.__pay_date
  if self.__observables <> None:
    for observable in self.__observables:
      s += observable.__str__()
  return s
```

Analogous to the generate_libor_observables() function of section 6.1.1 and the generate_swap_observables() of section 6.1.2, the ppf.core.generate_flows module provides the function generate_flows() from which a flow collection can be generated from a high-level description.

```
import ppf.date_time
from flow import *

def generate_flows(
   start
 , end
 , period = 6
 , duration = ppf.date_time.months
 , notional = 10000000
 , accrual_basis = ppf.date_time.basis_act_360
 , pay_currency = "USD"
 , pay_shift_method =
     ppf.date_time.shift_convention.modified_following
 , pay_holiday_centres = None
 , accrual_shift_method =
     ppf.date_time.shift_convention.modified_following
 , accrual_holiday_centres = None
 , observables = None
 , *arguments
 , **keywords):

  i, day = 0, start
  flows = []
```

```
shift = ppf.date_time.shift
while day < end:
    roll_start = start + duration(i*period)
    roll_end = start + duration((i + 1)*period)
    accrual_start = shift(
            roll_start
        , accrual_shift_method, accrual_holiday_centres)
    accrual_end = shift(
            roll_end
        , accrual_shift_method, accrual_holiday_centres)
    pay = shift(
            roll_end
        , pay_shift_method, pay_holiday_centres)
    flows.append(
      flow(notional
        , pay_currency
        , accrual_start
        , accrual_end
        , accrual_basis
        , pay)
    )
    day = roll_end
    i += 1

if observables <> None:
  if len(observables) <> len(flows):
    raise RuntimeError, "too few or too many observables"
  for i in range(len(flows)):
    f = flows[i]
    obs = observables[i]
    f.set_observables(obs)
return flows
```

Here is an example of the generate_flows() function in action:

```
>>> flows = generate_flows(
...     start = date(2007, Jun, 29)
...     , end = date(2017, Jun, 29)
...     , period = 6
...     , duration = ppf.date_time.months
...     , notional = 1000000
...     , accrual_basis = basis_30360
...     , pay_currency = "JPY"
...     , pay_shift_method = shift_convention.modified_following)
>>> for f in flows:
...   print f
1000000.000000, JPY, [2007-Jun-29, 2007-Dec-31], basis_30360, 2007-
Dec-31,
1000000.000000, JPY, [2007-Dec-31, 2008-Jun-30], basis_30360, 2008-
Jun-30,
1000000.000000, JPY, [2008-Jun-30, 2008-Dec-29], basis_30360, 2008-
```

```
Dec-29,
1000000.000000, JPY, [2008-Dec-29, 2009-Jun-29], basis_30360, 2009-
Jun-29,
1000000.000000, JPY, [2009-Jun-29, 2009-Dec-29], basis_30360, 2009-
Dec-29,
1000000.000000, JPY, [2009-Dec-29, 2010-Jun-29], basis_30360, 2010-
Jun-29,
1000000.000000, JPY, [2010-Jun-29, 2010-Dec-29], basis_30360, 2010-
Dec-29,
1000000.000000, JPY, [2010-Dec-29, 2011-Jun-29], basis_30360, 2011-
Jun-29,
1000000.000000, JPY, [2011-Jun-29, 2011-Dec-29], basis_30360, 2011-
Dec-29,
1000000.000000, JPY, [2011-Dec-29, 2012-Jun-29], basis_30360, 2012-
Jun-29,
1000000.000000, JPY, [2012-Jun-29, 2012-Dec-31], basis_30360, 2012-
Dec-31,
1000000.000000, JPY, [2012-Dec-31, 2013-Jun-28], basis_30360, 2013-
Jun-28,
1000000.000000, JPY, [2013-Jun-28, 2013-Dec-30], basis_30360, 2013-
Dec-30,
1000000.000000, JPY, [2013-Dec-30, 2014-Jun-30], basis_30360, 2014-
Jun-30,
1000000.000000, JPY, [2014-Jun-30, 2014-Dec-29], basis_30360, 2014-
Dec-29,
1000000.000000, JPY, [2014-Dec-29, 2015-Jun-29], basis_30360, 2015-
Jun-29,
1000000.000000, JPY, [2015-Jun-29, 2015-Dec-29], basis_30360, 2015-
Dec-29,
1000000.000000, JPY, [2015-Dec-29, 2016-Jun-29], basis_30360, 2016-
Jun-29,
1000000.000000, JPY, [2016-Jun-29, 2016-Dec-29], basis_30360, 2016-
Dec-29,
1000000.000000, JPY, [2016-Dec-29, 2017-Jun-29], basis_30360, 2017-
Jun-29,
```

6.3 ADJUVANTS

A financial payoff can depend on constants that vary over time, such as a gearing or barrier level. The class adjuvant_table in module ppf.core.adjuvant_table provides a simple structure for storing these time-dependent constants. The class is constructed by taking a list of keys, or equivalently variable names, the dates on which they apply, and the values. Access to a particular constant at a specific time is provided via the function call operator.

```
class adjuvant_table:
  def __init__(self, keys, dates, values):
    if len(values.shape) <> 2:
      raise RuntimeError, "expected 2d array of values"
    if len(keys) <> values.shape[0] or len(dates) <>
    values.shape[1]:
      raise RuntimeError, "incorrect size of values array"
```

```
      self.__table = {}
      i = 0
      for key in keys:
        elem = {}
        j = 0
        for dt in dates:
          elem[dt.julian_day()] = values[i][j]
          j += 1
        self.__table[key] = elem
        i += 1

  def __call__(self, key, dt):
    if self.__table.has_key(key):
      elem = self.__table.get(key)
      if elem.has_key(dt.julian_day()):
        return elem.get(dt.julian_day())
      else:
        raise RuntimeError, \
          "unable to find date in adjuvant table"+" dt = "+str(dt)
    else:
      raise RuntimeError, "unable to find key in adjuvant table"

  def __str__(self):
    return self.__table.__str__()
```

A high-level generator for adjuvant tables is provided in the ppf.core.generate_adjuvant_table module.

```
def generate_adjuvant_table(
    keys
  , tenors
  , values
  , start_date
  , roll_period = 6
  , roll_duration = ppf.date_time.months
  , holiday_centres = None
  , shift_method = ppf.date_time.shift_convention.modified_following
  , *arguments
  , **keywords):
  if len(values.shape) <> 2:
    raise RuntimeError, "expected 2d array of values"
  if len(keys) <> values.shape[0] or len(tenors) <> values.shape[1]:
    raise RuntimeError, "incorrect size of values array"

  from ppf.date_time import days
  shift = ppf.date_time.shift

  day = 0
  dates = []
  indices = []
  cnt = 0
  start = start_date
```

```
for tenor in tenors:
  end = start_date+roll_duration(tenor)
  if end < day:
    raise RuntimeError, "tenors are not monotonically increasing"
  i = 0
  while day < end:
    roll_start = start+roll_duration(i*roll_period)
    roll_end = start+roll_duration((i+1)*roll_period)
    pay = shift(roll_end, shift_method, holiday_centres)
    day = pay
    dates.append(day)
    indices.append(cnt)
    i += 1
  cnt += 1
  start = end

import numpy
all_values = numpy.zeros((len(keys), len(dates)))
for i in range(len(keys)):
  for j in range(len(dates)):
    idx = indices[j]
    all_values[i][j] = values[i][idx]
return adjuvant_table(keys, dates, all_values)
```

A sample invocation of the `generate_adjuvant_table()` function is shown below:

```
>>> from ppf.date_time import *
>>> from numpy import *
>>> adjuvants = generate_adjuvant_table(
...       keys = ["spread","coupon"]
...     , tenors = [12,24,36]
...     , values = array([[0.005, 0.006, 0.007], [0.05, 0.06, 0.07]])
...     , start_date = date(2008, May, 1)
...     , roll_period = 6
...     , shift_method = shift_convention.modified_following)
>>> print adjuvants
{'coupon': {2455137: 0.06, 2455683: 0.07, 2454953: 0.05,
2455502: 0.07, 2454772: 0.05, 2455318: 0.06},
'spread': {2455137: 0.006, 2455683: 0.007,
2454953: 0.005, 2455502: 0.007,
2454772: 0.005, 2455318: 0.006}}
```

6.4 LEGS

In essence, a leg is simply a collection of flows. However, we also need to know whether the cash flows they represent are to be paid or received. The module `ppf.core.pay_recieve` encapsulates this concept:

```
PAY, RECEIVE = (-1, 1)
```

Furthermore, a leg will also depend on the Python class representing the actual payoff and the adjuvant table referenced in the payoff. Examples of concrete payoffs will be discussed in the forthcoming chapters. The class `leg` from module `ppf.core.leg` provides an implementation of the leg.

```
class leg:
  def __init__(self
                , flows
                , pay_or_receive
                , adjuvant_table = None
                , payoff = None):
    self.__flows = flows
    self.__pay_or_receive = pay_or_receive
    self.__adjuvant_table = adjuvant_table
    self.__payoff = payoff

  def flows(self):
    return self.__flows

  def pay_receive(self):
    return self.__pay_or_receive

  def has_adjuvant_table(self):
    return self.__adjuvant_table <> None

  def has_payoff(self):
    return self.__payoff <> None

  def adjuvant_table(self):
    if self.__adjuvant_table == None:
      raise RuntimeError, "Null adjuvant table"
    return self.__adjuvant_table

  def payoff(self):
    if self.__payoff == None:
      raise RuntimeError, "Null payoff"
    return self.__payoff
```

6.5 EXERCISES

Many financial structures have exercise decisions embedded in them. An exercise decision or opportunity is the right to exercise into or cancel a stream of cash flows at some point in time. Typically the writer of the option will require some notification of exercise and so an exercise decision is most generally associated with two dates: a notification date and an exercise date. It may also be written into the contract that the holder of the option must pay a fee upon exercise. These three data elements are bundled up into the class `exercise` in the module `ppf.core.exercise`.

```
class exercise:
  def __init__(self
                , notification_date
                , exercise_date
                , fee = None
                , fee_ccy = None):
```

```
    self._notification_date = notification_date
    self._exercise_date = exercise_date
    self._fee = fee
    self._fee_ccy = fee_ccy
    if fee <> None and fee_ccy == None:
        raise RuntimeError, "non-zero fee with no currency"

def notification_date(self): return self._notification_date
def exercise_date(self): return self._exercise_date
def fee(self): return self._fee
def fee_currency(self): return self._fee_ccy

def __str__(self):
    s = "%s, " % self._notification_date
    s += "%s, " % self._exercise_date
    if self._fee <> None:
        s += "%f, " %  self._fee
        s += "%s, " % self._fee_ccy
    return s
```

Exercise opportunities generally offer the holder the right to do one of two things: enter into a contract or cancel an existing contract. This classification of exercise opportunities is captured in the ppf.core.exercise_type module.

```
class exercise_type:
    callable, cancellable = (1, -1)
```

Like flows, exercise opportunities frequently come in collections. In a pattern that is no doubt familiar by now, the ppf.core.generate_exercise_table module offers the function generate_exercise_table() presented below.

```
import ppf.date_time
from exercise import *

def generate_exercise_table(
    start
  , end
  , period = 6
  , duration = ppf.date_time.months
  , shift_method = ppf.date_time.modified_following
  , basis = ppf.date_time.basis_act_360
  , holiday_centres = None
  , fee = None
  , fee_currency = None
  , *arguments
  , **keywords):
    i, day, exercises = 0, 0, []
    shift = ppf.date_time.shift
    while day < end:
        roll_start = start + duration(i*period)
        roll_end = start + duration((i+1)*period)
```

```
    exercise_date = shift(
        roll_start
      , shift_method, holiday_centres)
    # assume no notification lag
    exercises.append(
        exercise(exercise_date, exercise_date, fee, fee_currency))
    day = exercise_date
    i += 1
 return exercises
```

Below is an example of the usage of generate_exercise_table():

```
>>> ex_sched = generate_exercise_table(
...    start = date(2007, Jun, 29)
...  , end = date(2017, Jun, 29)
...  , duration = months
...  , period = 6
...  , fee = 1000000
...  , fee_currency = "EUR"
...  , shift_method = shift_convention.modified_following)
>>> for ex in ex_sched: print ex
2007-Jun-29, 2007-Jun-29, 1000000.000000, EUR,
2007-Dec-31, 2007-Dec-31, 1000000.000000, EUR,
2008-Jun-30, 2008-Jun-30, 1000000.000000, EUR,
2008-Dec-29, 2008-Dec-29, 1000000.000000, EUR,
2009-Jun-29, 2009-Jun-29, 1000000.000000, EUR,
2009-Dec-29, 2009-Dec-29, 1000000.000000, EUR,
2010-Jun-29, 2010-Jun-29, 1000000.000000, EUR,
2010-Dec-29, 2010-Dec-29, 1000000.000000, EUR,
2011-Jun-29, 2011-Jun-29, 1000000.000000, EUR,
2011-Dec-29, 2011-Dec-29, 1000000.000000, EUR,
2012-Jun-29, 2012-Jun-29, 1000000.000000, EUR,
2012-Dec-31, 2012-Dec-31, 1000000.000000, EUR,
2013-Jun-28, 2013-Jun-28, 1000000.000000, EUR,
2013-Dec-30, 2013-Dec-30, 1000000.000000, EUR,
2014-Jun-30, 2014-Jun-30, 1000000.000000, EUR,
2014-Dec-29, 2014-Dec-29, 1000000.000000, EUR,
2015-Jun-29, 2015-Jun-29, 1000000.000000, EUR,
2015-Dec-29, 2015-Dec-29, 1000000.000000, EUR,
2016-Jun-29, 2016-Jun-29, 1000000.000000, EUR,
2016-Dec-29, 2016-Dec-29, 1000000.000000, EUR,
2017-Jun-29, 2017-Jun-29, 1000000.000000, EUR,
```

6.6   TRADES

A trade is built from a collection of legs and possibly a schedule of exercise decisions. The
class trade in module ppf.core.trade encapsulates the concept of a trade.

```
class trade:
  def __init__(self, legs, exercise_info=None):
```

```
      self.__legs = legs
      self.__exercise_info = exercise_info

   def legs(self):
     return self.__legs

   def exercise_type(self):
     if not self.__exercise_info:
       raise RuntimeError, "missing exercise information"
     return self.__exercise_info[1]

   def exercise_schedule(self):
     if not self.__exercise_info:
       raise RuntimeError, "missing exercise information"
     return self.__exercise_info[0]

   def has_exercise_schedule(self):
     return self.__exercise_schedule != None
```

The following snippet shows a simple example of how to assemble a trade:

```
>>> #semi-annual flows
>>> flows = generate_flows(
...    start = date(2007, Jun, 29)
...    , end = date(2017, Jun, 29)
...    , duration = ppf.date_time.months
...    , period = 6
...    , shift_method = shift_convention.modified_following
...    , basis = "ACT/360")
>>> pay_leg = leg(flows, PAY)
>>> receive_leg = leg(flows, RECEIVE)
>>> #1y nc
>>> ex_sched = generate_exercise_table(
...    start = date(2008, Jun, 29)
... , end = date(2016, Jun, 29)
... , period = 1
... , duration = ppf.date_time.years
... , shift_method = shift_convention.modified_following)
>>> structure = trade([pay_leg, receive_leg], [ex_sched, \
                    exercise_type.callable])
>>> print ("callable", "cancellable")[structure.exercise_type()
== -1]
callable
```

6.7   TRADE UTILITIES

It is not uncommon to perform standard operations on the trade representation. For example, the writer of a pricing model may wish to insist upon the trade being single currency, or that the trade doesn't contain any exercise stubs. The module ppf.core.trade_utils is the repository for such standard operations. The final_important_date function, detailed below, determines the last important date of a trade. The last important date is determined by looping through the legs of a trade and for each flow in the leg keeping count of the most distant date in the future, be it the flow pay date or the last important date of the observables attached to the flow. The end result is the most distant date in the future contained in the trade representation.

```
def final_important_date(trd):
  final_date = date(1900, Jan, 1)
  for l in trd.legs():
    for f in l.flows():
      candidate_date = f.pay_date()
      observables = f.observables()
      if not observables:
        raise RuntimeError, "Missing observables"
      for o in observables:
        if o.last_important_date() > candidate_date:
          candidate_date = o.last_important_date()
      if candidate_date > final_date:
        final_date = candidate_date
  return final_date
```

Here is a demonstration of the `final_important_date()` function:

```
>>> libor_observables = generate_libor_observables(
...      start = date(2007, Jun, 29)
...      , end = date(2009, Jun, 29)
...      , roll_period = 6
...      , roll_duration = ppf.date_time.months
...      , reset_period = 3
...      , reset_duration = ppf.date_time.months
...      , reset_currency = "JPY"
...      , reset_basis = basis_act_360
...      , reset_shift_method = shift_convention.modified_following)
>>> coupon_observables = generate_fixed_coupon_observables(
...      start = date(2007, Jun, 29)
...      , end = date(2009, Jun, 29)
...      , roll_period = 6
...      , reset_currency = "JPY"
...      , coupon_shift_method = shift_convention.modified_following
...      , coupon_rate = 0.045)
>>> #semi-annual flows
>>> pay_flows = generate_flows(
...      start = date(2007, Jun, 29)
...      , end = date(2009, Jun, 29)
...      , duration = ppf.date_time.months
...      , period = 6
...      , shift_method = shift_convention.modified_following
...      , basis = "30/360"
...      , observables = coupon_observables)
>>> rcv_flows = generate_flows(
...      start = date(2007, Jun, 29)
```

```
...     , end = date(2009, Jun, 29)
...     , duration = ppf.date_time.months
...     , period = 6
...     , shift_method = shift_convention.modified_following
...     , basis = "A/360"
...     , observables = libor_observables)
>>> pay_leg = leg(pay_flows, PAY)
>>> receive_leg = leg(rcv_flows, RECEIVE)
>>> #1y nc
>>> ex_sched = generate_exercise_table(
...     start = date(2008, Jun, 29)
... , end = date(2009, Jun, 29)
... , period = 1
... , duration = ppf.date_time.years
... , shift_method = shift_convention.modified_following)
>>> structure = trade((pay_leg, receive_leg), (ex_sched, \
                exercise_type.callable))
>>> print final_important_date(structure)
2009-Sep-30
```

The enforce_single_currency function harvests all the currencies contained in the trade representation, whether they be pay currencies or observable currencies, and then enforces that the number of unique currencies must be 1.

```
def enforce_single_currency(trd):
  ccys = []
  for l in trd.legs():
    for f in l.flows():
      pay_ccy = f.pay_currency()
      observables = f.observables()
      if not observables:
        raise RuntimeError, "Missing observables"
      for o in observables:
        reset_ccy = o.reset_currency()
        if ccys.count(reset_ccy) == 0:
          ccys.append(reset_ccy)
      if ccys.count(pay_ccy) == 0:
        ccys.append(pay_ccy)
  if len(ccys) <> 1:
    raise RuntimeError, "expected one currency"
  return ccys[0]
```

Lastly, the enforce_no_exercise_stubs function asserts that the exercise dates, if there are any, must fall within the union of accrual start dates.

```
def enforce_no_exercise_stubs(trd):
  accrual_start_dates = []
  for l in trd.legs():
    for f in l.flows():
      accrual_start_dates.append(f.accrual_start_date())

  if trd.has_exercise_schedule():
```

```
exercises = trd.exercise_schedule()
for exercise in exercises:
  notification_date = exercise.notification_date()
  if accrual_start_dates.count(notification_date) == 0:
    raise RuntimeError, "exercise stub encountered"
```

All these utility functions will be used at various stages in the forthcoming chapters.

7

Timeline: Events and Controller

In the preceding chapter we looked at trade representation. This chapter covers a number of concepts that provide the glue between the trade representation and the pricing models. We will first discuss the concept of an event. Once we have a firm understanding of an event we will move onto the timeline, which is essentially a convenient container for a sequence of events. We finish the chapter by reviewing the idea of a controller. Of all the classes discussed in this chapter, the controller is the conduit through which pricing models communicate with the trade representation.

7.1 EVENTS

A fundamental concept of any pricing analytics is that of an event. So what does an event represent? In essence an event represents either a cash flow depending on some piece of financial information, such as a foreign exchange rate on a particular date for example, or an exercise decision. The module `ppf.core.event`, as outlined below, contains two core classes: `pay_event` and `exercise_event`. The class `pay_event` is constructed from a flow, a pay or receive flag, a leg id, and a reset id. The leg id enables clients to determine which leg of the trade the flow belongs to and the reset id informs clients which observable of the flow is represented by the event. The class `exercise_event` is constructed from an exercise and a flag representing the type of exercise, i.e. cancellable or callable. For completeness, two helper functions are provided for determining the event type. We will use these helper functions in the forthcoming chapters.

```
import string
class event_type:
    flow, exercise = (1, -1)

class pay_event:
  def __init__(
        self
      , flow
      , pay_rcv
      , leg_id
      , reset_id):
    self.__flow        \
  , self.__pay_rcv \
  , self.__leg_id \
  , self.__reset_id = flow, pay_rcv, leg_id, reset_id

  def flow(self) : return self.__flow
  def pay_recieve(self) : return self.__pay_rcv
  def leg_id(self) : return self.__leg_id
  def reset_id(self) : return self.__reset_id
  def pay_currency(self) : return self.__flow.pay_currency()
```

```
    def __str__(self) :
      s = "payment [%s, %s, %s, %s], " % \
            (self.__pay_rcv, self.__leg_id, self.__reset_id,
             str(self.__flow))
      return s

class exercise_event:
  def __init__(
        self
      , exercise_opportunity
      , exercise_type):
    self.__exercise_opportunity \
  , self.__exercise_type = exercise_opportunity, exercise_type
  def exercise_type(self) : return self.__exercise_type
  def exercise_opportunity(self) : return self.__exercise_opportunity
  def pay_currency(self) :
    return self.__exercise_opportunity.fee_currency()
  def __str__(self) :
      s = "exercise [%s, %s], " % \
            (self.__exercise_type, str(self.__exercise_opportunity))
      return s

def is_pay_event(event): return isinstance(event, pay_event)
def is_exercise_event(event): return isinstance(event, exercise_event)
```

7.2 TIMELINE

Now that we have a clear understanding of an event, we move on to the timeline. Any financial payoff can be interpreted as a sequence of cash flows and exercise decisions with potentially more than one cash flow occurring at any one point in time. The purpose of the class `timeline` from the `ppf.core.timeline` module is to transform the trade representation into a sequence of events. The actual transformation occurs in the constructor of the timeline. We begin by harvesting the observables from the trade to create instances of the `pay_event` and follow on by harvesting the exercises from the trade to create instances of the `exercise_event`. Once constructed, an instance of the timeline can be queried for a list of the times on which either a cash flow occurs or an exercise decision is made, and for a list of events occurring at a particular time.

```
from types import *
from trade import *
from leg import *
from flow import *
from exercise import *
from event import *

class timeline:
  def __add_event_(self, t, event):
    if not self.__events.has_key(t.julian_day()):
      self.__events[t.julian_day()] = []
    self.__events.get(t.julian_day()).append(event)
```

```python
def __init__(self, trade, pricing_date):
    self._events = {}

    # add events from legs
    leg_id = 0
    for l in trade.legs():
        pay_rcv = l.pay_receive()
        for f in \
            [f for f in l.flows()
             if f.pay_date() >= pricing_date]:
            observables = f.observables()
            if not observables:
                raise RuntimeError, "Missing observables"
            for o in observables:
                self._add_event_(
                    o.reset_date()
                    , pay_event(f, pay_rcv, leg_id, o.reset_id())))
        leg_id += 1

    # add events from exercise schedule
    if trade.has_exercise_schedule():
        ex_type = trade.exercise_type()
        for ex in \
            [ex for ex in trade.exercise_schedule()
             if ex.notification_date() > pricing_date]:
            self._add_event_(
                ex.notification_date()
                , exercise_event(ex, ex_type))

def times(self):
    return sorted(self._events.keys())

def events(self, t):
    return self._events[t]

def __str__(self):
    s = "events: \n"
    times = sorted(self._events.keys())
    for t in times:
        s += "\"%s\", " % t
        events = self._events[t]
        for event in events: s += str(event)
        s += '\n'
    return s
```

Construction of a timeline from a financial structure proceeds as per the following example:

```python
>>> from ppf.date_time import *
>>> from pay_receive import *
>>> from generate_flows import *
>>> from generate_observables import *
>>> from generate_exercise_table import *
```

```
>>> from exercise_type import *
>>> from leg import *
>>> from trade import *
>>> libor_observables = generate_libor_observables(
...      start = date(2007, Jun, 29)
...    , end  = date(2009, Jun, 29)
...    , roll_period = 6
...    , roll_duration = ppf.date_time.months
...    , reset_period = 3
...    , reset_duration = ppf.date_time.months
...    , reset_currency = "JPY"
...    , reset_basis = basis_act_360
...    , reset_shift_method = shift_convention.modified_following)
>>> coupon_observables = generate_fixed_coupon_observables(
...      start = date(2007, Jun, 29)
...    , end  = date(2009, Jun, 29)
...    , roll_period = 6
...    , reset_currency = "JPY"
...    , coupon_shift_method = shift_convention.modified_following
...    , coupon_rate = 0.045)
>>> #semi-annual flows
>>> pay_flows = generate_flows(
...    start = date(2007, Jun, 29)
...    , end  = date(2009, Jun, 29)
...    , duration = ppf.date_time.months
...    , period = 6
...    , shift_method = shift_convention.modified_following
...    , basis = "30/360"
...    , observables = coupon_observables)
>>> rcv_flows = generate_flows(
...    start = date(2007, Jun, 29)
...    , end  = date(2009, Jun, 29)
...    , duration = ppf.date_time.months
...    , period = 6
...    , shift_method = shift_convention.modified_following
...    , basis = "A/360"
...    , observables = libor_observables)
>>> pay_leg = leg(pay_flows, PAY)
>>> receive_leg = leg(rcv_flows, RECEIVE)
>>> #1y nc
>>> ex_sched = generate_exercise_table(
...    start = date(2008, Jun, 29)
...  , end  = date(2009, Jun, 29)
...  , period = 1
...  , duration = ppf.date_time.years
...  , shift_method = shift_convention.modified_following)
>>> structure = trade((pay_leg, receive_leg), (ex_sched,
    exercise_type.callable))
>>> pricing_date = date(2007, Jan, 29)
>>> tline = timeline(structure, pricing_date)
```

7.3 CONTROLLER

As already discussed in the introduction, the controller provides the main glue between the trade representation (or more correctly its transformation into events) and the pricing models. Essentially the controller is constructed from the trade, the model and the market environment. The final argument of the constructor is used to control how historical discount factors are treated and we defer further discussion on this point to later chapters. The main job of the controller is to maintain a dictionary of variables whose values will be updated and retrieved by the pricing models. The controller is also the conduit for the pricing models to evaluate the payoffs in the trade representation. The payoffs are evaluated by first setting the event followed by an invocation of the function call operator. The following excerpt from the ppf.core.controller module illustrates the essential details of the controller class.

```
class controller:
  def __init__(self, trade, model, env, historic_df):
    self.__trade = trade
    self.__model = model
    self.__env = env
    self.__historical_df = historical_df
    self.__symbol_table = {}
    self.__event = None

  def get_trade(self):
    return self.__trade

  def get_model(self):
    return self.__model

  def get_environment(self):
    return self.__env

  def get_event(self):
    return self.__event

  def set_event(self, event):
    self.__event = event

  def insert_symbol(self, name, at):
    self.__symbol_table[name] = \
      (at, self.__model.state().create_variable())

  def update_symbol(self, name, symbol, at):
    self.__symbol_table[name] = (at, symbol)

  def retrieve_symbol(self, name):
    if not self.__symbol_table.has_key(name):
      raise RuntimeError, "name not found in symbol table"
    return self.__symbol_table.get(name)[1]

  def retrieve_symbol_update_time(self, name):
```

```
if not self.__symbol_table.has_key(name):
  raise RuntimeError, "name not found in symbol table"
return self.__symbol_table.get(name)[0]
```

In the body of the __call__ method we retrieve the leg corresponding to the event from the trade, the payoff from the leg and determine whether the leg is pay or receive. The payoff is then evaluated by calling the function call operator on the payoff class, passing in the controller as an argument.

```
class controller:
  def __call__(self, t):
    leg = self.__trade.legs()[self.__event.leg_id()]
    payoff = leg.payoff()
    pay_rcv = leg.pay_receive()
    return pay_rcv*payoff(t, self)
```

In the following chapters we will provide concrete examples of payoff classes. For the time being all we insist upon is that the payoff class provides an implementation of the function call operator with the correct signature.

In later chapters, we will return to the controller to add more methods. In contrast to strongly typed programming languages such as C++, the addition of more methods on the controller doesn't create an (compile/link dependency) implementation bottleneck. If a call onto a controller method results in invoking a call on a method of a particular model that hasn't been implemented, all we get is a runtime error. To achieve this kind of flexibility in C++ requires more effort but can be reasonably dealt with by interface based programming paradigms such as one finds in COM.[1]

---

[1] COM (Component Object Model) is explained in Chapter 12.

8

The Hull–White Model

The purpose of this chapter is to develop a fully functional Hull–White model in Python. We will separate the characteristic features of the Hull–White model into functionally orthogonal components, thereby fostering code re-use and facilitating rapid model development. The Hull–White model has been chosen because it is both simple and rich enough to illustrate the power of component-based programming in Python.

In finance there are broadly speaking two approaches to pricing financial instruments: (a) deriving analytic or semi-analytic formulae; or (b) applying numerical techniques. Which approach is chosen depends upon the complexity of the financial instrument. For example, for many so-called 'vanilla' financial instruments there exist commonly accepted pricing formulae. However, exotic or hybrid financial instruments generally require the application of numerical techniques in their valuation. Both 'vanilla' and 'exotic' financial instruments can be split into two categories: (a) non-path dependent, where the payoff only depends of the asset price(s) at the present moment in time; and (b) path dependent, where the pay-off depends on some property of the asset price(s) history as well as the asset price(s) at the present moment in time. Path dependent financial instruments can be further categorised into 'weakly' and 'strongly' path dependent. An example of a 'weakly' path dependent financial instrument is a barrier option where the option is triggered if the asset price(s) hits a prescribed barrier level at any time prior to option expiry. An Asian option provides us with an example of a 'strongly' path dependent financial instrument. In this contract, the payoff depends on the average asset price(s) over the period from inception to expiry. To price 'strongly' path dependent financial instruments one is forced to introduce one extra state variable for every property of the asset price path influencing the payoff. Obviously adding extra state variables increases the overall dimensionality of the pricing problem, leaving the model developer having to decide between pricing the problem on a tree, or equivalently lattice, or pricing the problem using the Monte-Carlo method.

The component-based design discussed in this chapter has been developed to faciliate the writing and implementation of models for pricing financial instruments using numerical techniques. For models with analytic or semi-analytic pricing formulae, the core components are still applicable but the numerical components would need to be replaced. An all-encompassing design for both analytic and numerical based models is beyond the scope of this book.

8.1 A COMPONENT-BASED DESIGN

In this section we introduce the components (or building blocks) that together form the Hull–White model. We dedicate a subsection to each of the identified components with the emphasis on the implementation rather than the mathematics. Details of the mathematics can be found in the appendices.

8.1.1   Requestor

Every model is dependent on market information; for example, market rates or asset spot prices. This primary information is normally fed into the calibration routine for the model. The purpose of the calibration is to ensure that the model prices back the liquid market instruments that the trader would buy or sell on a regular basis to mitigate the risks of being long or short a more complex financial instrument. By saying pricing back, we simply mean that the model price of a market instrument matches the market price within an acceptable tolerance, usually a small fraction of the market bid–offer spread. The output of the calibration is a set of model parameters or variables, termed secondary information, that normally completely specifies the model. Furnished with these model parameters we can then go on to price the complex financial instrument in question. As we have already mentioned in the introductory section, there are typically a number of approaches to pricing; however they all have one thing in common in that they will require certain transformations of the model parameters during the process of pricing. The *requestor* component encapsulates the need for a model pricer to gain access to both primary and secondary information: in essence a model pricer makes 'requests' of the model for this information.

In the case of the Hull–White model there are only a few pieces of information required: a discount factor, a local volatility and a term volatility. In the language of Appendix C, the term volatility is simply $\sqrt{\int_0^t C^2(s)ds}$ and the local volatility is $\phi(t) - \phi(T)$. Note that, taken together with the relevant discount factors, any zero coupon bond can be written in terms of the local volatility and the term volatility. What we actually store in the environment for the term volatility is the following

$$\sqrt{\frac{\int_0^t C^2(s)ds}{\int_0^t \exp(2\lambda s)ds}}. \tag{8.1}$$

The reason for this is that the above variable is more natural to use when calibrating the model to market prices. The requestor for the Hull–White model can be found in the `ppf.model.hull_white.requestor` module as detailed below:

```
class requestor:
  def discount_factor(self, t, ccy, env):
      key = "zc.disc."+ccy
      curve = env.retrieve_curve(key)
      return curve(t)

  def term_vol(self, t, ccy, env):
      key = "ve.term."+ccy+".hw"
      surf = env.retrieve_surface(key)
      term_var = surf(t, 0)
      key = "cv.mr."+ccy+".hw"
      mr = env.retrieve_constant(key)
      if mr <> 0:
        term_var *= (math.exp(2.0*mr*t)-1.0)/(2.0*mr)
      else:
        term_var *= t
      return math.sqrt(term_var)
```

```
def local_vol(self, t, T, ccy, env):
    assert t <= T
    key = "cv.mr."+ccy+".hw"
    mr = env.retrieve_constant(key)
    return math.exp(-mr*t)-math.exp(-mr*T)
```

The requestor class uses the `class environment` implemented in the `ppf.market.environment` module. The purpose of this class is to provide access to market data objects such as yield curves, volatility surfaces, correlation surfaces, etc. Refer to section 5.3 for the details. The following code snippets illustrate how to construct a requestor and make a request for a discount factor and a term volatility:

```
>>> import math
>>> import ppf.market
>>> from ppf.math.interpolation import loglinear
>>> times = [0.0, 0.5, 1.0, 1.5, 2.0]
>>> factors = [math.exp(-0.05*t) for t in times]
>>> c = ppf.market.curve(times, factors, loglinear)
>>> env = ppf.market.environment()
>>> key = "zc.disc.eur"
>>> env.add_curve(key, c)
>>> r = requestor()
>>> t = 1.5
>>> print r.discount_factor(t, "eur", env)
0.927743486329

>>> import math
>>> import ppf.market
>>> from numpy import zeros
>>> expiries = [0.1, 0.5, 1.0, 1.5, 2.0, 3.0, 4.0, 5.0]
>>> tenors = [0, 90]
>>> values = zeros((8, 2))
>>> values.fill(0.04)
>>> surf = ppf.market.surface(expiries, tenors, values)
>>> env = ppf.market.environment()
>>> key = "ve.term.eur.hw"
>>> env.add_surface(key, surf)
>>> key = "cv.mr.eur.hw"
>>> env.add_constant(key, 0.0)
>>> r = requestor()
>>> t = 0.25
>>> print r.term_vol(t, "eur", env)
0.1
```

8.1.2 State

When pricing a financial instrument we frequently need to know about the state of the world – the world being both defined and modelled by the chosen model. For example, when pricing a target redemption note in a Monte-Carlo framework under the Hull–White model in the spot measure, we need to know at every simulation time t the current state of the short rate $r(t)$. A similar requirement arises when pricing a Bermudan on a lattice in the terminal measure:

in this case we need to know at every exercise time the current state of the stochastic variable $\int_0^t C(s)dW(s)$. The *state* component encapsulates the need for both Monte-Carlo and lattice pricers to have knowledge of the state of the world at various points in time. An implementation of a state component suitable for lattice pricing in the Hull–White model can be found in the `ppf.model.hull_white.lattice.state` module and the details are shown below.

```
class state:
  def __init__(self, ccy, n = 31, stddev = 5.5):
    self.__ccy = ccy
    self.__n = n
    self.__stddev = stddev

  def fill(self, t, req, env):
    term_vol = req.term_vol(t, self.__ccy, env)
    f = normal_distribution(0, term_vol)

    return f.state(self.__stddev, self.__n)

  def __incremental_vol(self, t, T, req, env):
    term_volt = req.term_vol(t, self.__ccy, env)
    term_volT = req.term_vol(T, self.__ccy, env)
    term_vartT = term_volT*term_volT-term_volt*term_volt
    if term_vartT < 0:
      raise RuntimeError,\
        "incremental variance is negative"+" t = "+str(t)+ \
        " T = "+str(T)
    term_voltT = math.sqrt(term_vartT)
    return term_voltT

  def incremental_fill(self, t, T, req, env):
    term_voltT = self.__incremental_vol(t, T, req, env)
    f = normal_distribution(0, term_voltT)
    return f.state(self.__stddev, self.__n)

  def incremental_distribution(self, t, T, req, env):
    term_voltT = self.__incremental_vol(t, T, req, env)
    return normal_distribution(0, term_voltT)

  def create_variable(self):
    var = numpy.zeros(self.__n)
    return var
```

Note that we also use the state component for both the creation of variables and the construction of the underlying distribution of the current state of the world. An example invocation of the state component is given below.

```
>>> import math
>>> import numpy
>>> import ppf.market
>>> from ppf.math.normal_distribution import *
>>> expiries = [0.1, 0.5, 1.0, 1.5, 2.0, 3.0, 4.0, 5.0]
```

```
>>> tenors = [0, 90]
>>> from numpy import zeros
>>> values = zeros((8, 2))
>>> values.fill(0.04)
>>> surf = ppf.market.surface(expiries, tenors, values)
>>> env = ppf.market.environment()
>>> key = "ve.term.eur.hw"
>>> env.add_surface(key, surf)
>>> key = "cv.mr.eur.hw"
>>> env.add_constant(key, 0.01)
>>> r = ppf.model.hull_white.requestor()
>>> s = state("eur", 11, 3.5)
>>> x = s.fill(1.25, r, env)
>>> for i in range(11): print x[i]
-0.787540762658
-0.630032610127
-0.472524457595
-0.315016305063
-0.157508152532
0.0
0.157508152532
0.315016305063
0.472524457595
0.630032610127
0.787540762658
```

Although it is common among practitioners to write the Monte-Carlo version of their Hull–White model in the spot measure, for the sake of brevity our implementation is in the terminal measure. The implementation of a state component suitable for Monte-Carlo pricing shown below has been taken from the module ppf.model.hull_white.monte_carlo.state.

```
class state:
  def __init__(self, num_sims):
    self.__num_sims = num_sims
    self.__variates = numpy.zeros((num_sims))

  def num_sims(self):
    return self.__num_sims

  def fill(self, t, req, env):
    return self.__variates

  def set_variates(self, variates):
    if len(variates.shape) <> 1:
      raise RuntimeError, 'expected a 1d array of variates'
    if variates.shape[0] <> self.__num_sims:
      raise RuntimeError, 'mismatched number of simulations'
    self.__variates = variates

  def get_variates(self):
    return self.__variates
```

```
def create_variable(self):
    var = numpy.zeros(self.__num_sims)
    return var
```

Note that both the lattice state class and the Monte-Carlo state class have an implementation of the `fill` method as this enables us to use the same payoff classes in both the lattice pricers and Monte-Carlo pricers.

8.1.3 Filler

Another important requirement of any model is to provide values for market indices such as LIBOR rates, swap rates, equity forwards, inflation rates, etc. In other words values for the variables we usually choose to directly model. It is the job of the *filler* component to perform this function. Obviously to be able to carry out this function the filler component needs to have knowledge of both the market and the state of the world. Therefore, although it is our stated aim to provide functionally orthogonal components, certain components have to depend on more fundamental or core components. Both authors firmly believe that this isn't a limitation of the design but a natural consequence of any attempt to break up what we mean by a model into separate functional components. Indeed, both authors have extensive experience of applying the design to a broad spectrum of pricing problems and have generally found the framework to be extremely flexible and conducive to fast model implementation. An implementation of a fill component suitable for lattice pricing in the Hull–White model can be found in the `ppf.model.hull_white.fill` module and the details are shown below.

```
class fill:
    def __init__(self, terminal_T):
        self.__terminal_T = terminal_T

    def numeraire_rebased_bond(self, t, T, ccy, env, requestor, state):
        if t > T:
            raise RuntimeError, 'time beyond maturity of bond'
        if T > self.__terminal_T:
            raise RuntimeError, \
              'bond maturity after terminal measure bond
               maturity'
        if len(state.shape) <>1:
            raise RuntimeError, 'expected one dimensional arrays'
        dfTN = 1.0
        dfT = requestor.discount_factor(T, ccy, env)
        gt = requestor.term_vol(t, ccy, env)
        phiTTN = requestor.local_vol(T, self.__terminal_T, ccy, env)
        scale = dfT/dfTN*math.exp(-0.5*gt*gt*phiTTN*phiTTN)
        n = state.shape[0]
        ret = numpy.zeros(n)
        for i in range(n):
            x = state[i]
            ret[i] = scale*math.exp(phiTTN*x)
        return ret

    def numeraire(self, t, ccy, env, requestor, state):
```

```python
    if t > self.__terminal_T:
      raise RuntimeError, \
       'time beyond terminal measure bond maturity'
    ptt = self.numeraire_rebased_bond(t, t, ccy, env, requestor,
                                       state)
    n = state.shape[0]
    ret = numpy.zeros(n)
    ret.fill(1.0)
    ret = ret/ptt
    return ret

  def libor(self, t, libor_obs, env, requestor, state):
    if len(state.shape) <>1:
      raise RuntimeError, 'expected one dimensional array'
    n = state.shape[0]
    fix = libor_obs.fix()
    if fix.is_fixed():
      ret = numpy.zeros(n)
      for i in range(n):
        ret[i] = fix.value()
      return ret

    proj_start_date = libor_obs.proj_start_date()
    proj_end_date = libor_obs.proj_end_date()
    dcf = libor_obs.year_fraction()
    dfs = self.numeraire_rebased_bond(t, \
        env.relative_date(proj_start_date)/365.0,\
        libor_obs.reset_currency(),\
         env, requestor, state)
    dfe = self.numeraire_rebased_bond(t, \
        env.relative_date(proj_end_date)/365.0,\
        libor_obs.reset_currency(),\
        env, requestor, state)
    ret = numpy.zeros(n)
    for i in range(n):
       ret[i] = (dfs[i]/dfe[i]-1.0)/dcf
    return ret

  def swap(self, t, swap_obs, env, requestor, state):
    if len(state.shape) <> 1:
      raise RuntimeError, 'expected one dimensional array'
    n = state.shape[0]
    fix = swap_obs.fix()
    if fix.is_fixed():
      ret = numpy.zeros(n)
      for i in range(n):
        ret[i] = fix.value()
      return ret

    fixed_flows = swap_obs.fixed_flows()
    fixed_pv = numpy.zeros(n)
```

```
for f in fixed_flows:
    pay_date, dcf = \
      (f.pay_date(), f.year_fraction())
    dfp = self.numeraire_rebased_bond(t, pay_date,\
          swap_obs.reset_currency(), env,\
          requestor, state)
    for i in range(n):
        fixed_pv[i] += dcf*dfp[i]
float_flows = swap_obs.float_flows()
float_pv = numpy.zeros(n)
for f in float_flows:
    obs = f.observables()[0]
    proj_start, proj_end, reset_dcf = \
            (obs.proj_start_date(), obs.proj_end_date(), obs.
            year_fraction())
    dfs = self.numeraire_rebased_bond(t, proj_start,\
          swap_obs.reset_currency(), env,\
          requestor, state)
    dfe = self.numeraire_rebased_bond(t, proj_end,\
          swap_obs.reset_currency(), env,\
          requestor, state)
    pay_date, dcf = \
      (f.pay_date(), f.year_fraction())
    dfp = self.numeraire_rebased_bond(t, pay_date,\
          swap_obs.reset_currency(), env,\
          requestor, state)
    for i in range(n):
        float_pv[i] += (dfs[i]/dfe[i]-1.0)/reset_dcf*dcf*dfp[i]
ret = numpy.zeros(n)
for i in range(n):
    ret[i] = float_pv[i]/fixed_pv[i]
return ret
```

For completeness we also provide sample snippets for using the filler component to get a numeraire-rebased bond (i.e. $P(t, T)/P(t, T_N)$) and a LIBOR rate.

```
>>> from ppf.math.interpolation import loglinear
>>> times = [0.0, 0.5, 1.0, 1.5, 2.0]
>>> factors = [math.exp(-0.05*t) for t in times]
>>> c = ppf.market.curve(times, factors, loglinear)
>>> expiries = [0.1, 0.5, 1.0, 1.5, 2.0, 3.0, 4.0, 5.0]
>>> tenors = [0, 90]
>>> values = numpy.zeros((8, 2))
>>> surf = ppf.market.surface(expiries, tenors, values)
>>> env = ppf.market.environment()
>>> key = "zc.disc.eur"
>>> env.add_curve(key, c)
>>> key = "ve.term.eur.hw"
>>> env.add_surface(key, surf)
>>> key = "cv.mr.eur.hw"
>>> env.add_constant(key, 0.0)
```

```
>>> r = ppf.model.hull_white.requestor()
>>> s = ppf.model.hull_white.state("eur", 11, 3.5)
>>> sx = s.fill(0.25, r, env)
>>> f = fill(2.0)
>>> PtT = f.numeraire_rebased_bond(0.25, 1.5, "eur", env, r, sx)
>>> for i in range(11): print PtT[i]
1.02531512052
1.02531512052
1.02531512052
1.02531512052
1.02531512052
1.02531512052
1.02531512052
1.02531512052
1.02531512052
1.02531512052
1.02531512052


>>> from ppf.math.interpolation import loglinear
>>> times = [0.0, 0.5, 1.0, 1.5, 2.0]
>>> factors = [math.exp(-0.05*t) for t in times]
>>> c = ppf.market.curve(times, factors, loglinear)
>>> expiries = [0.1, 0.5, 1.0, 1.5, 2.0, 3.0, 4.0, 5.0]
>>> tenors = [0, 90]
>>> values = numpy.zeros((8, 2))
>>> surf = ppf.market.surface(expiries, tenors, values)
>>> from ppf.date_time import *
>>> pd = date(2008, 01, 01)
>>> env = ppf.market.environment(pd)
>>> key = "zc.disc.eur"
>>> env.add_curve(key, c)
>>> key = "ve.term.eur.hw"
>>> env.add_surface(key, surf)
>>> key = "cv.mr.eur.hw"
>>> env.add_constant(key, 0.0)
>>> rd = date(2008, 07, 01)
>>> libor_obs = ppf.core.libor_rate(None, 0, 0, rd, "eur",\
    rd, shift(rd+months(6), modified_following),\
    basis_act_360, ppf.core.fixing(False))
>>> r = ppf.model.hull_white.requestor()
>>> s = ppf.model.hull_white.state("eur", 11, 3.5)
>>> sx = s.fill(0.25, r, env)
>>> f = fill(2.0)
>>> libortT = f.libor(0.25, libor_obs, env, r, sx)
>>> for i in range(11): print libortT[i]
0.0499418283138
0.0499418283138
0.0499418283138
0.0499418283138
0.0499418283138
```

```
0.0499418283138
0.0499418283138
0.0499418283138
0.0499418283138
0.0499418283138
0.0499418283138
```

8.1.4 Rollback

As discussed at the beginning of this section, there are two main numerical techniques commonly used in the pricing of financial instruments: namely lattice methods and Monte-Carlo methods. In this section we concentrate on the component required for pricing financial instruments using a lattice method. In any lattice method we constantly need to perform expectations of the form $\mathbb{E}^{\mathbb{P}}[N_t^{-1}V_t|\mathcal{F}_s]$ where V_t is the price of the financial instrument at t, N_t is the numeraire in the measure $\mathbb{P}$ and $\mathcal{F}_s$ is the filtration at $s < t$. In laymen's terms the expectation is just saying find the expected value of the discounted value of the financial instrument at time t given the information about the market at an earlier term s. It is common among practitioners to call this operation either a 'rollback' or 'drag'. We also need to calculate expectations of the form $\mathbb{E}^{\mathbb{P}}[\max\left(N_t^{-1}V_t, 0\right)|\mathcal{F}_s]$ and this type of operation is commonly called a 'rollback max' or 'drag max'. So the purpose of the *rollback* component is to enscapsulate the calculation of these expectations. The rollback component for the Hull–White model is implemented in the `ppf.model.hull_white.lattice.rollback` module as shown below.

```
class rollback:
  def __init__(self, ccy):
      self.__ccy = ccy
      self.__integrator = semi_analytic_domain_integrator()

  def rollback(self, t, T, state, req, env, yT):
      xt = state.fill(t, req, env)
      xT = state.fill(T, req, env)
      xtT = state.incremental_fill(t, T, req, env)
      ftT = state.incremental_distribution(t, T, req, env)
      return self.__integrator.rollback(t, T, xt, xT, xtT, ftT, yT)

  def rollback_max(self, t, T, state, req, env, yT):
      xt = state.fill(t, req, env)
      xT = state.fill(T, req, env)
      xtT = state.incremental_fill(t, T, req, env)
      ftT = state.incremental_distribution(t, T, req, env)
      return self.__integrator.rollback_max(t, T, xt, xT, xtT, ftT, yT)
```

To perform the actual expectation, the rollback component delegates to the semi-analytic domain space integrator implemented in the `ppf.math.semi_analytic_domain_integrator` module. The following snippet illustrates a sample usage of the rollback component.

```
>>> import math
>>> from ppf.math import semi_analytic_domain_integrator
>>> from ppf.math.interpolation import loglinear
>>> times = [0.0, 0.5, 1.0, 1.5, 2.0]
```

```
>>> factors = [math.exp(-0.05*t) for t in times]
>>> import ppf.market
>>> c = ppf.market.curve(times, factors, loglinear)
>>> from numpy import zeros
>>> expiries = [0.0, 0.5, 1.0, 1.5, 2.0, 3.0, 4.0, 5.0]
>>> tenors = [0, 90]
>>> values = zeros((8, 2))
>>> values.fill(0.04)
>>> surf = ppf.market.surface(expiries, tenors, values)
>>> env = ppf.market.environment()
>>> key = "zc.disc.eur"
>>> env.add_curve(key, c)
>>> key = "ve.term.eur.hw"
>>> env.add_surface(key, surf)
>>> key = "cv.mr.eur.hw"
>>> env.add_constant(key, 0.01)
>>> r = ppf.model.hull_white.requestor()
>>> s = ppf.model.hull_white.lattice.state(21, 3.5)
>>> sx = s.fill("eur", 1.0, r, env)
>>> f = ppf.model.hull_white.fill(2.0)
>>> PtT = f.numeraire_rebased_bond(1.0, 1.5, "eur", env, r, sx)
>>> roll = rollback("eur")
>>> yt = roll.rollback(0.5, 1.0, s, r, env, PtT)
>>> y0 = roll.rollback(0.0, 0.5, s, r, env, yt)
>>> for i in range(21): print y0[i]
0.922022844448
0.922022844448
0.922022844448
0.922022844448
0.922022844448
0.922022844448
0.922022844448
0.922022844448
0.922022844448
0.922022844448
0.922022844448
0.922022844448
0.922022844448
0.922022844448
0.922022844448
0.922022844448
0.922022844448
0.922022844448
0.922022844448
0.922022844448
0.922022844448
```

Further unit tests are provided in the module ppf.test.test_hull_white. Each separate test is represented by a method on the class rollback_tests. For example the first method on the class is test_discounted_libor_rollback and checks that the discounted value of the LIBOR at some future date is equal to the forward value today as calculated off the discount curve. Note that the LIBOR rates in the Hull–White model are only martingales if the pay date for the LIBOR rate matches the projection end date.

```
def test_discounted_libor_rollback(self):
    from ppf.date_time \
        import date, shift, modified_following, basis_act_360, months
    pd = date(2008, 01, 01)
    env = ppf.market.environment(pd)
    times = numpy.linspace(0, 6, 10)
    factors = numpy.array([math.exp(-0.05*t) for t in times])
    env.add_curve("zc.disc.eur"
        , ppf.market.curve(times, factors, ppf.math.interpolation.
          loglinear))
    expiries, tenors = [0.0, 0.5, 1.0, 1.5, 2.0, 3.0, 4.0, 5.0, 6.0], \
                       [0, 90]
    values = numpy.zeros((9, 2))
    values.fill(0.001)
    env.add_surface("ve.term.eur.hw"
                  , ppf.market.surface(expiries, tenors, values))
    env.add_constant("cv.mr.eur.hw", 0.01)
    r = ppf.model.hull_white.requestor()
    s = ppf.model.hull_white.lattice.state("eur", 41, 4.5)
    f = ppf.model.hull_white.fill(5.0)
    rd = date(2011, 01, 01)
    libor_obs = \
      ppf.core.libor_rate( \
          None #attributes
        , 0      #flow-id
        , 0      #reset-id
        , rd     #reset-date
        , "eur" #reset-currency
        , rd     #proj-start-date
        , shift(rd + months(6), modified_following) #proj-end-date
        , basis_act_360#proj-basis
        , ppf.core.fixing(False))# fixing (and no spread)
    t = env.relative_date(libor_obs.proj_start_date())/365.0
    T = env.relative_date(libor_obs.proj_end_date())/365.0
    sx = s.fill(t, r, env)
    libort = f.libor(t, libor_obs, env, r, sx)
    ptT = f.numeraire_rebased_bond(t, T, "eur", env, r, sx)
    pv = libort*ptT*libor_obs.year_fraction()
    roll = ppf.model.hull_white.lattice.rollback("eur")
    intermediate_pv = roll.rollback(0.5*t, t, s, r, env, pv)
    actual = \
        roll.rollback(0.0, 0.5*t, s, r, env, intermediate_pv).mean()
    expected = \
        r.discount_factor(t, "eur", env)-r.discount_factor (T, "eur", env)
    _assert_seq_close([expected],[actual],1.0e-6)
```

The next method on the class `test_bond_option` verifies that the price for a bond option computed numerically matches the analytic price. Note that because the numeraire-rebased zero coupon bond is a lognormal martingale, the price of a bond option is simply given by the famous Black–Scholes option pricing formula.

```
def test_bond_option(self):
  from ppf.date_time \
       import date, shift, modified_following, basis_act_360, months
  pd = date(2008, 01, 01)
  env = ppf.market.environment(pd)
  times = numpy.linspace(0, 6, 10)
  factors = numpy.array([math.exp(-0.05*t) for t in times])
  env.add_curve("zc.disc.eur"
     , ppf.market.curve(times, factors, ppf.math.interpolation.
       loglinear))
  expiries, tenors = [0.0, 0.5, 1.0, 1.5, 2.0, 3.0, 4.0, 5.0, 6.0], \
                     [0, 90]
  values = numpy.zeros((9, 2))
  values.fill(0.001)
  env.add_surface("ve.term.eur.hw"
              , ppf.market.surface(expiries, tenors, values))
  env.add_constant("cv.mr.eur.hw", 0.01)
  r = ppf.model.hull_white.requestor()
  s = ppf.model.hull_white.lattice.state("eur", 41, 4.5)
  f = ppf.model.hull_white.fill(5.0)
  t = 3.0
  T = 4.0
  terminal_T = 5.0
  sx = s.fill(t, r, env)
  ptT = f.numeraire_rebased_bond(t, T, "eur", env, r, sx)
  k = 0.9
  pv = ptT-k
  roll = ppf.model.hull_white.lattice.rollback("eur")
  actual = roll.rollback_max(0.0, t, s, r, env, pv).mean()
  volt = r.term_vol(t, "eur", env)* \
         r.local_vol(T, terminal_T, "eur", env)
  F = r.discount_factor(T, "eur", env)
  d1 = math.log(F/k)/volt+0.5*volt
  d2 = d1-volt
  expected = F*ppf.math.N(d1)-k*ppf.math.N(d2)
  _assert_seq_close([expected],[actual],1.0e-5)
```

The last method `test_constant` checks that the conditional expectation of a constant is equal to the constant.

```
def test_constant(self):
  from ppf.date_time \
       import date, shift, modified_following, basis_act_360, months
  pd = date(2008, 01, 01)
  env = ppf.market.environment(pd)
  times = numpy.linspace(0, 6, 10)
  factors = numpy.array([math.exp(-0.05*t) for t in times])
  env.add_curve("zc.disc.eur"
     , ppf.market.curve( \
```

```
            times, factors, ppf.math.interpolation.loglinear))
    expiries, tenors = [0.0, 0.5, 1.0, 1.5, 2.0, 3.0, 4.0, 5.0, \
                        6.0], [0, 90]
    values = numpy.zeros((9, 2))
    values.fill(0.001)
    env.add_surface("ve.term.eur.hw"
                    , ppf.market.surface(expiries, tenors, values))
    env.add_constant("cv.mr.eur.hw", 0.01)
    r = ppf.model.hull_white.requestor()
    s = ppf.model.hull_white.lattice.state("eur", 41, 5.5)
    f = ppf.model.hull_white.fill(5.0)
    t = 3.0
    T = 4.0
    terminal_T = 5.0
    sx = s.fill(t, r, env)
    yT = numpy.zeros(41)
    yT.fill(1)
    roll = ppf.model.hull_white.lattice.rollback("eur")
    yt = roll.rollback(t, T, s, r, env, yT)
    _assert_seq_close(yt, yT, 1.0e-5)
```

8.1.5 Evolve

In this subsection we discuss the component required for pricing financial instruments using Monte-Carlo methods. We call this component the *evolve*. Essentially the evolve component has the responsibility of evolving forwards in time any stochastic variables needed by the model to carry out the functionality provided by the fill component. As already mentioned, in the interest of brevity we stay in the terminal measure. In particular this means that we can re-use the fill component already discussed for the Monte-Carlo model.

In the terminal measure there is only one state variable that needs to be evolved: namely, $\int_0^t C(s)dW(s)$. In a typical application, the evolve step will be peformed on a discrete set of contiguous times. In other words, suppose we have the discrete times $\{T_1, T_2, \ldots, T_i\}$ with the time today denoted by T_0, then the simulation of $\int_0^{T_i} C(s)dW(s)$ is carried out as the discrete sum shown below

$$\int_0^{T_i} C(s)dW(s) = \sum_{k=0}^{i} \sqrt{\int_{T_k}^{T_{k+1}} C^2(s)ds}\, Z_K \qquad (8.2)$$

with $Z_1, Z_2, \ldots$ independent, identical distributed normal variates with distribution $N(0, 1)$.

The evolve component of the Hull–White model is implemented in the `ppf.model.hull_white.monte_carlo.evolve` module as shown below.

```
class evolve:
    def __init__(self, ccy, seed = 1234, antithetic = True):
        self.__ccy = ccy
        self.__seed = seed
        self.__antithetic = antithetic

    def evolve(self, t, T, state, req, env):
```

```
if t > T:
  raise RuntimeError, 'attempting to evolve backwards'
if t == T:
  return
variates = state.get_variates()
num_sims = variates.shape[0]
if self.__antithetic:
    raise RuntimeError, \
       'expected number of simulations to be even with' \
       'antithetic'
  num_sims /= 2
volt = req.term_vol(t, self.__ccy, env)
volT = req.term_vol(T, self.__ccy, env)
vartT = volT*volT-volt*volt
if vartT < 0:
  raise RuntimeError, 'negative incremental variance'
voltT = math.sqrt(vartT)
generator = random.Random(self.__seed)
for i in range(num_sims):
  z = generator.gauss(0, 1.0)
  variates[i] = variates[i]+voltT*z
  if self.__antithetic:
    variates[num_sims+i] = variates[num_sims+i]-voltT*z
state.set_variates(variates)
self.__seed = self.__seed+1
```

The evolve component is constructed by passing in the currency, the start seed for the random generator and a boolean to control whether we wish to have antithetic variates. We delegate to a random number generator in the Python `random` module to generate the normal variates. The generated variates are then pushed into the state component. The `evolve` method provides the functionality necessary to carry out the evolve step. Provided `t` is not equal to `T`, then every time the `evolve` method is called, the underlying seed for the random generator is incremented by 1. This ensures that the variates for each evolve step are as independent as possible.

In more complicated models it is normal to fix the discretisation of the time axis over which the model is evolved and then use a combination of interpolation and/or a Brownian bridge to fill in the gaps when we come to request the state of the world at times other than the discretisation times. There are many reasons for wanting to fix the discretisation of the time axis but the main reason is that many stochastic differential equations do not have analytic solutions, which means that the equations have to be discretised (e.g. using the Euler's scheme) in order to solve them. Naturally any discretisation scheme is approximate and the writer of the model will want to control the discretisation error by fixing the size of the evolution step. The authors have found that the aforementioned abstractions of the model into core components works extremely well, even for sophisticated models like the Libor Market Model with stochastic volatility, which requires a non-trivial discretisation scheme in order to evolve the state variables of the model forwards in time. The following snippet illustrates a typical application of the evolve component.

```
>>> import ppf.market
>>> from numpy import zeros
```

```
>>> expiries = [0.0, 0.5, 1.0, 1.5, 2.0, 3.0, 4.0, 5.0]
>>> tenors = [0, 90]
>>> values = zeros((8, 2))
>>> values.fill(0.001)
>>> surf = ppf.market.surface(expiries, tenors, values)
>>> env = ppf.market.environment()
>>> key = "ve.term.eur.hw"
>>> env.add_surface(key, surf)
>>> key = "cv.mr.eur.hw"
>>> env.add_constant(key, 0.01)
>>> r = ppf.model.hull_white.requestor()
>>> s = ppf.model.hull_white.monte_carlo.state(10000)
>>> e = evolve("eur")
>>> e.evolve(0.0,0.5,s,r,env)
```

Once again unit tests are provided in the module ppf.test.test_hull_white. The first method test_mean_and_variance on the class evolve_tests verifies that the state of the world after two evolve steps, each of half a year, has the expected distribution.

```
def test_mean_and_variance(self):
  from ppf.date_time \
      import date, shift, modified_following, basis_act_360, months
  pd = date(2008, 01, 01)
  env = ppf.market.environment(pd)
  times = numpy.linspace(0, 6, 10)
  factors = numpy.array([math.exp(-0.05*t) for t in times])
  env.add_curve("zc.disc.eur"
      , ppf.market.curve(times, factors, ppf.math.interpolation.
        loglinear))
  expiries, tenors = [0.0, 0.5, 1.0, 1.5, 2.0, 3.0, 4.0, 5.0, \
                    6.0], [0, 90]
  values = numpy.zeros((9, 2))
  values.fill(0.01)
  env.add_surface("ve.term.eur.hw"
              , ppf.market.surface(expiries, tenors, values))
  env.add_constant("cv.mr.eur.hw", 0.01)
  r = ppf.model.hull_white.requestor()
  s = ppf.model.hull_white.monte_carlo.state(10000)
  e = ppf.model.hull_white.monte_carlo.evolve("eur")
  e.evolve(0.0,0.5,s,r,env)
  e.evolve(0.5,1.0,s,r,env)
  variates = s.get_variates()
  mean = variates.sum()/10000
  assert(math.fabs(mean) < 1.0e-4)
  tmp = variates*variates
  variance = tmp.sum()/10000
  vol = r.term_vol(1.0,"eur",env)
  assert(math.fabs(variance-vol*vol) < 1.0e-4)
```

The second method test_bond confirms that the expected value of a numeraire-rebased zero coupon bond after a single evolve step matches the value today.

```
def test_bond(self):
  from ppf.date_time \
      import date, shift, modified_following, basis_act_360, months
  pd = date(2008, 01, 01)
  env = ppf.market.environment(pd)
  times = numpy.linspace(0, 6, 10)
  factors = numpy.array([math.exp(-0.05*t) for t in times])
  env.add_curve("zc.disc.eur"
      , ppf.market.curve(times, factors, ppf.math.interpolation.
      loglinear))
  expiries, tenors = [0.0, 0.5, 1.0, 1.5, 2.0, 3.0, 4.0, 5.0, \
                  6.0], [0, 90]
  values = numpy.zeros((9, 2))
  values.fill(0.001)
  env.add_surface("ve.term.eur.hw"
              , ppf.market.surface(expiries, tenors, values))
  env.add_constant("cv.mr.eur.hw", 0.01)
  r = ppf.model.hull_white.requestor()
  s = ppf.model.hull_white.monte_carlo.state(10000)
  e = ppf.model.hull_white.monte_carlo.evolve("eur")
  e.evolve(0.0,3.0,s,r,env)
  f = ppf.model.hull_white.fill(5.0)
  t = 3.0
  T = 4.0
  sx = s.fill(t, r, env)
  ptT = f.numeraire_rebased_bond(t, T, "eur", env, r, sx)
  actual = ptT.mean()
  expected = r.discount_factor(T, "eur", env)
  assert(math.fabs(actual-expected) < 1.0e-3)
```

8.1.6 Exercise

To price callable structures using Monte-Carlo methods we need to be able to estimate the exercise boundary, or equivalently, the probability of exercise. The exercise boundary is expressed as a function (to be estimated) of variables, such as a LIBOR rate or a swap rate; the variables are usually referred to as explanatory variables. The exercise component encapsulates the need to be able to calculate explanatory variables as part of any algorithm for estimating the exercise boundary. We have implemented an exercise component suitable for single currency callable LIBOR exotics such as Bermudans, inverse floaters and cap floaters. The exercise component of the Hull–White model can be found in the `ppf.model.hull_white.monte_carlo.cle_exercise` module and is illustrated below. The constructor of the exercise component takes in a leg and the component supplies two methods: the `num_explanatory_variables` method for determining the number of explanatory variables; and the function call operator whose job it is to calculate the explanatory variables at a particular point in time. In the body of the function call operator we first harvest the remaining active flows and subsequently use them to build both the LIBOR rate and the swap rate. The explanatory variables are then returned to the client.

```
class cle_exercise:
  def __init__(self, l):
    self.__leg = l
```

```
def num_explanatory_variables(self):
  return 2
def __call__(self, t, fill, state, requestor, env):
  # harvest active flows
  all_flows = self.__leg.flows()
  flows = []
  for flow in all_flows:
    accrual_start_days = env.relative_date(
      flow.accrual_start_date())
    if accrual_start_days >= t*365.0:
      flows.append(flow)
  if len(flows) < 1:
    raise RuntimeError, "no active flows remaining"

  # explanatory variables
  num_sims = state.shape[0]
  evs = numpy.zeros((num_sims, self.num_explanatory_variables()))
  pv01 = numpy.zeros(num_sims)
  notl_exchange = numpy.zeros(num_sims)
  cnt = 0
  for flow in flows:
    Ts = env.relative_date(flow.accrual_start_date())/365.0
    Te = env.relative_date(flow.accrual_end_date())/365.0
    Tp = env.relative_date(flow.pay_date())/365.0
    dfp = fill.numeraire_rebased_bond(t, Tp, flow.pay_currency()\
                                     , env, requestor, state)
    pv01 += flow.year_fraction()*dfp
    if cnt == 0:
      dfs = fill.numeraire_rebased_bond(t, Ts, flow.pay_currency()\
                                       , env, requestor, state)
      notl_exchange = dfs
      dfe = fill.numeraire_rebased_bond(t, Te, flow.pay_currency()\
                                       , env, requestor, state)
      evs[:, 0] = (dfs/dfe-1.0)/flow.year_fraction()
    elif cnt == len(flows)-1:
      notl_exchange -= fill.numeraire_rebased_bond(t, Te,
                       flow.pay_currency(), env,
                       requestor, state)
    cnt = cnt+1

  evs[:, 1] = notl_exchange/pv01

  return evs
```

Note that the above component is model independent and therefore could be re-used for other models.

Unit tests for the exercise component are provided in the module ppf.test.test_hull_white. The method test_explanatory_variables on the class exercise_tests checks that the computed explanatory variables, the LIBOR and swap rates, match the corresponding rates taken from the yield curve for the case when the Hull–White volatilities are all zero.

```
def test_explanatory_variables(self):
    from ppf.math.interpolation import loglinear
    times = [0.0, 0.5, 1.0, 1.5, 2.0, 2.5, 3.0]
    factors = [math.exp(-0.05*t) for t in times]
    c = ppf.market.curve(times, factors, loglinear)
    expiries = [0.0, 0.5, 1.0, 1.5, 2.0, 3.0, 4.0, 5.0]
    tenors = [0, 90]
    values = numpy.zeros((8, 2))
    surf = ppf.market.surface(expiries, tenors, values)
    from ppf.date_time \
         import date, shift_convention, modified_following, \
         basis_act_360, months
    pd = date(2008, 01, 01)
    env = ppf.market.environment(pd)
    key = "zc.disc.eur"
    env.add_curve(key, c)
    key = "ve.term.eur.hw"
    env.add_surface(key, surf)
    key = "cv.mr.eur.hw"
    env.add_constant(key, 0.0)
    r = ppf.model.hull_white.requestor()
    s = ppf.model.hull_white.monte_carlo.state(10)
    sx = s.fill(0.25, r, env)
    f = ppf.model.hull_white.fill(3.0)
    flows = ppf.core.generate_flows(
              start  = date(2008, 01, 01)
            , end    = date(2010, 01, 01)
            , duration = months
            , period = 6
            , shift_method = shift_convention.modified_following
            , basis = "ACT/360"
            , pay_currency = "EUR")
    lg = ppf.core.leg(flows, ppf.core.PAY)
    ex = ppf.model.hull_white.monte_carlo.cle_exercise(lg)
    t = env.relative_date(flows[1].accrual_start_date())/365.0
    T = env.relative_date(flows[1].accrual_end_date())/365.0
    ret = ex(t, f, sx, r, env)
    dft = c(t)
    dfT = c(T)
    expected_libor = (dft/dfT-1.0)/flows[1].year_fraction()
    pv01 = 0.0
    for fl in flows[1:]:
      T = env.relative_date(fl.pay_date())/365.0
      dfT = c(T)
      pv01 += fl.year_fraction()*dfT
    T = env.relative_date(flows[-1].accrual_end_date())/365.0
    dfT = c(T)
    expected_swap = (dft-dfT)/pv01
```

```
expected_libors = numpy.zeros(10)
expected_libors.fill(expected_libor)
expected_swaps = numpy.zeros(10)
expected_swaps.fill(expected_swap)
actual_libors = ret[:, 0]
actual_swaps = ret[:, 1]

_assert_seq_close(actual_libors, expected_libors)
_assert_seq_close(actual_swaps, expected_swaps)
```

8.2   THE MODEL AND MODEL FACTORIES

The model class brings all the components from the preceding sections together into one place. The module ppf.model.model is illustrated below. A model is constructed by passing the components into the constructor. An exception is thrown if both the evolve component and the rollback component are null or both the evolve and rollback components are non-null. Accessor methods to the contained components are also provided.

```
class model:
  def __init__(self, requestor, state, fill, rollback = None,
               evolve = None\ , exercise = None):
    self.__requestor = requestor
    self.__state = state
    self.__fill = fill
    self.__rollback = rollback
    self.__evolve = evolve
    self.__exercise = exercise
    # check that either the evolve or rollback policy isn't None
    if self.__rollback == None and self.__evolve == None:
      raise RuntimeError, \
       "either the 'rollback' or 'evolve' must be defined"
    if self.__rollback <> None and self.__evolve <> None:
      raise RuntimeError, \
       "either the 'rollback' or 'evolve' must be defined"
    # check that the exercise policy can only be bound with the
      evolve
    if self.__exercise <> None and self.__rollback <> None:
      raise RuntimeError, \
       "the 'exercise' cannot be bound to the 'rollback'"

  def requestor(self):
    return self.__requestor

  def state(self):
    return self.__state

  def fill(self):
    return self.__fill

  def rollback(self):
    if self.__rollback == None:
```

```
      raise RuntimeError, "'rollback' component is undefined"
    return self.__rollback

  def evolve(self):
    if self.__evolve == None:
      raise RuntimeError, "'evolve' component is undefined"
    return self.__evolve

  def exercise(self):
    if self.__exercise == None:
      raise RuntimeError, "'exercise' component is undefined"
    return self.__exercise
```

The final missing components in the model framework are classes for managing the construction of all the model components. Such classes are commonly referred to as factory classes. An example of a factory class for the Hull–White lattice model can be found in the module `ppf.model.model_factories` as shown below. The factory supports the function call operator with a signature consisting of the trade, the environment and optional model arguments. The model arguments is simply a Python dictionary. Stepping through the implementation we see that we first of all ensure that the financial instrument is single currency. The next step is to determine the last important date of the trade: this will typically be either the final payment date or the final important date of the last observable. This date will be interpreted as the terminal measure bond maturity in the constructor of the fill component. If the model arguments are non-null, then the `num states` and the `num std dev` are retrieved from the dictionary, otherwise default values are provided. Finally all the components for a Hull–White lattice model are constructed and passed into the constructor of the model, which is then returned to the client.

```
class hull_white_lattice_model_factory:
  def __call__(self, trd, env, model_args = None):
    ccy = ppf.core.enforce_single_currency(trd)
    terminal_T = env.relative_date(ppf.core.final_important_date(trd))/
              365.0
    n = 31
    if model_args <> None and model_args.has_key("num states"):
      n = model_args["num states"]
    std_dev = 4.5
    if model_args <> None and model_args.has_key("num std dev"):
      std_dev = model_args["num std dev"]
    s = lattice.state(ccy, n, std_dev)
    rb = lattice.rollback(ccy)
    f = fill(terminal_T)
    r = requestor()
    return model(r, s, f, rb)
```

From the Python command line, a Hull–White model can be created using the above factory as follows:

```
>>> pd = date(2008, 05, 01)
>>> from ppf.market import environment
>>> env = environment(pd)
```

```
>>> from ppf.date_time import *
>>> from pay_receive import *
>>> from generate_flows import *
>>> from generate_observables import *
>>> from generate_exercise_table import *
>>> from exercise_type import *
>>> from leg import *
>>> from trade import *
>>> libor_observables = generate_libor_observables(
...      start = date(2007, Jun, 29)
...      , end  = date(2009, Jun, 29)
...      , roll_period = 6
...      , roll_duration = ppf.date_time.months
...      , reset_period = 3
...      , reset_duration = ppf.date_time.months
...      , reset_currency = "JPY"
...      , reset_basis = basis_act_360
...      , reset_shift_method = shift_convention.modified_following)
>>> coupon_observables = generate_fixed_coupon_observables(
...      start = date(2007, Jun, 29)
...      , end  = date(2009, Jun, 29)
...      , roll_period = 6
...      , reset_currency = "JPY"
...      , coupon_shift_method = shift_convention.modified_following
...      , coupon_rate = 0.045)
>>> #semi-annual flows
>>> pay_flows = generate_flows(
...      start = date(2007, Jun, 29)
...      , end  = date(2009, Jun, 29)
...      , duration = ppf.date_time.months
...      , period = 6
...      , shift_method = shift_convention.modified_following
...      , basis = "30/360"
...      , pay_currency = "JPY"
...      , observables = coupon_observables)
>>> rcv_flows = generate_flows(
...      start = date(2007, Jun, 29)
...      , end  = date(2009, Jun, 29)
...      , duration = ppf.date_time.months
...      , period = 6
...      , shift_method = shift_convention.modified_following
...      , basis = "A/360"
...      , pay_currency = "JPY"
...      , observables = libor_observables)
>>> pay_leg = leg(pay_flows, PAY)
>>> receive_leg = leg(rcv_flows, RECEIVE)
>>> #1y nc
>>> ex_sched = generate_exercise_table(
...      start = date(2008, Jun, 29)
... , end  = date(2009, Jun, 29)
... , period = 1
```

```
... , duration = ppf.date_time.years
... , shift_method = shift_convention.modified_following)
>>> structure = trade((pay_leg, receive_leg), (ex_sched,
                exercise_type.callable))
>>> factory = hull_white_lattice_model_factory()
>>> hwmodel = factory(structure, env)
```

The corresponding factory for the Hull–White Monte-Carlo model is shown below. The details are almost identical to the factory for the Hull–White lattice model. The main differences are that the model argument dictionary is used to control the values of the number of simulations and start seed, and instead of a rollback component being constructed we construct an evolve component. We finish off by constructing an exercise component for the case when the trade is callable.

```
class hull_white_monte_carlo_model_factory:
  def __call__(self, trd, env, model_args = None):
    ccy = ppf.core.enforce_single_currency(trd)
    terminal_T = env.relative_date(ppf.core.final_important_date(trd))/
                365.0
    num_sims = 1000
    if model_args <> None and model_args.has_key("num sims"):
      num_sims = model_args["num sims"]
    seed = 1234
    if model_args <> None and model_args.has_key("seed"):
      seed = model_args["seed"]
    s = monte_carlo.state(num_sims)
    ev = monte_carlo.evolve(ccy, seed)
    f = fill(terminal_T)
    r = requestor()
    ex = None
    id = 0
    if model_args <> None and \
     model_args.has_key("explanatory variables leg id"):
      id = model_args["explanatory variables leg id"]
    if trd.has_exercise_schedule():
      ex = monte_carlo.cle_exercise(trd.legs()[id])
    return model(r, s, f, None, ev, ex)
```

8.3   CONCLUDING REMARKS

By splitting the concept of a model into functionally orthogonal pieces we have been able to design an extremely flexible framework within which it is easy to develop new models. In particular, the design promotes code re-use. The idea of breaking complex concepts into simpler more fundamental orthogonal pieces is not new in programming. What we have done is nothing more than composition in the language of C++. More recently a number of authors have developed the idea further. One example, from [1], is the concept of policies. A policy defines a class interface or class template interface with the emphasis firmly on behaviour or functionality. The core theme of [1] is the idea of bringing together many different policies to produce a functionally richer interface. The inspiration for the design developed in this chapter has come from the idea of policy-based programming.

The design pattern for the model can be transferred over to C++ and indeed in any business application the bulk of the core code would be in C++ for reasons of efficiency. At this point, the developer has two choices: either to use a mix of composition and class inheritance hierarchies or a policy-based design. Both authors have found the latter to be a better choice because the advantage of compile-time checking easily outweighs the marginal increase in compile-time overhead. As this book is about the application of Python to financial programming, the emphasis has been on Python rather than C++. However the techniques required to carry out the migration are discussed in Chapter 11.

Pricing using Numerical Methods

As the demand for ever more complex financial structures grows and the trend towards multi-asset products accelerates, quantitative analysts will resort more and more to numerical methods to solve their pricing problems. The two most common approaches currently in use are Monte-Carlo simulation and lattice integration schemes, for example finite difference. In this chapter we will develop a general framework for both approaches that can be used to price a large set of pricing problems. The ultimate goal of the chapter is to arrive at a design where the pricing frameworks are invariant over the pricing model used.

9.1 A LATTICE PRICING FRAMEWORK

Let us begin this section by outlining the domain of problems the lattice pricing framework to be developed will be able to handle. Firstly, the pricing model needs to be a low-dimensional Markovian model otherwise the time taken to price becomes prohibitive; and, secondly, the financial instrument must not be path-dependent. If these two criteria are satisfied, then the following framework is applicable. The second criterion can be relaxed, through the introduction of state-variables, to include only strongly path-dependent instruments. However this next step is beyond the scope of the book and we leave it as an exercise for the reader.

The aforementioned criteria restrict the universe of pricing problems to a class of instruments commonly referred to as 'vanilla' callable LIBOR exotics. A typical instrument is made up of two legs, a funding leg and an exotic coupon leg, together with an exercise schedule. The funding leg is simply a strip of cash flows at regular intervals paying LIBOR plus a spread. The exotic coupon leg consists of a strip of cash flows at regular intervals paying some function of LIBOR, for example a LIBOR collar. The exercise schedule gives the holder of the financial instrument the right to cancel or call the trade, again at regular intervals. Typically the exercise decision dates fall on one of the reset dates of the cash flows – otherwise a stub payment usually has to be paid if an exercise decision falls mid-way through the accrual period of a cash flow. We will restrict ourselves to the case of no stub flows. Note that the combination of the funding leg and exotic coupon leg is referred to as a swap because the holder usually pays, or receives, the exotic coupon cash flows in exchange for receiving, or paying, the funding cash flows.

Let us denote the pricing date by T_0, the exercise decision dates by $T_1 < T_2 < \ldots < T_M$, the pricing numeraire by N_{T_i} and the expectation in the pricing measure by $\mathbb{E}$. The price of the callable trade can be written as follows

$$N_{T_i}^{-1} V_{T_i}^{\text{call}} = \max(\mathbb{E}[N_{T_{i+1}}^{-1} V_{T_{i+1}}^{\text{call}} | \mathcal{F}_{T_i}], N_{T_i}^{-1} V_{T_i}^{\text{swap}}) \tag{9.1}$$

with boundary condition

$$V_{T_{M+1}}^{call} = 0 \tag{9.2}$$

Here $V_{T_i}^{call}$ represents the price of the callable structure at T_i and similarly $V_{T_i}^{swap}$ denotes the price of the underlying swap at T_i. In other words we iterate backwards through the list of exercise decision dates, evaluating equation (9.1) on each exercise decision date until we reach T_0, the pricing date. Next we denote the union of the cash-flow payment dates by $t_1 < t_2 < \ldots < t_N$ and the value of the cash flow payments at t_i by $V_{t_i}^{cf}$. Then the price of the underlying swap at T_i is given by the summation

$$V_{T_i}^{swap} = N_{T_i} \sum_{k=n(T_i)}^{N} \mathbb{E}[N_{t_k}^{-1} V_{t_k}^{cf} | \mathcal{F}_{T_i}] \qquad (9.3)$$

with $T_i \leq t_k \forall k \geq n(T_i)$. The conditional expectations, in the equations above, are calculated on the lattice of the pricing model. Note that the price of the cancellable trade is simply the price of the underlying swap plus the price of the callable on the reverse of the underlying swap (i.e. with the pay and receive legs swapped around).

Now that we understand how to price the trades we need to set about writing a pricer to price them. Fortunately we already have all the fundamental building blocks to hand. Before we discuss the implementation of the pricer in detail, we must first return to the controller and add a few more methods. The following code excerpt from ppf.core.controller contains the new methods. When pricing we need to maintain the state of various symbols required in the calculation, for example a symbol for the value of the underlying. We also need to know when the symbol was last updated – this is necessary during arithmetic operations on the values of two symbols, such as addition. Before carrying out the arithmetic operation we must first ensure that the two symbols are synchronised, that is they were last updated at the same time. If one of the symbols was last updated at a later time (recall we iterate backwards in time), then we need to rollback, or equivalently perform a conditional expectation on, the value of the symbol to the time of the other symbol. The method retrieve_symbols_to_rollback() on the controller queries the symbol table for all symbols with a last update time later than the specified time at. The remaining two methods, rollback() and rollback_max(), rollback a symbol or the maximum of two symbols from time T to time t. The actual calculation of the conditional expecations is carried out by the rollback component of the model stored in the controller.

```
class controller:
  def retrieve_symbols_to_rollback(self, at):
    symbols = []
    for symbol in self.__symbol_table:
      pair = self.__symbol_table.get(symbol)
      if pair[0] > at:
        symbols.append(symbol)
    return symbols

  def rollback(self, T, t, symbol):
    requestor = self.__model.requestor()
    state = self.__model.state()
    return self.__model.rollback().rollback(t, T, state
        , requestor, self.__env, symbol)

  def rollback_max(self, T, t, symbol_one, symbol_two):
    requestor = self.__model.requestor()
    state = self.__model.state()
```

```
      res1 = self.__model.rollback().rollback(t, T, state
                   , requestor, self.__env, symbol_one)
      res2 = self.__model.rollback().rollback_max(t, T, state
                   , requestor, self.__env, symbol_two-symbol_one)
      return res1+res2
```

The following excerpt from `ppf.pricer.lattice_pricer` illustrates the details of
the lattice pricer. The pricer is constructed by passing in the trade, the model, the market
environment and an optional object called a symbol table listener. In the body of the constructor
itself we check that the trade contains no stubs and then construct the timeline from the trade
and the pricing date.

```
class lattice_pricer:
  def __init__(self, trade, model, env, symbol_table_listener = None):
    self.__trade = trade
    self.__model = model
    self.__env = env
    self.__symbol_table_listener = symbol_table_listener
    # check no stubs
    trade_utils.enforce_no_exercise_stubs(trade)
    # create timeline
    self.__timeline = timeline(trade, env.pricing_date())
  def __symbol_listener_(self, t, symbol, value):
    if self.__symbol_table_listener:
      self.__symbol_table_listener(t, symbol, value, self.__model,
      self.__env)
```

The main method of the pricing framework is the function call operator: it is this method that
performs the actual pricing. We will step through this method line by line highlighting the
main features. The first thing we do is construct a controller – recall that this is the class that
provides the conduit between the pricing framework and the pricing model. We then retrieve
the dates on which conditional expectations need to be calculated. We do this by calling the
`times` method on the timeline: on each of these times a collection of events will have been
registered during the construction of the timeline. We conclude the set up, phase of the pricing
by injecting the symbols 'underlying', 'berm', 'leg0', 'leg1', ... into the symbol table of the
controller. Each of these symbols has an initial value of zero.

```
class lattice_pricer:
  def __call__(self):
    # create controller
    ctr = controller(self.__trade, self.__model, self.__env)
    times = self.__timeline.times()
    from_ = self.__env.relative_date(times[-1])/365.0
    # initialise symbols
    ctr.insert_symbol("underlying", from_)
    ctr.insert_symbol("berm", from_)
    cnt = 0
    for l in self.__trade.legs():
      symbol = "leg"+str(cnt)
      ctr.insert_symbol(symbol, from_)
```

```
cnt += 1
.
.
.
```

We now come to the main loop. Here we iterate backwards through the list of times from the timeline, maintaining two time variables from_ and to_. The variable from_ denotes the current time, as a year fraction, at which the events are to be evaluated, and to_ denotes either the next time (in the timeline) or the pricing date, again as a year fraction. At each time we again query the timeline for the collection of events registered at the current time. Once we have the list of events we iterate through them in the order they were registered. The event to be evaluated is passed into the controller via the set_event method. If the event is a pay event, i.e. a cash flow, we delegate to the function call operator of the controller to perform the actual evaluation. After evaluating the pay event, the corresponding symbol for the present value of the leg is retrieved from the symbol table and its value is incremented by the current value of the event. On completion of the evaluation, the value of the corresponding leg symbol is updated in the symbol table. If the event represents an exercise decision, then we compute the underlying by retrieving the values of the leg symbols and adding them together. The value of the callable, denoted by berm, is then computed via an invocation of the rollback_max method on the controller. Finally the underlying is also rolled back using the rollback method on the controller and both the value of the underlying and that of the callable are updated in the symbol table. Note that the underlying is multiplied by the exercise type of the trade prior to performing the calculation of the Bermudan. This way we can evaluate both callable and cancellable instruments within a uniform framework.

```
class lattice_pricer:
  def __call__(self):
    .
    .
    .
    # reverse iterate through the timeline
    for i in range(len(times)-1,-1,-1):
      time = times[i]
      to_ = 0
      if i <> 0:
        to_ = self.__env.relative_date(times[i-1])/365.0
      events = self.__timeline.events(time)
      for event in events:
        # set event on controller
        ctr.set_event(event)
        # evaluate
        if is_pay_event(event):
          # evaluate payoff
          cpn = ctr(from_)
          # rollback symbol
          symbol = "leg"+str(event.leg_id())
          leg_pv = ctr.retrieve_symbol(symbol)
          leg_pv += cpn
          self.__symbol_listener_(from_, symbol, leg_pv)
          ctr.update_symbol(symbol, leg_pv, to_)
```

```
      else:
        # evaluate underlying
        underlying = ctr.retrieve_symbol("underlying")
        underlying *= 0 # not pretty
        cnt = 0
        for l in self._trade.legs():
          underlying += ctr.retrieve_symbol("leg"+str(cnt))
          cnt += 1
        self._symbol_listener_(from_, "underlying"\
           , self._trade.exercise_type()*underlying)
        # rollback berm
        berm = ctr.retrieve_symbol("berm")
        self._symbol_listener_(from_, "berm", berm)
        berm = ctr.rollback_max(from_, to_, berm\
           , self._trade.exercise_type()*underlying)
        # rollback underlying
        underlying = ctr.rollback(from_, to_, underlying)
        # update symbols
        ctr.update_symbol("underlying", underlying, to_)
        ctr.update_symbol("berm", berm, to_)
   .
   .
   .
```

After all the events at a particular time have been evaluated we have to retrieve all the symbols in the symbol table that haven't yet been rolled back to `to_` and roll them back. The computation of the symbols requiring a roll back operation is carried out by the `retrieve_symbols_to_rollback` method of the controller. The final phase of the pricer is the calculation of the present value of the trade. The only complication here is to decide whether the trade has an exercise schedule and, if so, whether the exercise type is callable or cancellable. In the case of the exercise type being cancellable, the present value is the sum of the mean of the callable value and the mean of the underlying value, otherwise the present value is simply the mean of the callable value. If the trade has no exercise schedule, then the present value is just the mean of the underlying value. Note that the mean is calculated using the mean method on the NumPy array.

```
class lattice_pricer:
  def __call__(self):
    .
    .
    .
    # rollback any symbols in symbol table not already
    # rolled back
    symbols = ctr.retrieve_symbols_to_rollback(to_)
    for symbol in symbols:
      from_ = ctr.retrieve_symbol_update_time(symbol)
      value = ctr.retrieve_symbol(symbol)
      value = ctr.rollback(from_, to_, value)
      ctr.update_symbol(symbol, value, to_)
    from_ = to_
  # calculate pv
```

```
underlying = ctr.retrieve_symbol("underlying")
underlying *= 0
cnt = 0
for l in self.__trade.legs():
  underlying += ctr.retrieve_symbol("leg"+str(cnt))
  cnt += 1
ctr.update_symbol("underlying", underlying, to_)
pv = 0
if self.__trade.has_exercise_schedule():
  if self.__trade.exercise_type() == exercise_type.callable:
    pv = ctr.retrieve_symbol("berm").mean()
  else:
    pv = ctr.retrieve_symbol("underlying").mean() \
           + ctr.retrieve_symbol("berm").mean()
else:
  pv = ctr.retrieve_symbol("underlying").mean()
return pv
```

It needs to be emphasised that in the above pricing framework there is theoretically no restriction on the dimensionality of the model. Everything will flow through just as well for a multidimensional model, albeit more slowly, as it would do for a one-dimensional model. The only assumption being made on the underlying numerical container is that it has the arithmetic operators overloaded and a mean operator.

To conclude this section, we note that sometimes it is useful for diagnostics purposes to be able to listen to the symbols at various stages of the calculation. The optional symbol_table_listener argument in the constructor provides this functionality. A concrete example, provided in the test module ppf.test.test_lattice_pricer, is given below:

```
class european_symbol_table_listener:
  def __init__(self):
    self.__symbols = []
  def __call__(self, t, symbol, value, model, env):
    if symbol == "underlying":
      requestor = model.requestor()
      state = model.state()
      self.__symbols.append(
        model.rollback().rollback_max(
          0.0, t, state, requestor, env, value).mean())

  def retrieve_symbols(self):
    return self.__symbols
```

The purpose of the above listener is to store the European option prices at various stages of the pricing. The listened symbols can then be retrieved via an invocation of the retrieve_symbols method on the listener.

9.2   A MONTE-CARLO PRICING FRAMEWORK

Our aim in this section is to develop a Monte-Carlo pricing framework similar in spirit to the lattice-pricing framework already developed. Suppose Y is a random variable, the core idea behind Monte-Carlo pricing is to simulate the value of Y many times and approximate the expectation of Y by the following discrete sum

$$\mathbb{E}[Y] \approx \sum_{i=1}^{n} w_i Y_i \qquad (9.4)$$

where Y_i denotes the ith simulation (or draw) of the value of Y and w_i denotes the associated weight. In most applications the weights are uniform and set to $1/n$. By Kolmogorov's strong law of large numbers, as $n \rightarrow \infty$ the above approximation becomes exact.

It should come as no surprise that we need to add a method onto the controller. The new method is called `evolve` and is detailed below. The implementation is simple, with the actual evolve operation being delegated to the evolve component on the model.

```
def evolve(self, t, T):
  requestor = self.__model.requestor()
  state = self.__model.state()
  self.__model.evolve().evolve(t, T, state, requestor, self.__env)
```

In the next two subsections we develop the pricing framework for pricing both non-callable and callable structures, beginning with non-callable structures.

9.2.1 Pricing Non-callable Trades

The implementation of the Monte-Carlo pricer is in the `ppf.pricer.monte_carlo_pricer` module. To simplify the exposition we only concentrate on those pieces of code from the module needed for pricing non-callable trades. Like the lattice pricer, the Monte-Carlo pricer is constructed by passing in the trade, the model, the environment and an optional symbol table listener.

```
class monte_carlo_pricer:
  def __init__(self, trade, model, env, symbol_table_listener = None):
    self.__trade = trade
    self.__model = model
    self.__env = env
    self.__symbol_table_listener = symbol_table_listener
    # check no stubs
    trade_utils.enforce_no_exercise_stubs(trade)
    # create timeline
    self.__timeline = timeline(trade, env.pricing_date())

  def __symbol_listener__(self, t, symbol, value):
    if self.__symbol_table_listener:
      self.__symbol_table_listener(t, symbol, value, self.__model,
      self.__env)
```

The actual pricing is carried out by the function call operator. Again we step through the implementation of the function call operator line by line. We start by creating the controller. Then we query the timeline for the list of times on which events have been registered. After initialising the `berm`, `underlying`, `leg0`, `leg1`, ... variables to zero and the time `from_` to zero, we come to the main loop.

```
class monte_carlo_pricer:
  def __call__(self, symbol_value_pairs_to_add = None):
    # create controller
    ctr = controller(self.__trade, self.__model, self.__env)
    times = self.__timeline.times()
    from_ = 0.0
    # initialise symbols
    ctr.insert_symbol("underlying", from_)
    ctr.insert_symbol("berm", from_)
    # add extra symbols
    if symbol_value_pairs_to_add:
      for symbol_value_pair in symbol_value_pairs_to_add:
        symbol, value = symbol_value_pair
        ctr.insert_symbol(symbol, value)
    cnt = 0
    for l in self.__trade.legs():
      symbol = "leg"+str(cnt)
      ctr.insert_symbol(symbol, from_)
      cnt += 1
      .
      .
      .
```

In the main loop we iterate forwards in time through the list of times. At each time we invoke the `evolve` operator on the controller to evolve from time `from_` to time `to_` all state variables, required by the model to calculate the payoff, forwards in time. At each time we loop through the events registered at that time and invoke the function call operator on the controller to calcluate the payoff. The corresponding leg variable is retrieved from the symbol table, incremented by the value of the cash flow and pushed back into the symbol table. At the end of the events loop we update the time `from_` to `to_`. The calculation of the present value (pv) returned by the function call operator is exactly the same as for the lattice pricer and needs no further comment.

```
class monte_carlo_pricer:
  def __call__(self, symbol_value_pairs_to_add = None):
      .
      .
      .
    # forward iterate through the timeline
    for time in times:
      to_ = self.__env.relative_date(time)/365.0
      # evolve
      ctr.evolve(from_, to_)
      events = self.__timeline.events(time)
      for event in events:
        # set event on controller
        ctr.set_event(event)
        # evaluate
```

```
        if is_pay_event(event):
            # evaluate payoff
            cpn = ctr(from_)
            symbol = "leg"+str(event.leg_id())
            leg_pv = ctr.retrieve_symbol(symbol)
            leg_pv += cpn
            self.__symbol_listener_(to_, symbol, leg_pv)
            ctr.update_symbol(symbol, leg_pv, to_)
        else:
            raise RuntimeError, 'callables not yet implemented'
      from_ = to_
  # calculate pv
  pv = 0
  if self.__trade.has_exercise_schedule():
      if self.__trade.exercise_type() == exercise_type.callable:
        pv = ctr.retrieve_symbol("berm").mean()
      else:
        pv = ctr.retrieve_symbol("underlying").mean()\
               +ctr.retrieve_symbol("berm").mean()
  else:
    cnt = 0
    for l in self.__trade.legs():
      leg_pv = ctr.retrieve_symbol("leg"+str(cnt))
      pv += leg_pv.mean()
      cnt += 1
  return pv
```

Before moving on to the pricing of callable structures, we note that the signature of the function call operator for the Monte-Carlo pricer differs from that of the lattice pricer. The function call operator now takes an optional list of tuples representing symbol-value pairs that need to be inserted into the symbol table prior to the evaluation taking place. The reason for this addition is down to the strongly path-dependent nature of the type of payoffs evaluated by the Monte-Carlo pricing framework. The strongly path-dependent nature implies the existence of variables whose history influences the payoff and such variables need to be initialised to some starting values.

9.2.2 Pricing Callable Trades

The pricing of callable structures entails finding the optimal exercise rule by solving an optimal stopping time problem. Once the optimal stopping time rule has been discovered, the pricing of a structure simply involves the computation of the expected discounted payoff, subject to the stopping time rule. Let $V(t)$ denote the discounted payoff from exercise at time t and T be the class of stopping times with values in $[0, T]$, where T is the last exercise time. The problem then becomes to find the optimal expected discounted payoff

$$\sup_{\tau \in T} \mathbb{E}[V(t)]. \tag{9.5}$$

There exist many algorithms for estimating the optimal stopping time. However, all algorithms of practical use result in either low-bias estimators or high-bias estimators. A low-bias estimator gives a price for the callable that is bounded above by the true price. In a similar fashion, a high-bias estimator gives a price for the callable that is bounded below by the true price (see [9] for further details). We have implemented a low-bias estimator in terms of the pickup value. The pickup value at a given exercise time is just the difference between the immediate exercise value and the value of holding on to the option. Further details on the exact algorithm for estimating the stopping time can be found in Appendix D but, broadly speaking, at each exercise time we approximate the pickup value as a linear sum of functions of an arbitrary number of explanatory variables and estimate the coefficients in the sum using generalised least squares. The choice of a linear sum of functions for the approximation is standard, but other forms have been mooted in the literature – see [11] for an example applied to the pricing of Bermudan swaptions.

The implementation of our low-bias estimator is taken from the `ppf.math.exercise_regressions` module. Stepping through the code, we begin by defining a number of functors to represent the constant function, the linear function and the quadratic function. Next we define a wrapper class for all the functions used in the approximation of the pickup value. The class is called n_quadratic_fo and the constructor takes in the number of explanatory variables and builds up a list of function objects. For example, if we have two explanatory variables X and Y, then the function call operator of n_quadratic_fo simply mimics the function

$$f(X, Y) = \alpha_1 + \alpha_2 X + \alpha_3 X^2 + \alpha_4 XY + \alpha_5 Y + \alpha_6 Y^2. \qquad (9.6)$$

The final class, fitted_fo, is simply an adaptor of the class n_quadratic_fo with the purpose of providing a function call operator with a single argument.

```
class unit_fo:
  def __call__(self, x):
    return 1.0
class linear_fo:
  def __init__(self, i):
    self.__i = i
  def __call__(self, x):
    return x[self.__i]
class quadratic_fo:
  def __init__(self, i, j):
    self.__i = i
    self.__j = j
  def __call__(self, x):
    return x[self.__i]*x[self.__j]

class n_quadratic_fo:
  def __init__(self,num_expl_vars):
    self.__fos = []
    self.__fos.append(unit_fo())
    for i in range(num_expl_vars):
      self.__fos.append(linear_fo(i))
      for j in range(i, num_expl_vars):
        self.__fos.append(quadratic_fo(i, j))
    self.__n = len(self.__fos)
  def __call__(self, alphas, x):
    y = 0.0
    for i in range(self.__n):
```

```
      y += alphas[i]*self.__fos[i](x)
    return y
  def fit_fos(self):
    return self.__fos

class fitted_fo:
  def __init__(self, alphas, fo):
    self.__alphas = alphas
    self.__fo = fo
  def __call__(self, x):
    return self.__fo(self.__alphas, x)
```

The actual fitting of the approximate sum to the pickup value is carried out by the free function `fit` which, in turn, delegates to the generalised least squares algorithm implemented in `ppf.math.generalised_least_square`. The free function takes in the explanatory variables x and the values to be fitted y and returns an instance of the class `fitted_fo`.

```
def fit(x, y):
  if len(x.shape) <> 2:
    raise RuntimeError, "Expected 'x' to be 2d array"
  if len(y.shape) <> 1:
    raise RuntimeError, "Expected 'y' to be 1d array"
  num_obs = x.shape[0]
  num_expl_vars = x.shape[1]
  if num_obs <> y.shape[0]:
    raise RuntimeError, "'y' array has wrong size"

  fo = n_quadratic_fo(num_expl_vars)
  sig = numpy.zeros(num_obs)
  sig.fill(1.0)
  alphas = generalised_least_squares_fit(y, x, sig, fo.fit_fos())
  return fitted_fo(alphas, fo)
```

Given a fitted function, we need to be able to evaluate it. The free function `evaluate_regression`, taking in the explanatory variables x and the fitted function fo, does this for us.

```
def evaluate_regression(x, fo):
  if len(x.shape) <> 2:
    raise RuntimeError, "Expected 'x' to be a 2d array"
  num_obs = x.shape[0]
  y = numpy.zeros(num_obs)
  for i in range(num_obs):
    y[i] = fo(x[i, :])
  return y
```

Finally, the actual implementation of the pickup regression algorithm is provided in the free function `pickup_value_regression` and follows closely the mathematics in Appendix D.

```
# max for numpy arrays
max = numpy.vectorize(lambda x, y: (x, y)[x < y])
```

```
def pickup_value_regression(ies, ns, vs):
  if len(ies.shape) <> 2:
    raise RuntimeError, "Expected 'immediate exercise" \
                        "values' to be a 2d array"
  if len(ns.shape) <> 2:
    raise RuntimeError, "Expected 'numeraires' to be a 2d array"
  if len(vs.shape) <> 3:
    raise RuntimeError, "Expected 'explanatory" \
    "variables' to be a 3d array"

  num_times = ies.shape[0]
  num_obs = ies.shape[1]
  num_expl_vars = vs.shape[2]

  if ns.shape[0] <> num_times or ns.shape[1] <> num_obs:
    raise RuntimeError, "'numeraires' array has wrong size"
  if vs.shape[0] <> num_times or vs.shape[1] <> num_obs:
    raise RuntimeError, \
      "'explanatory variables' array has wrong size"

  fitted_fos = []
  zero = numpy.zeros(num_obs)
  H = numpy.zeros(num_obs) # holding value
  for i in range(num_times-1,-1,-1):
    x = vs[i, :, :]
    n = ns[i, :]
    pv = n*(ies[i, :]-H) # reinflate by numeraire
    fit_fo = fit(x, pv)
    temp = evaluate_regression(x, fit_fo) # pickup value regression
    fitted_fos.insert(0, fit_fo)
    H += max_(temp/n, zero) # deflate by numeraire

  return fitted_fos
```

Armed with the pickup value regressions we can define a stopping time rule, the details of which are in Appendix D. The class below from the module ppf.pricer.monte_carlo_helper manages the life cycle of the stopping time rule. In the constructor we initialise the indicator on all paths to minus 1, where minus 1 means don't exercise.

```
class exercise_helper:
  def __init__(self, num_sims):
    self.__num_sims = num_sims
    self.__last_cfs = numpy.zeros((num_sims))
    self.__indicator = numpy.zeros((num_sims))
    self.__indicator.fill(-1)
```

In the update_indicator method we update the value of the indicator to the current exercise time, represented by at, on all paths where the pickup value from the regression is positive.

```
class exercise_helper:
  def update_indicator(self, at, vs, fo):
```

```
    regression_value = evaluate_regression(vs, fo)
    for i in range(self.__num_sims):
      if self.__indicator[i] < 0:
        if regression_value[i] > 0:
          self.__indicator[i] = at
        else:
          self.__indicator[i] = -1
```

The class also provides an implementation of the max operator. At each exercise time, at, the max operator does nothing more than check to see if we have exercised on or before the exercise time. On those paths where this is true we return the previous holding value, hv, plus the intermediate cash flows between the current exercise time and the previous exercise time; otherwise we return the holding value.

```
class exercise_helper:
  def max(self, at, cfs, hv):
    res = numpy.zeros((self.__num_sims))
    for i in range(self.__num_sims):
      value = 0.0
      if self.__indicator[i] > 0 and self.__indicator[i] <= at + 0.01:
        # cash flow(s) between exercise dates
        value = cfs[i]-self.__last_cfs[i]
      res[i] = hv[i]+value
    self.__last_cfs = cfs.copy() # deep copy
    return res
```

Because we move forwards in time when pricing using Monte-Carlo, the handling of the cash flows is a bit tricky. We begin by initialising the cash flows to the sum of all cash flows paying on or before the first exercise date. This can be done by invoking the set_last_cfs method.

```
class exercise_helper:
  def set_last_cfs(self, cfs):
    self.__last_cfs = cfs.copy() # deep copy
```

Then at the end of every call to max we update the values of the cash flows to the new sum of all cash flows paying on or before the next exercise date(or the end of the trade). Note that since we need to maintain a copy of the value of cash flows we have to use the copy method of NumPy arrays, otherwise we would just get a reference.

In extending the Monte-Carlo pricing to handle callable instruments we have had to add two more methods to the controller class. The methods are illustrated below. The first method, numeraire, delegates to the fill component of the model to calculate the numeraire at a specified time t. Similarly, the second method, explanatory_variables, delegates to the exercise component of the model to calculate the explanatory variables at a specified time t. One thing to note is the use of the pay_currency method on the event. This method either returns the pay currency for a flow event or the fee currency for an exercise event.

```
  def numeraire(self, t):
    if t < 0:
      raise RuntimeError, \
        "attempting to call numeraire in the past"
    fill = self.__model.fill()
```

```
    requestor = self.__model.requestor()
    state = self.__model.state().fill(t, requestor, self.__env)
    return fill.numeraire(t, self.__event.pay_currency(), self.__env\
                          , requestor, state)

  def explanatory_variables(self, t):
    if t < 0:
      raise RuntimeError, \
        "attempting to call 'explanatory_variables' in the past"
    fill = self.__model.fill()
    requestor = self.__model.requestor()
    state = self.__model.state().fill(t, requestor, self.__env)
    exercise = self.__model.exercise()
    return exercise(t, fill, state, requestor, self.__env)
```

The full unedited version of the Monte-Carlo pricer is in the ppf.pricer.monte_carlo_pricer module. For pricing callable structures you need two instances of the model: one for use in the exercise boundary estimation; and the other for pricing. Both instances will have different seeds for the random number generator(s) to prevent any foresight bias, (see [6] for more details). Furthermore, the estimation of the exercise boundary is usually carried out using fewer paths than the actual pricing, so the models will normally have a different number of simulations. As a consequence of the need for two models, the constructor of the Monte-Carlo pricer has been altered to take in an optional second model used in the estimation of the exercise boundary.

```
class monte_carlo_pricer:
  def __init__(self, trade, model, env, symbol_table_listener = None\
    , regression_model = None):
    self.__trade = trade
    self.__model = model
    self.__env = env
    self.__symbol_table_listener = symbol_table_listener
    self.__regression_model = regression_model
    self.__fitted_fos = None
    self.__exercise_helper = None
    # check no stubs
    trade_utils.enforce_no_exercise_stubs(trade)
    # create timeline
    self.__timeline = timeline(trade, env.pricing_date())
    # check regression model present if callable
    if self.__trade.has_exercise_schedule() \
      and self.__regression_model == None:
      raise RuntimeError, \
        "exercise schedule present but no 'regression model'"

  def __symbol_listener_(self, t, symbol, value):
    if self.__symbol_table_listener:
      self.__symbol_table_listener(t, symbol, value, self.__model,
      self.__env)
```

The main new block of code is in the `__exercise_boundary_regression` method. This method only gets called if a second model is present. If the method is called, then we begin by constructing the controller, initialising some symbols in the symbol table and inserting the symbols contained in `symbol_value_pairs_to_add` into the symbol table.

```
class monte_carlo_pricer:
  def __exercise_boundary_regression(self, symbol_value_pairs_to_add):
    num_expl_vars = \
     self.__regression_model.exercise().num_explanatory_variables()
    num_sims = self.__regression_model.state().num_sims()
    num_exercises = self.__timeline.number_of_exercises()
    # create controller
    ctr = controller(self.__trade, self.__regression_model, self.__env,
         1.0)
    times = self.__timeline.times()
    from_ = 0.0
    # initialise symbols
    ctr.insert_symbol("underlying", from_)
    # add extra symbols
    if symbol_value_pairs_to_add:
      for symbol_value_pair in symbol_value_pairs_to_add:
        symbol, value = symbol_value_pair
        ctr.insert_symbol(symbol, value)
    cnt = 0
    for l in self.__trade.legs():
      symbol = "leg"+str(cnt)
      ctr.insert_symbol(symbol, from_)
      cnt += 1
    .
    .
    .
```

Then we evolve along the timeline calculating the cash flows on the way; storing at each exercise time the sum of the cash flows up to that time, the numeraire and explanatory variables.

```
class monte_carlo_pricer:
  def __exercise_boundary_regression(self, symbol_value_pairs_to_add):
    .
    .
    .
    # forward iterate through the timeline
    vs = numpy.zeros([num_exercises, num_sims, num_expl_vars])
    ies = numpy.zeros([num_exercises, num_sims])
    # for fees - ignored for present
    ns = numpy.zeros([num_exercises, num_sims])
    normalisation = 1.0/self.__trade.legs()[0].flows()[0].notional()
    ex_cnt = 0
    for time in times:
      to_ = self.__env.relative_date(time)/365.0
      # evolve
      ctr.evolve(from_, to_)
```

```
events = self._timeline.events(time)
# evaluate explanatory variables and immediate exercise values
for event in events:
    # set event on controller
    ctr.set_event(event)
    # evaluate
    if is_exercise_event(event):
        # evaluate underlying
        underlying = ies[ex_cnt, :]
        cnt = 0
        for l in self._trade.legs():
            underlying += ctr.retrieve_symbol("leg"+str(cnt))
            cnt += 1
        underlying *= self._trade.exercise_type()
        underlying *= normalisation
        # evaluate explanatory variables and numeraire
        ns[ex_cnt, :] = ctr.numeraire(to_)
        vs[ex_cnt, :] = ctr.explanatory_variables(to_)
        ex_cnt += 1
# evaluate cash flows
for event in events:
    # set event on controller
    ctr.set_event(event)
    # evaluate
    if is_pay_event(event):
        # evaluate payoff
        cpn = ctr(to_)
        symbol = "leg"+str(event.leg_id())
        leg_pv = ctr.retrieve_symbol(symbol)
        leg_pv += cpn
        self._symbol_listener_(to_, symbol, leg_pv)
        ctr.update_symbol(symbol, leg_pv, to_)
from_ = to_
.
.
.
```

Once we have all of this information we compute the immediate exercise values by subtracting from the total sum of all cash flows each of the stored sum of cash flows in turn. The regression is then carried out via an invocation of the free function pickup_value_regression. The method ends with the creation of an instance of the exercise_helper class, which will be used in the actual pricing of the callable structure.

```
class monte_carlo_pricer:
    def _exercise_boundary_regression(self, symbol_value_pairs_to_add):
        .
        .
        .
        # final immediate exercise value
        underlying = ctr.retrieve_symbol("underlying")
        cnt = 0
```

```
for l in self.__trade.legs():
  underlying += ctr.retrieve_symbol("leg"+str(cnt))
  cnt += 1
underlying *= self.__trade.exercise_type()
underlying *= normalisation
# subtract immediate exercise values from final
for i in range(num_exercises):
  ies[i, :]=underlying-ies[i, :]
# perform regression
self.__fitted_fos = pickup_value_regression(ies, ns, vs)
# create helper class for dealing with exercise indicator -
# note number of simulations
self.__exercise_helper = \
  exercise_helper(self.__model.state().num_sims())
```

The function call operator hasn't had to change too much from the non-callable version. The main differences are the careful order in which we handle the different event types and the subsequent calls onto the instance of the `exercise_helper` class to determine whether to exercise or not. Again we will step through the code highlighting the main features of interest. Just like before, we begin by constructing the controller, initialising some symbols in the symbol table and inserting the symbols contained in `symbol_value_pairs_to_add` into the symbol table.

```
def __call__(self, symbol_value_pairs_to_add = None):
  # do regression if required
  if self.__regression_model:
    self.__exercise_boundary_regression(symbol_value_pairs_to_add)
  # create controller
  ctr = controller(self.__trade, self.__model, self.__env, 1.0)
  times = self.__timeline.times()
  from_ = 0.0
  # initialise symbols
  ctr.insert_symbol("underlying", from_)
  ctr.insert_symbol("berm", from_)
  # add extra symbols
  if symbol_value_pairs_to_add:
    for symbol_value_pair in symbol_value_pairs_to_add:
      symbol, value = symbol_value_pair
      ctr.insert_symbol(symbol, value)
  cnt = 0
  for l in self.__trade.legs():
    symbol = "leg"+str(cnt)
    ctr.insert_symbol(symbol, from_)
    cnt += 1
    .
    .
    .
```

Next we evolve through the timeline calculating the cash flows on the way. The difference now is that we have to initialise the instance of the `exercise_helper` class with the sum of cash flows paid on or before the first exercise time. Consequently we have split what was a single loop over all events at a particular time on the timeline into three separate loops. In the first loop we check for the first exercise event.

```python
def __call__(self, symbol_value_pairs_to_add = None):
    .
    .
    .
    # forward iterate through the timeline
    ex_cnt = 0
    for time in times:
        to_ = self.__env.relative_date(time)/365.0
        # evolve
        ctr.evolve(from_, to_)
        events = self.__timeline.events(time)
        # set initial immediate exercise value
        # - sum of all flows before exercise date
        for event in events:
            if is_exercise_event(event):
                # evaluate underlying
                underlying = ctr.retrieve_symbol("underlying")
                underlying *= 0
                cnt = 0
                for l in self.__trade.legs():
                    underlying += ctr.retrieve_symbol("leg"+str(cnt))
                    cnt += 1
                if ex_cnt == 0:
                    self.__exercise_helper.set_last_cfs(\
                        self.__trade.exercise_type()*underlying)
                self.__symbol_listener_(to_, "underlying", underlying)
    .
    .
    .
```

In the second loop we calculate the cash flows as before:

```python
def __call__(self, symbol_value_pairs_to_add = None):
    .
    .
    .
    # evaluate cash flows
    for event in events:
        # set event on controller
        ctr.set_event(event)
        # evaluate
        if is_pay_event(event):
            # evaluate payoff
            cpn = ctr(to_)
            symbol = "leg"+str(event.leg_id())
            leg_pv = ctr.retrieve_symbol(symbol)
            leg_pv += cpn
            self.__symbol_listener_(to_, symbol, leg_pv)
```

```
ctr.update_symbol(symbol, leg_pv, to_)
       .
       .
       .
```

and in the final loop we check to see if we have exercised or not by calling the update_indicator method of the instance of the exercise_helper class. The max method is also invoked in the final loop, thereby updating the callable value with the cash flows paid between the current exercise time and the previous exercise time.

```
def __call__(self, symbol_value_pairs_to_add = None):
     .
     .
     .

   # evaluate exercise using regression
   for event in events:
     # set event on controller
     ctr.set_event(event)
     # evaluate
     if is_exercise_event(event):
       # evaluate underlying
       underlying = ctr.retrieve_symbol("underlying")
       underlying *= 0
       cnt = 0
       for l in self.__trade.legs():
         underlying += ctr.retrieve_symbol("leg"+str(cnt))
         cnt += 1
       # explanatory variables and numeraire
       ns = ctr.numeraire(to_) # for fees but not used at present
       vs = ctr.explanatory_variables(to_)
       # evaluate regression
       self.__exercise_helper.update_indicator(
         to_, vs, self.__fitted_fos[ex_cnt])
       berm = ctr.retrieve_symbol("berm")
       berm = self.__exercise_helper.max(
         to_, self.__trade.exercise_type()*underlying, berm)
       # update symbols
       ctr.update_symbol("underlying", underlying, to_)
       ctr.update_symbol("berm", berm, to_)
       ex_cnt = ex_cnt+1
     from_ = to_
   .
   .
   .
```

At the end of the loop over the timeline we have to call the max operator of the exercise_helper class once more to ensure that the final cash flows paying after the last exercise time are added to the callable value, the symbol berm, on those paths that have exercised before the end of the trade.

```
def __call__(self, symbol_value_pairs_to_add = None):
  .

  .

  .
  # calculate pv
  underlying = ctr.retrieve_symbol("underlying")
  underlying *= 0
  cnt = 0
  for l in self.__trade.legs():
    underlying += ctr.retrieve_symbol("leg"+str(cnt))
    cnt += 1
  self.__symbol_listener_(to_, "underlying", underlying)
  ctr.update_symbol("underlying", underlying, to_)
  if self.__regression_model:
    berm = ctr.retrieve_symbol("berm")
    berm = self.__exercise_helper.max(to_, \
            self.__trade.exercise_type()*underlying, berm)
    ctr.update_symbol("berm", berm, to_)
  pv = 0
  if self.__trade.has_exercise_schedule():
    if self.__trade.exercise_type() == exercise_type.callable:
      pv = ctr.retrieve_symbol("berm").mean()
    else:
      pv = ctr.retrieve_symbol("underlying").mean() \
            +ctr.retrieve_symbol("berm").mean()
  else:
    pv = ctr.retrieve_symbol("underlying").mean()
  return pv
```

The above pricing framework is generic and makes few assumptions on either the model or the underlying numerical container. One obvious caveat to this is that the pricing framework doesn't handle stubs, the treatment of which is beyond the scope of this book. As a final comment, the inclusion of fees into the framework is left as an exercise for the reader.

9.3   CONCLUDING REMARKS

In this chapter we have developed two pricing frameworks: a lattice pricing framework for pricing non-path-dependent callable structures; and a Monte-Carlo pricing framework for pricing both non-callable and callable path-dependent structures. Throughout the exposition we have only concentrated on the pricing and not the risk. By risk we mean the greeks. It is well known in financial mathematics that any poor treatment of discontinuties in the payoff is amplified in the greeks, usually to such an extent that the noise in the greeks renders them of no practical use. Consequently, many papers have been published on this topic by both academics and practitioners.

When discussing the integrator used in the lattice pricing framework to perform the conditional expectations, we took great care in the way we dealt with discontinuities. It is possible to extend the semi-analytic lattice integrator to multidimensions provided we introduce a way of splitting the lattice into portions with the function being continuous on each portion. Typically the way this is achieved is by introducing an algebra on indicator functions. The management of these indicators is quite complicated. An alternative, and perhaps simpler, approach is to use PDE techniques. As in the semi-analyic lattice integrator case, we would still need to provide a mechanism whereby the payoff could be parsed for information about where potential discontinuities may occur, but once we have the information we can refine the PDE mesh around the discontinuities. For more information on the application of PDE techniques to finance consult [4] and [13].

Similarly discontinuities must be treated carefully when pricing using Monte-Carlo. Many algorithms have been proposed: pathwise derivatives and likelihood ratio methods to name a few. A form of likelihood ratio method, called a *partial proxy scheme*, suitable for use with the Libor Market Model, can be found in [7]. In [8] the authors apply the *partial proxy scheme* to target redemption notes and demonstrate that the scheme produces extremely accurate greeks. An application of the pathwise derivatives method for computing delta is demonstrated in [17] together with the so-called *sausage Monte-Carlo* method for smoothing the greeks.

10

Pricing Financial Structures
in Hull–White

In this chapter we bring everything we have developed in the preceding chapters together and apply it to the pricing of a number of financial structures: namely Bermudans and target redemption notes. The structures have been chosen for two reasons: firstly, they are fairly straightforward; and, secondly, they demonstrate the need for both lattice and Monte-Carlo pricing algorithms. For each trade type we begin by defining the structure before moving on to the actual pricing. Test cases have been written for both trade types and are discussed in detail in the following sections.

10.1 PRICING A BERMUDAN

In this section we illustrate how we can use the model components described in the preceding chapters to price a Bermudan swaption. First of all we need to understand what we mean by a Bermudan swaption. A Bermudan swaption gives the holder the right to exercise into an underlying vanilla swap at regular intervals. The underlying vanilla swap of a Bermudan receiver swaption, is structured so that the holder, upon exercise, pays LIBOR plus a spread in exchange for a fixed coupon at regular intervals until the end of the swap. For a Bermudan payer swaption, the legs of the underlying vanilla swap are the other way around.

The payoff class from module `ppf.pricer.payoffs.fixed_leg_payoff` encapsulates the fixed leg of the underlying swap. In mathematical terms the discounted value at time `t` of the fixed coupon payment at time `T` is given by (per unit notional)

$$\frac{V_t}{P_{tT_N}} = \mathbb{E}^{T_N}\left[c \times \delta \times \frac{1}{P_{TT_N}} | \mathcal{F}_t\right] \tag{10.1}$$

where T_N denotes the maturity of the terminal bond, $\mathbb{E}^{T_N}$ the expectation in the terminal measure, P_{tT_N} the price of the terminal bond at time t, c the fixed coupon rate, δ the accrual period year fraction and $\mathcal{F}_t$ the filtration at time t. Since $1/P_{TT_N}$ is a martingale in the terminal measure, the above conditional expectation reduces to the equation

$$\frac{V_t}{P_{tT_N}} = c \times \delta \times \frac{P_{tT}}{P_{tT_N}}. \tag{10.2}$$

Let us step through, line by line, the body of the function call operator of the `fixed_leg_payoff` class. We begin by querying the event for its flow and reset identifier. Armed with these two pieces of information we can then retrieve the observable from the flow. In this instance the observable will be a fixed coupon observable. Such an observable has the method `fixed_rate` for gaining access to the fixed coupon. Next we query the model for the requestor and state components. The current state of the world is then calculated by calling the `fill` method on the state component. Finally we are in a position to compute the value of the fixed coupon payment. The second from last line of the implementation is the code representation of the above formula.

```
class fixed_leg_payoff:
  def __call__(self, t, controller):
    event = controller.get_event()
    flow = event.flow()
    id = event.reset_id()
    obs = flow.observables()[id]
    model = controller.get_model()
    env = controller.get_environment()
    fixed_rate = obs.coupon_rate()
    requestor = model.requestor()
    state = model.state().fill(t, requestor, env)
    cpn = fixed_rate*flow.notional()*flow.year_fraction()\
       *controller.pay_df(t, state)
    return cpn
```

Note that we delegate to the controller for the actual calculation of the zero coupon bond. The implementation of the `pay_df` method on the controller class is given below:

```
def pay_df(self, t, state):
  if t < 0:
    historical_df = self.__model.state().create_variable()
    historical_df = self.__historical_df
    return historical_df
  else:
    flow = self.__event.flow()
    fill = self.__model.fill()
    requestor = self.__model.requestor()
    T = self.__env.relative_date(flow.pay_date())/365.0
    return fill.numeraire_rebased_bond(t, T, flow.pay_currency()\
       , self.__env, requestor, state)
  endif
```

In a pattern that should be familiar, the fill component of the model is called upon to perform the calculation of the numeraire-rebased zero coupon bond. It should also be noted that the implementation returns a value for discount factors in the past; the value being determined by the `historical_df` argument passed in at construction time of the controller. For most applications the historical discount factor will be set to zero but in the next section we give an example where it has a value of one.

In a similar fashion the payoff class contained in the module `ppf.pricer.payoffs.float_leg_payoff` encapsulate the funding leg coupon. Let t denote the setting time of the LIBOR rate, then using no-arbitrage arguments one can show that the value of the LIBOR rate at time t with projection period (T_s, T_e) is given by

$$L_{t T_s T_e} = \left(\frac{P_{t T_s}}{P_{t T_e}} - 1 \right) / \delta' \tag{10.3}$$

where δ' denotes the projection period year fraction. The discounted value of the funding coupon payment is then

$$\frac{V_t}{P_{tT_N}} = \mathbb{E}^{T_N}\left[L_{tT_sT_e} \times \delta \times \frac{1}{P_{TT_N}}|\mathcal{F}_t\right] \qquad (10.4)$$

with the same interpretation for the symbols as before. Once again, because $L_{tT_sT_e}$ is known at time t, the conditional expectation reduces to the following equation

$$\frac{V_t}{P_{tT_N}} = L_{tT_sT_e} \times \delta \times \frac{P_{tT}}{P_{tT_N}}. \qquad (10.5)$$

The details of the implementation are essentially the same as for the fixed leg coupon. The second from last line of the implementation represents the above formula in code form. Note that we use the adjuvant table to store the spread – an exception will be raised if the symbol is not found in the symbol table.

```
class float_leg_payoff:
  def __call__(self, t, controller):
    event = controller.get_event()
    flow = event.flow()
    id = event.reset_id()
    obs = flow.observables()[id]
    model = controller.get_model()
    env = controller.get_environment()
    adjuvant_table = controller.get_adjuvant_table()
    # lookup 'spread' in adjuvant table at flow pay date
    spread = adjuvant_table("spread"+str(id), flow.pay_date())
    requestor = model.requestor()
    state = model.state().fill(t, requestor, env)
    cpn = flow.notional()*flow.year_fraction()* \
          (controller.libor (t, state) +spread)*controller.pay_df(t,
          state)
    return cpn
```

We delegate to the controller to determine both the LIBOR rate and the zero coupon bond. The code excerpt below details the implementation of the `libor` method on the controller. Most of the implementation should be self-explanatory but one point to highlight is the treatment of LIBOR fixings in the past: if there is no fixing an exception will be raised, otherwise the value of the fixing is returned.

```
  def libor(self, t, state):
    flow = self.__event.flow()
    id = self.__event.reset_id()
    obs = flow.observables()[id]
    if t < 0:
      fix = obs.fix()
      if fix.is_fixed():
        fixing = self.__model.state().create_variable()
        fixing = fix.value()
      return fixing
    else:
      raise RuntimeError, 'libor in the past with no fixing'
```

```
      endif
     else:
      fill = self._model.fill()
      requestor = self._model.requestor()
      return fill.libor(t, obs, self._env, requestor, state)
     endif
```

For completeness we also provide the implementation of the get_adjuvant_table method on the controller which is invoked in the script for the floating leg payoff.

```
def get_adjuvant_table(self):
   leg = self._trade.legs()[self._event.leg_id()]
   adjuvant_table = None
   if leg.has_adjuvant_table():
     adjuvant_table = leg.adjuvant_table()
   return adjuvant_table
```

Before proceeding on to the actual pricing of the Bermudan swaption we need to once again emphasise that the above payoffs are completely generic. By generic we mean they are not model specific. The only constraints imposed on the model are that it understands how to interpret zero coupon bonds and LIBOR rates. The actual dimensionality of the model is completely irrelevant from the perspective of the payoffs – provided that the numerical containers returned by the methods on the fill component have overloaded arithmetic operations, everything will flow through.

With the definition of the underlying coupon payments making up the swap out of the way, we now turn our attention to the pricing of the Bermudan swaption. In section 9.1 we discussed a generic framework for pricing 'vanilla' callable LIBOR exotics. Since a Bermudan swaption belongs to this class of financial instruments, we can employ the framework to compute the price. In the module ppf.test.test_lattice_pricer we have written a number of unit tests to verify both the pricing framework and all the model components. The first test class verifies that the pricing framework prices back the underlying swap to market, where by market we mean the market as defined by the curve in the market environment. The two functions below calculate the market price of both the fixed coupon leg and the funding leg, and should be self-explanatory.

```
def _fixed_leg_pv(leg, env):
  pv = 0.0
  for f in leg.flows():
    obs = f.observables()[0]
    key = "zc.disc."+f.pay_currency()
    curve = env.retrieve_curve(key)
    T = env.relative_date(f.pay_date())/365.0
    dfT = curve(T)
    pv += obs.coupon_rate()*f.notional()*f.year_fraction()*dfT
  return pv*leg.pay_receive()

def _funding_leg_pv(leg, env):
  pv = 0.0
  for f in leg.flows():
    obs = f.observables()[0]
```

```
    key = "zc.disc."+f.pay_currency()
    curve = env.retrieve_curve(key)
    T = env.relative_date(f.pay_date())/365.0
    dfT = curve(T)
    pv += obs.forward(env.pricing_date(), curve)\
        *f.notional()*f.year_fraction()*dfT
  return pv*leg.pay_receive()
```

The actual unit test for the underlying swap is detailed below. The functions _create_fixed_leg and _create_funding_leg create the fixed and funding legs respectively. _create_environment creates a test market environment suitable for the Hull–White model. The lattice pricer is created in the function _create_pricer. The price from the lattice pricer is compared with the market price and an assert is made to ensure that the prices (divided by the notional) are within a basis point (i.e. 10^{-4}).

```
class swap_tests(unittest.TestCase):
  def test_value(self):
    fixed_leg = _create_fixed_leg()
    funding_leg = _create_funding_leg()
    env = _create_environment()
    swap = ppf.core.trade((fixed_leg, funding_leg))
    pricer = _create_pricer(swap, env)
    actual = pricer()
    expected = _fixed_leg_pv(fixed_leg, env)+ \
               _funding_leg_pv(funding_leg, env)
    _assert_seq_close([actual/10000000], [expected/10000000], 1.0e-4)
```

In the _create_pricer function we use the Hull–White lattice model factory to create the Hull–White pricer. Note that the model arguments dictionary is set so that the number of states equals 41 and the number of standard deviations equals 5.5.

```
def _create_pricer(trade, env, listener = None):
  model_args = {"num states": 41, "num std dev": 5.5}
  factory = ppf.model.hull_white_lattice_model_factory()
  model = factory(trade, env, model_args)
  pricer = ppf.pricer.rollback_pricer(trade, model, env, listener)
  return pricer
```

There are two unit tests for the Bermudan swaption. The first unit test checks that the value of the Bermudan swaption is at least as large in magnitude as the most valuable European swaption. To perform this test we use a symbol table listener to store the European swaption prices. The code for the unit test is shown below. Again we use functions defined in the module to create both the legs and the exercise schedule. The values of the European swaption prices are retrieved by invoking the retrieve_symbol method on the listener after the pricing of the berm has been completed.

```
class bermudan_tests(unittest.TestCase):
  def test_value(self):
    fixed_leg = _create_fixed_leg()
    funding_leg = _create_funding_leg()
    ex_sch = _create_exercise_schedule()
```

```
env = _create_environment()
berm = ppf.core.trade((fixed_leg, funding_leg)\
   , (ex_sch, ppf.core.exercise_type.callable))
listener = european_symbol_table_listener()
pricer = _create_pricer(berm, env, listener)
actual = pricer()
europeans = listener.retrieve_symbols()
for european in europeans:
   assert(actual >= european)
```

The second unit test verifies that both deeply-out-of-the-money Bermudans price back to zero and deeply-in-the-money Bermudans have the same value as the underlying swap. The code excerpt for the moneyness tests is given below. The moneyness of the underlying swap is controlled by changing the coupon on the fixed leg from large positive (deeply-out-of-the-money) to large negative (deeply-in-the-money).

```
class moneyness_tests(unittest.TestCase):
   def deep_in_the_money_test(self):
      fixed_leg = _create_fixed_leg(-1.0)
      funding_leg = _create_funding_leg()
      ex_sch = _create_exercise_schedule()
      env = _create_environment()
      berm = ppf.core.trade((fixed_leg, funding_leg)\
         , (ex_sch, ppf.core.exercise_type.callable))
      pricer = _create_pricer(berm, env)
      actual = pricer()
      expected = _fixed_leg_pv(fixed_leg, env)+_funding_leg_pv
                  (funding_leg, env)
      _assert_seq_close([actual/10000000], [expected/10000000], 1.0e-4)
   def deep_out_the_money_test(self):
      fixed_leg = _create_fixed_leg(1.0)
      funding_leg = _create_funding_leg()
      ex_sch = _create_exercise_schedule()
      env = _create_environment()
      berm = ppf.core.trade((fixed_leg, funding_leg)\
         , (ex_sch, ppf.core.exercise_type.callable))
      pricer = _create_pricer(berm, env)
      actual = pricer()
      expected = 0.0
      _assert_seq_close([actual/10000000], [expected/10000000], 1.0e-4)
```

For completeness we also provide test cases for the Bermudan pricing using the Monte-Carlo pricing framework developed in section 9.2. The test cases are to be found in the ppf.test. test_monte_carlo_pricer module. In the _create_callable_pricer function two models are created using the Hull–White Monte-Carlo factory. One model is used for the regression and the other for the actual pricing. Note that the seeds are different and we have to provide an extra model argument, explanatory variables leg id, so that the exercise component of the model knows which leg to use in the calculation of the explanatory variables.

```
def _create_callable_pricer(trade, env, listener = None):
   regression_model_args = {"num sims": 3000, "seed": 12345,
```

```
                    "explanatory variables leg id": 0}
factory = ppf.model.hull_white_monte_carlo_model_factory()
regression_model = factory(trade, env, regression_model_args)
model_args = {"num sims": 6000, "seed": 1234
              , "explanatory variables leg id": 0}
model = factory(trade, env, model_args)
pricer = ppf.pricer.monte_carlo_pricer(trade, model, env,
        listener, regression_model)
return pricer
```

Three unit tests are provided. The two moneyness tests are identical to those for the lattice pricer and will not be mentioned further. The remaining test shown below checks that the value of the Bermudan swaption is bounded below by the most valuable European swaption price. The values of the European swaptions are calculated in the 'for' loop, from trades with only a single exercise date.

```
class bermudan_tests(unittest.TestCase):
  def test_value(self):
    fixed_leg = _create_fixed_leg()
    funding_leg = _create_funding_leg()
    ex_sch = _create_exercise_schedule()
    env = _create_environment()
    berm = ppf.core.trade((fixed_leg, funding_leg)\
          , (ex_sch, ppf.core.exercise_type.callable))
    pricer = _create_callable_pricer(berm, env)
    actual = pricer()
    europeans = []
    for exercise in ex_sch:
      european_ex_sch = _create_exercise_schedule(\
        exercise.exercise_date(), exercise.exercise_date())
      european = ppf.core.trade((fixed_leg, funding_leg)\
                , (european_ex_sch, ppf.core.exercise_type.callable))
      pricer = _create_callable_pricer(european, env)
      europeans.append(pricer())
    for european in europeans:
      print actual, european
      assert(actual >= european)
```

Note that the number of exercises created in the exercise schedule is controlled by passing in both the start and end dates, as can be seen in the code snippet below.

```
def _create_exercise_schedule(sd = ppf.date_time.date(2007, 06, 29)\
                            , ed = ppf.date_time.date(2009, 06, 29)):
  from ppf.date_time \
      import date, shift_convention, modified_following,
      basis_act_360, months
  sched = ppf.core.generate_exercise_table(
    start  = sd
    , end  = ed
    , period = 1
    , duration = ppf.date_time.years
```

```
    , shift_method = shift_convention.modified_following
    , fee_currency = "USD")
  return sched
```

10.2   PRICING A TARN

In this section we illustrate how we can use the components to price a Target Redemption Note, commonly referred to as a TARN. We will use the code developed in section 9.2 to do the actual pricing. So what is a TARN? A TARN is a swap consisting of a funding leg paying LIBOR plus a spread in exchange for an exotic coupon leg receiving a coupon of the form

$$c_t = \max\left(f, c + g \times L_{tT_sT_e}\right) \tag{10.6}$$

with f the floor, c a fixed coupon amount, g the leverage and $L_{tT_sT_e}$ the LIBOR rate for the period (T_s, T_e) observed at $t \in \{T_1, T_2, \ldots, T_n\}$, a discrete set of times. The whole contract knocks out if the total accrued coupon reaches a predefined target. Typically if the swap hasn't triggered before it ends, then the holder of the TARN receives a guaranteed accrued amount called the redemption floor. In addition, if the swap triggers, then the holder receives an accrued amount no greater than the redemption cap. In most TARN structures both the redemption floor and redemption cap are equal to the target.

Before moving on to discuss the payoff classes for the TARN, it is helpful to first look at the mathematical form of the exotic coupon in more detail. The exotic coupon, denoted by C_t in the formulae below, can be split into two parts. The first part can be expressed as

$$C_t = \left(1 - \mathbb{1}_{\sum_{t-1} \geq \text{target}}\right)\left\{\mathbb{1}_{\sum_t \geq \text{target}}\right.$$
$$\times \left(\delta c_t - \max\left(\sum_t - \text{redemption cap}, 0\right)\right)$$
$$+ \left(1 - \mathbb{1}_{\sum_t \geq \text{target}}\right)\delta c_t\right\} \tag{10.7}$$

with $\mathbb{1}_A$ representing the probability of an event A; the accrued coupon, denoted by $\sum_t$, is computed via the relation

$$\sum_t = \sum_{t-1} + \delta\, c_t. \tag{10.8}$$

with $\sum_t = 0$ for $t = 0$; and δ represents the accrual year fraction for the coupon period. The second part of the exotic coupon payoff represents what is paid in the event that the target is never reached, and in mathematical terms is equal to

$$C_{t_n} = C_{t_n} + \left(1 - \mathbb{1}_{C_{t_n} \geq \text{target}}\right)$$
$$\times \max\left(\text{redemption floor} - \sum_{t_n}, 0\right) \tag{10.9}$$

with t_n denoting the reset date on the final flow.

The `tarn_coupon_leg_payoff` class from the module `ppf.pricer.payoffs.tarn_coupon_leg_payoff` represents the exotic coupon leg of the TARN. At the beginning of the module we have implemented a simple pointwise min and max operator for NumPy arrays, denoted by `min_` and `max_` respectively, using the lambda statement of Python. The max_ operator is used in the calculation of the coupon, whereas we invoke the min_ when updating the variable representing whether the contract has been triggered.

```
# max for numpy arrays
max_ = numpy.vectorise(lambda x, y: (x, y)[x < y])
# min for numpy arrays
min_ = numpy.vectorise(lambda x, y: (x, y)[x > y])
```

Stepping through the implementation of the function call operator, we see that a number of variables used in the computation of the coupon payoff are retrieved from the adjuvant table associated with the leg: the state of the target_indicator, i.e. whether the target has been reached or not, and the accrued_coupon. If the writer of the TARN pricer has not populated the symbol tables with these symbols, then a runtime exception will be raised. It should be easy to see that the actual implementation of the exotic coupon in the code excerpt below follows the above equations faithfully and consequently requires only a few comments. Firstly, the is_last_flow function from the module ppf.core.trade_utils is used to determine if we have reached the last flow of the trade; and, secondly, we note that both the state of the target_indicator and the accrued_coupon are updated prior to returning control back to the client.

```
class tarn_coupon_leg_payoff:
  def __call__(self, t, controller):
    event = controller.get_event()
    flow = event.flow()
    id = event.reset_id()
    obs = flow.observables()[id]
    model = controller.get_model()
    env = controller.get_environment()
    adjuvant_table = controller.get_adjuvant_table()
    # lookup 'floor', 'fixed_rate', 'leverage', 'target',
    # 'redemption_floor' and 'redemption_cap'
    floor = adjuvant_table("floor"+str(id), flow.pay_date())
    fixed_rate = adjuvant_table("fixed_rate"+str(id), flow.pay_date())
    leverage = adjuvant_table("leverage"+str(id), flow.pay_date())
    target = adjuvant_table("target"+str(id), flow.pay_date())
    redemption_floor = adjuvant_table("redemption_floor"+str(id),
                    flow.pay_date())
    redemption_cap = adjuvant_table("redemption_cap"+str(id),
                   flow.pay_date())
    requestor = model.requestor()
    state = model.state().fill(t, requestor, env)
    cpn = flow.year_fraction()*max_(floor \
        , fixed_rate+leverage*controller.libor(t, state))
    # retrieve symbol representing target indicator
    indicator = controller.retrieve_symbol("target_indicator")
    # retrieve symbol representing accrued coupon
    accrued_cpn = controller.retrieve_symbol("accrued_coupon")
    accrued_cpn += cpn
    # actual coupon assuming a redemption cap and a redemption floor
    # potentially different from the target
    actual_cpn = model.state().create_variable()
```

```
local_indicator = accrued_cpn >= target
actual_cpn = (1-indicator)*local_indicator\
  *(cpn-max_(accrued_cpn-redemption_cap,0.0)) \
  +(1-indicator)*(1-local_indicator)*cpn
leg_id = event.leg_id()
if is_last_flow(controller.get_trade().legs()[leg_id], flow):
    actual_cpn += (1-local_indicator)*max_(redemption_floor-
                    accrued_cpn, 0.0)
actual_cpn *= flow.notional()*controller.pay_df(t, state)

# update indicator - probability of triggering
# addition of logicals is equivalent of 'or'
indicator = min_(indicator+local_indicator, 1)
# update symbols
at = env.relative_date(flow.pay_date())/365.0
controller.update_symbol("accrued_coupon", accrued_cpn, at)
controller.update_symbol("target_indicator", indicator, at)

return actual_cpn
```

Similarly the payoff class from module `ppf.pricer.payoffs.tarn_funding_leg_payoff` illustrated below encapsulates the funding leg of the TARN. The only complication is that the funding payment is still due immediately after the trigger is breached. The simplest way to ensure that this happens is to put the funding leg before the exotic coupon leg when defining the trade representing the TARN. We will see shortly that this is the case for all the test cases written for the TARN.

```
class tarn_funding_leg_payoff:
  def __call__(self, t, controller):
    event = controller.get_event()
    flow = event.flow()
    id = event.reset_id()
    obs = flow.observables()[id]
    model = controller.get_model()
    env = controller.get_environment()
    adjuvant_table = controller.get_adjuvant_table()
    # lookup 'spread' in adjuvant table at flow pay date
    spread = adjuvant_table("spread"+str(id), flow.pay_date())
    requestor = model.requestor()
    state = model.state().fill(t, requestor, env)
    cpn = flow.notional()*flow.year_fraction()*( \
      controller.libor (t, state) +spread)* \
        controller.pay_df(t, state)
    # retrieve symbol representing target indicator
    indicator = controller.retrieve_symbol("target_indicator")
    return cpn*(1-indicator)
```

Once again it cannot be overstated that the above two payoffs are generic and would work for any model provided that the required components have been implemented.

In the module `ppf.test.test_monte_carlo_pricer` we have written a number of tests for the pricing of the TARN. The first test verifies that the two legs cancel each other out if the target is never reached and the exotic coupon just pays LIBOR. The functions _create_tarn_coupon_leg and _create_tarn_funding_leg create the exotic coupon and funding legs respectively of the TARN. The function _create_environment creates a test market environment suitable for the Hull–White model. The Monte-Carlo pricer is created in the function _create_pricer. A list of symbol value pairs is built for the symbols accrued_coupon and target_indicator and then passed through to the function call operator of the pricer. The price from the Monte-Carlo pricer is compared with the market price and an assert is made to ensure that the prices (divided by the notional) are within a basis point (i.e. 10^{-4}).

```
class tarn_tests(unittest.TestCase):
  def no_trigger_limit_test(self):
    floor = -100
    fixed_rate = 0.0
    leverage = 1.0
    target = 10000
    redemption_floor = -100
    redemption_cap = -100
    coupon_leg = _create_tarn_coupon_leg(floor, fixed_rate, leverage\
      , target, redemption_floor, redemption_cap)
    funding_leg = _create_tarn_funding_leg()
    env = _create_environment()
    tarn = ppf.core.trade((funding_leg, coupon_leg)) # note the
                                                     # ordering
    pricer = _create_pricer(tarn, env)
    symbol_value_pairs_to_add = []
    symbol_value_pairs_to_add.append(
      ("accrued_coupon", numpy.zeros(5000)))
    symbol_value_pairs_to_add.append(
      ("target_indicator", numpy.zeros(5000)))
    actual = pricer(symbol_value_pairs_to_add)
    _assert_seq_close([actual/10000000], [0.0], 1.0e-4)
```

In the _create_pricer function we use the Hull–White Monte-Carlo model factory to create the Hull–White pricer. Note that the model arguments dictionary is set so that the number of simulation equals 5000 and the seed for the variate generator equals 1234.

```
def _create_pricer(trade, env, listener = None):
  model_args = {"num sims": 5000, "seed": 1234}
  factory = ppf.model.hull_white_monte_carlo_model_factory()
  model = factory(trade, env, model_args)
  pricer = ppf.pricer.monte_carlo_pricer(trade, model, env, listener)
  return pricer
```

The next test checks that if the target is set so that the target will be reached after the first flow, then the result should be equal to a simple swaplet. The code snippet below details the test case. To guarantee the target being reached after the first flow, the target is set to zero, and, unlike in the previous test case, the exotic coupon leg now pays a fixed coupon rate of 5%.

```
class tarn_tests(unittest.TestCase):
  def trigger_after_first_flow_test(self):
    floor = -100
    fixed_rate = 0.05
```

```
leverage = 0.0
target = 0.0
redemption_floor = -100
redemption_cap = 100
coupon_leg = _create_tarn_coupon_leg(floor, fixed_rate, leverage\
  , target, redemption_floor, redemption_cap)
funding_leg = _create_tarn_funding_leg()
env = _create_environment()
tarn = ppf.core.trade((funding_leg, coupon_leg)) # note the
                                                 # ordering

pricer = _create_pricer(tarn, env)
symbol_value_pairs_to_add = []
symbol_value_pairs_to_add.append(
  ("accrued_coupon", numpy.zeros(5000)))
symbol_value_pairs_to_add.append(
  ("target_indicator", numpy.zeros(5000)))
actual = pricer(symbol_value_pairs_to_add)
expected = _exotic_first_flow_pv(coupon_leg, env)\
  +_funding_first_flow_pv(funding_leg, env)
_assert_seq_close([actual/10000000], [expected/10000000], 1.0e-4)
```

Note that we have used the functions _exotic_first_flow_pv and _funding_first_flow_pv from the same module to compute the present value of the swaplet.

The last test case shown below checks that an out-of-the-money TARN swap becomes more out-of-the-money as the target is increased.

```
class tarn_tests(unittest.TestCase):
  def monotonic_with_target_test(self):
    floor = -100
    fixed_rate = 0.025
    leverage = 2.0
    redemption_floor = -100
    redemption_cap = 100
    prev = 1 # out-of-the-money
    targets = [0.075, 0.1, 0.125, 0.15, 0.175, 0.2]
    for target in targets:
      coupon_leg = _create_tarn_coupon_leg(floor, fixed_rate, leverage\
        , target, redemption_floor, redemption_cap)
      funding_leg = _create_tarn_funding_leg()
      env = _create_environment()
      tarn = ppf.core.trade((funding_leg, coupon_leg)) # note the
                                                       # ordering

      pricer = _create_pricer(tarn, env)
      symbol_value_pairs_to_add = []
      symbol_value_pairs_to_add.append(
        ("accrued_coupon", numpy.zeros(5000)))
      symbol_value_pairs_to_add.append(
        ("target_indicator", numpy.zeros(5000)))
      curr = pricer(symbol_value_pairs_to_add)
      assert(curr < prev)
      prev = curr
```

Before finishing this section one final point needs to be made. Some path-dependent trades may involve path variables dependent on the pay discount factor and, for seasoned trades, the path variables still need to be calculated even though they are in the past. For this reason, the instances of the `controller` classes in the Monte-Carlo pricing framework set the `historical_df` to unit.

10.3   CONCLUDING REMARKS

We have successfully applied the pricing frameworks developed in Chapter 9 to the pricing of both Bermudan swaptions and target redemption notes. In any real business application the main body of code would be in C++, which would then call out to Python to perform the evaluation of the payoff. For efficiency reasons, you would not wish to do this for every Monte-Carlo path because the cost of crossing the C++/Python boundary is too punitive – indeed you would have to cross the boundary for every simulation (or, equivalently, path). If instead you pass the current state of the world at a particular time, then you only cross the boundary as many times as there are flows (for each leg). Moreover, by passing the state of the world through gives the writer of the Python payoff the opportunity to employ parallelisation techniques when performing arithmetic operations within the payoff class. The authors have found, even in a system entirely implemented in C++, that it is approximately 40% faster to pass the state of the world through to the payoff functionals than calling the functionals once for each simulation – in this case the cost of the function call alone becomes punitive. The remaining question then is: should the memory be allocated on the C++ or Python side. There is no clear answer to this question but in any case Chapters 3 and 11 cover the necessary techniques for doing either approach.

During our treatment of the TARN payoff we were forced to carry out tricky indicator logic to handle the 'if-else' clauses. It would be much better if the Python 'if' statement understood NumPy arrays, i.e. if we could write `if m_array > 0` .... Indeed, if we were to write everything in C++, including our own payoff language interpreter, then this is almost certainly the approach we would adopt. To get this to work in Python would require hacking into the Python interpreter, which is well beyond the scope of this book.

## 11

Hybrid Python/C++ Pricing Systems

In Chapter 3, we saw how we may extend Python with modules written in C++. Specifically, we studied case examples of reflecting types from the Boost.Date_Time library into Python. Further, in section 3.1.1 we developed functionality in Python making use of those reflected types to compute IMM dates. In this chapter we aim to show how we can exercise that functionality from C++. What is the relevance of this? Well, it demonstrates the possibility of 'hybrid pricing systems'. That is, systems formed from a mix of both C++ and Python. Such potential will likely be of no small interest to those institutions that already have a considerable investment in C++. By using the techniques about to be presented, organisations with pricing frameworks in C++ can enjoy the many benefits Python offers while seamlessly integrating these efforts with their existing C++ frameworks.

11.1 nth_imm_of_year REVISITED

Our goal will be to exercise the Python code for IMM date computation functionality, presented in section 3.1.1 from C++. As the first step in seeing how to achieve that, it is necessary for us to review the implementation of the Python class nth_imm_of_year and examine in closer detail its relationship with the C++ code on which it rests.

```
from ppf_date_time import    \
    weekdays                  \
    , months_of_year          \
    , nth_kday_of_month        \
    , year_based_generator

class nth_imm_of_year(year_based_generator):
  '''Calculate the nth IMM date for a given year

  '''
  # ...
```

We see that this class inherits from the ppf.date_time type class year_based_generator. The class year_based_generator is served up to Python in the C++ Python extension module ppf_date_time.pyd and is in fact a Boost.Date_Time defined base type for year-based generators, or, in other words, a base class for polymorphic function objects that take a year and produce a concrete date. In synopsis:

```
template<typename date_type>
class year_based_generator {
public:
  // types
  typedef date_type::calendar_type calendar_type;
  typedef calendar_type::year_type year_type;

  // construct/copy/destruct
```

```
    year_based_generator();
    ~year_based_generator();

    // public member functions
    virtual date_type get_date(year_type) const;
    virtual std::string to_string() const;
};
```

In the `ppf_date_time.pyd` source file 'register_date_more.cpp', can be found the following code describing the instantiation of this class template over class `boost::gregorian::date` to Python:

```
namespace ppf { namespace date_time {

struct year_based_generator_wrap
  : boost::date_time::
      year_based_generator<boost::gregorian::date>
  , boost::python::wrapper<
      boost::date_time::
      year_based_generator<boost::gregorian::date> >
{
  boost::gregorian::date
    get_date(boost::gregorian::date::year_type y) const
    {
      return this->get_override("get_date")(y);
    }

  std::string to_string() const
    {
      return this->get_override("to_string")();
    }
};

void register_date_more()
{
  using namespace boost::python;
  namespace bg = boost::gregorian;
  namespace bd = boost::date_time;

  // ...

  class_<year_based_generator_wrap
        , boost::noncopyable>("year_based_generator")
    .def("get_date", pure_virtual(&bd::year_based_generator<bg::date>:
    :get_date))
    .def("to_string", pure_virtual(&bd::year_based_generator<bg::date>
    ::to_string))
    ;

  // ...
}

}} // namespace ppf::date_time
```

11.2   EXERCISING nth_imm_of_year FROM C++

We turn our attention now to 'embedding' a Python interpreter in a C++ program. We have seen how to call C++ code from Python. Here we aim to do the reverse: call Python code from C++. To do this we use a mix of Python C API routines together with helper types and functions in the Boost.Python library:

```
#include <boost/detail/lightweight_test.hpp>
#include <boost/python.hpp>
#include <boost/date_time/gregorian/gregorian.hpp>

int main()
{
  namespace bd = boost::date_time;
  namespace bg = boost::gregorian;
  namespace python = boost::python;
  typedef bd::year_based_generator<bg::date> ybd_t;

  Py_Initialise();

  try
  {
    //extract the ppf.date_time.nth_imm_of_year class
    //object
    python::object main_module = python::import("__main__");
    python::object global(main_module.attr("__dict__"));
    python::object result =
      python::exec("from ppf.date_time import *\n", global, global);
    python::object nth_imm_of_year_class = global["nth_imm_of_year"];

    //use the class object to create instances of
    //nth_imm_of_year
    python::object first_imm_ = nth_imm_of_year_class(bg::Mar);
    python::object second_imm_ = nth_imm_of_year_class(bg::Jun);
    python::object third_imm_ = nth_imm_of_year_class(bg::Sep);
    python::object fourth_imm_ = nth_imm_of_year_class(bg::Dec);

    //get references to boost date_time year_based_generators
    //from the newly created objects
    ybd_t& first_imm  = python::extract<ybd_t&>(first_imm_);
    ybd_t& second_imm = python::extract<ybd_t&>(second_imm_);
    ybd_t& third_imm  = python::extract<ybd_t&>(third_imm_);
    ybd_t& fourth_imm = python::extract<ybd_t&>(fourth_imm_);

    //check imm dates for 2005
    BOOST_TEST(first_imm.get_date (2005) == bg::date(2005,
    bg::Mar, 16));
    BOOST_TEST(second_imm.get_date (2005) == bg::date(2005,
    bg::Jun, 15));
    BOOST_TEST(third_imm.get_date  (2005) == bg::date(2005,
    bg::Sep, 21));
    BOOST_TEST(fourth_imm.get_date (2005) == bg::date(2005,
```

```
  bg::Dec, 21)));
}
catch(python::error_already_set const&)
{
   PyErr_Print();
}
catch(std::runtime_error const& e)
{
   std::cerr << e.what() << std::endl;
}
catch(...)
{
   std::cerr << "unexpected exception" << std::endl;
}

return boost::report_errors();
}
```

The significant steps in the above program are as follows: first, the Python interpreter is initialised with the call to the Python C API function `Py_Initialise()`. Among other things, this has the effect of creating the fundamental ''_main_'' module. The following statements

```
python::object main_module = python::import("_main_");
python::object global(main_module.attr("_dict_"));
```

import the _main_ module and obtain a reference to its namespace. With these the context for executing Python code has been obtained and we execute

```
python::object result =
   python::exec("from ppf.date_time import *\n", global, global);
```

to cause Python to import all types and functions in the `ppf.date_time` module into the global namespace. In particular, we are interested in the `nth_imm_of_year` class object which we retrieve with

```
python::object nth_imm_of_year_class = global["nth_imm_of_year"];
```

With the class object at our disposal, we use it to produce `nth_imm_of_year` class instances

```
python::object first_imm_ = nth_imm_of_year_class(bg::Mar);
python::object second_imm_ = nth_imm_of_year_class(bg::Jun);
python::object third_imm_ = nth_imm_of_year_class(bg::Sep);
python::object fourth_imm_ = nth_imm_of_year_class(bg::Dec);
```

This is the point at which things get interesting. Since `nth_imm_of_year` IS_A year_based_generator<date> we can manipulate them through a year_based_generator<date> reference or pointer

```
ybd_t& first_imm =  python::extract<ybd_t&>(first_imm_);
ybd_t& second_imm = python::extract<ybd_t&>(second_imm_);
ybd_t& third_imm =  python::extract<ybd_t&>(third_imm_);
ybd_t& fourth_imm = python::extract<ybd_t&>(fourth_imm_);
```

Finally, invoking the virtual function `get_date` on these references calls out to Python for the implementation

```
BOOST_TEST(first_imm.get_date   (2005)  == bg::date(2005,
bg::Mar, 16));
BOOST_TEST(second_imm.get_date  (2005)  == bg::date(2005,
bg::Jun, 15));
BOOST_TEST(third_imm.get_date   (2005)  == bg::date(2005,
bg::Sep, 21));
BOOST_TEST(fourth_imm.get_date  (2005)  == bg::date(2005,
bg::Dec, 21));
```

The net effect is that this shows how we can implement classes in Python and have them behave as first-class C++ types in C++, a very powerful technique indeed!

Python Excel Integration

The use of Microsoft Excel in financial institutions practising Quantitative Analysis is simply too widespread to be overlooked. Python, or more specifically, the Win32 Python extensions, make it easy to access Python functionality from Microsoft Excel. To do so, we dip into the world of COM.[1] We won't attempt to teach COM here, it is too broad a subject for this book, but will instead focus on how we can write simple COM servers in Python and COM clients in Microsoft Excel VBA.[2] For richer details regarding Python/COM integration beyond those presented here, readers are strongly recommended to consult Hammond & Robinson's *Python Programming on Win32* [19]. For those readers who are interested in acquiring a deeper understanding of COM beyond the specific field of Python/COM integration we recommend Don Box's *Essential COM* [3].

12.1 BLACK–SCHOLES COM SERVER

To illustrate the basic ideas of publishing COM servers in Python we'll jump straight in with a COM component exposing the functionality of the `ppf.core.black_scholes` module. The code presented below can be found in the `ppf.com.black_scholes` module.

```
class BlackScholes:
  _public_methods_ = ["OptionPrice"]
  _reg_clsid_ = "{14B40B3E-DC9A-4E07-A512-F65DA07BDC09}"
  _reg_progid_ = "ppf.black_scholes"

  def OptionPrice(self, spot, strike, rate, vol, time, call_put):
    from win32com.server.exception import COMException
    from ppf.core import black_scholes
    try:
      return black_scholes(
        S=spot, K=strike, r=rate, sig=vol, T=time, CP=call_put)
    except RuntimeError, e:
      raise COMException(
        desc="ppf error : \""+str(e)+"\"", scode=0x80040201)

if __name__ == "__main__":
  print "Registering \"BlackScholes\" server... ",
  import win32com.server.register
  win32com.server.register.UseCommandLine(BlackScholes)
  print  "done!"
```

The first thing to note about the code above is that the Black–Scholes COM server is really nothing more than a decorated Python class. The Python Win32 framework does most of

---

[1] COM is an acronym standing for the 'Component Object Model', a (partially standardised) technology from the Microsoft Windows family of operating systems.

[2] VBA is an acronym for 'Visual Basic for Applications'.

the work that relates to COM specifically (argument conversions between the Win32 `VARI-ANT` data-type and native Python data-types for example). The `class BlackScholes` COM component exposes one function, `OptionPrice`, which is a wrapper around the `ppf.core.black_scholes` function. The intention of publishing the `OptionPrice` function in the `BlackScholes` interface is expressed by adding the name of the function to the class static data member `_public_methods_`. Although not shown here, additional functions that the class may have, unless added to this list, will not form part of the COM interface offered by the class. In COM, class IDs(CLSID) are 128-bit globally unique identifiers (GUID) associated with COM objects. The `_reg_clsid_` class data member assigns to our `class BlackScholes` the value '*14B40B3E-DC9A-4E07-A512-F65DA07BDC09*'. These CLSIDs should never be copied. Instead they can and should be generated for each new COM component developed in the following way:

```
>>> import pythoncom
>>> print str(pythoncom.CreateGuid())
{1C8D8011-01D9-492A-974B-7B5CE3F3DF43}
```

In addition to naming COM objects by their CLSIDs, COM allows for text-based aliases called programmatic IDs or ProgIDs. These are usually in the form *library-name.classname.version*. Our `class BlackScholes` is assigned the ProgID given by the value of the `_reg_progid_` class variable, that is, '*ppf.black_scholes*'.

If run from the command line, the `_main_` function takes care of registering the `BlackScholes` component with COM (Figure 12.1). We'll skip the details of precisely what that involves and ultimately means, but, in short, a collection of values are written to the Windows registry based on the information provided by the class data members just covered that enables operating system calls at runtime to discover our `BlackScholes` class and allow instances of them to be created in the calling process (COM (late-bound automation) clients – we'll get on to examples below).

Before we present an automation client that exercises the functionality provided by our `BlackScholes` component, we will quickly cover the definition of the `OptionPrice` function. As noted earlier, it's a simple wrapper around the `ppf.core.black_scholes` function. One important responsibility of the wrapper is to trap any Python exceptions that may result from the call to the `ppf.core.black_scholes` function and translate them into `win32.com.server.exception.COMException` exception objects. The Python COM framework takes charge of phrasing such exceptions in terms that the calling environment (automation clients,) can deal with. This is important since such environments will in general know nothing about how to deal with raw Python exceptions (in fact, the code

```
raise COMException(
        desc="ppf error : \""+str(e)+"\"", scode=0x80040201)
```

is creating a `COMException` with a custom error code).

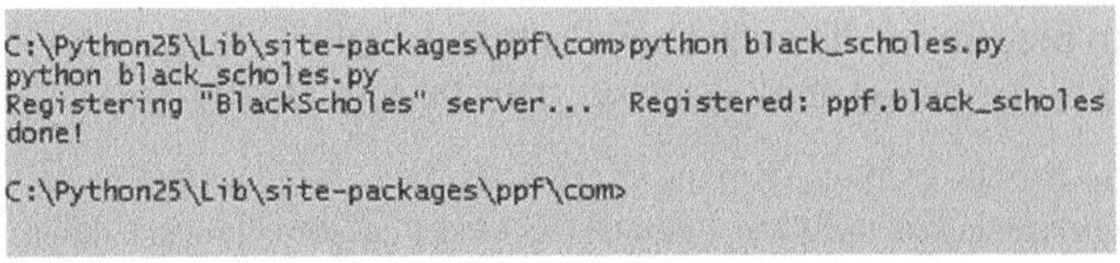

Figure 12.1 Registering the PPF Black–Scholes COM server.

```
C:\live\trunk\ppf\example>cscript test_black_scholes.vbs
cscript test_black_scholes.vbs
Microsoft (R) Windows Script Host Version 5.6
Copyright (C) Microsoft Corporation 1996-2001. All rights reserved.

4.75942193530954

C:\live\trunk\ppf\example>
```

Figure 12.2   Invoking the PPF Black–Scholes function from VBScript.

12.1.1   VBS client

COM is all about getting objects in different languages talking to each other. We'll put that to the test now by implementing a client of the `BlackScholes` server from the preceding section in Microsoft VBScript that is intended to be executed under the Microsoft Windows Scripting Host environment offered by the command line interpreter `cscript.exe`. The code can be found in the 'example' directory of the code accompanying the book in the file 'test_black_scholes.vbs'.

```
On Error Resume Next

Dim Pricer : Set Pricer = CreateObject("ppf.black_scholes")
Dim spot: spot = 42.
Dim strike: strike = 40.
Dim r: r = 0.1
Dim sig: sig = 0.2
Dim T: T= 0.5
Dim european_call: european_call = 1

Dim price : price = \
  Pricer.OptionPrice(spot, strike, r, sig, T, european_call)

If Err.Number <> 0 Then
  WScript.Echo "Automation error : " & vbCr & Err.Number & _
               " (" & Hex(Err.Number) & ")" & vbCr & Err.Description
  Err.Clear
Else
  WScript.Echo price
End If

Set Pricer = Nothing
```

Figure 12.2 shows the result of executing the client script.

12.1.2   VBA Client

The following Microsoft Excel VBA code implements a Black–Scholes client suitable for use in Microsoft Excel. Figure 12.3 shows an example session exercising the client on an Excel worksheet.

```
Public Function PPF_BlackScholes( _
   Spot As Double, _
   Strike As Double, _
   Rate As Double, _
```

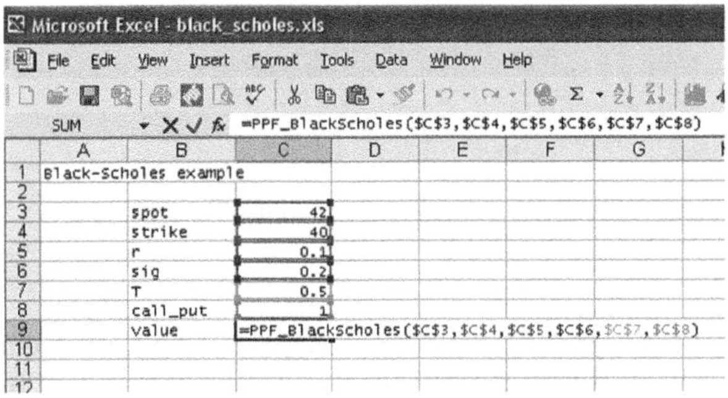

Figure 12.3   Invoking the PPF Black–Scholes function from Microsoft Excel.

```
   Vol As Double, _
   T As Double, _
   CallPut As Double) As Variant
 On Error Resume Next
 Dim Pricer As Object
 Set Pricer = CreateObject("ppf.black_scholes")
 PPF_BlackScholes = Pricer.OptionPrice(_
   Spot, Strike, Rate, Vol, T, CallPut)
 If Err.Number <> 0 Then
    PPF_BlackScholes = "#err: " & Err.Description
    Err.Clear
 End If
 Set Pricer = Nothing
End Function
```

12.2   NUMERICAL PRICING WITH PPF IN EXCEL

Armed with the understanding of the basic principles of publishing Python COM components from the preceding section, we now consider how we can assemble such components into a broader example to provide numerical pricing capabilities using PPF in Excel. Specifically, our goal will be to enable Bermudan swaption pricing on a Hull–White lattice.

12.2.1   Common Utilities

Before going on, we will find, in implementing the COM servers for this example, some code that is common among all the servers that it is helpful to factor out (to aid clarity and reduce unnecessary code repetition). The simple utilities presented here all reside in the the ppf.com.utils module.

Date Conversion

The to_ppf_date function converts a Win32 COM date into a ppf.date_time.date representation. It is frequently used at the boundary between the COM servers and 'pure' ppf Python:

```
def to_ppf_date(t):
  import ppf.date_time
  return ppf.date_time.date(t.year, t.month, t.day)
```

COM Class Registration

Although no great saving as stated, the `register_com_class` function does abstract away the details of COM server registration and provides a convenient hook for associating other actions at the time of COM class registration in the future.

```
def register_com_class(classobj):
  import win32com.server.register
  win32com.server.register.UseCommandLine(classobj)
```

COM Exceptions

A simple function abstracting away the details of raising `win32.server.exception.COMExceptions`.

```
def raise_com_exception(e):
  from win32com.server.exception import COMException
  raise COMException(
    desc="ppf error : \""+str(e)+"\"", scode=0x80040201)
```

Symbol Retrieval

We will see an application for the following function in the next section. It is a function that works as follows: given the name of a module ('module'), the name of a class object('server'), the name of a symbol ('tag') and the name of a dictionary ('what'), the function attempts to retrieve the value associated with the key 'tag' from the dictionary `module.server._what`, raising an exception in the event that the operation cannot be fulfilled.

```
def retrieve(module, server, tag, what):
  exec("from %s import %s "% (module, server))
  table=eval(server+"._"+what)
  if not table.has_key(tag):
    raise RuntimeError, "\""+tag+"\" not found"
  return table[tag]
```

12.2.2   Market Server

The first step in numerical pricing is a need to construct the market data environment in which to price. In this section we introduce the `class MarketServer` COM component, the code for which resides in the `ppf.com.market_server` module. The responsibility of this component is to wrap the services provided by the `ppf.market.enviroment` module (the `ppf.market` package was covered in Chapter 5) using the code:

```
import ppf.market import utils

class MarketServer(object):
  _reg_progid_ = "ppf.market"
  _reg_clsid_ = "{CAFAEEDF-E876-4DD6-9B6F-7038EDA25BCD}"
  _public_methods_ = \
```

```
[
    "CreateEnvironment"
            , "AddCurve"
            , "AddSurface"
            , "AddConstant"
]
_environments = {}

retrieve = staticmethod(
    lambda tag, which :
        utils.retrieve('market_server', 'MarketServer', tag, which))

def CreateEnvironment(self, tag, t):
    try:
        MarketServer._environments[tag] = \
            ppf.market.environment(utils.to_ppf_date(t))
        return tag
    except RuntimeError, e: utils.raise_com_exception(e)

def AddCurve(self, tag, name, curve, interp):
    try:
        import ppf.math.interpolation
        interp = eval("ppf.math.interpolation."+interp)
        times, factors = [x[1] for x in curve[1:]],[x[2] for x in
                        curve[1:]]
        MarketServer.retrieve(tag, 'environments').add_curve(
            str(name), ppf.market.curve(times, factors, interp))
    except RuntimeError, e: utils.raise_com_exception(e)

def AddConstant(self, tag, name, value):
    try:
        MarketServer.retrieve(tag, 'environments').add_constant(
            str(name), value)
    except RuntimeError, e: utils.raise_com_exception(e)

def AddSurface(self, tag, name, expiries, tenors, values):
    try:
        import numpy
        exp, ten = expiries[1:], tenors[1:]
        surface = [x[1:] for x in values[1:]]
        MarketServer.retrieve(tag,'environments').add_surface(
            str(name),
            ppf.market.surface(exp, ten, numpy.array-(surface)))
    except RuntimeError, e: utils.raise_com_exception(e)

if _name_ == "_main_": utils.register_com_class(MarketServer)
```

To begin our explanation of the above code, note the existence of the class 'static' member _environments. This data member will be used to contain class environment instances (from the ppf.market.environment module), each of which will be associated with a user provided 'name'. Access to the _environments member is given by the class static method `retrieve` implemented easily using the `ppf.com.utils.retrieve` function, the Python built in `staticmethod` function and partial function application achieved with a λ expression (isn't Python wonderfully expressive?). The `retrieve` method is not part of the COM interface of `class MarketServer`, it is there for interaction between the servers, on the Python side. The use of a class static data member to hold the environments makes the design of `class MarketServer` an example of a 'mono-state' pattern; all instances share the same state and are therefore equivalent. Excepting the `retrieve` function, the remaining methods of `class MarketServer` satisfy its COM interface.

CreateEnvironment

The `CreateEnvironment` method takes a user-supplied name for an environment, a COM date (the pricing date for the market), creates an empty `class environment` instance, stores it in the `_environments` dictionary for later retrieval and simply returns the user provided name for the environment to indicate success. Should the operation fail for any reason, the Python exception is caught and a COM exception raised by means of the `ppf.com.utils.raise_com_exception` function. This exception handling idiom at the Python/COM boundary (explained in section 12.1) will be the same for every COM interface method and we will refrain from remarking on it again going forward.

AddCurve

The `AddCurve` function 'injects' a user-supplied curve into the named market environment. We will look at this function in a little more detail:

```
def AddCurve(self, tag, name, curve, interp):
   try:
      import ppf.math.interpolation
      interp = eval("ppf.math.interpolation."+interp)
      times, factors = [x[1] for x in curve[1:]],[x[2] for x in
curve[1:]]
      MarketServer.retrieve(tag, 'environments').add_curve(
          str(name), ppf.market.curve(times, factors, interp))
   except RuntimeError, e: utils.raise_com_exception(e)
```

The `tag` parameter indicates the name of the environment in which the curve is to be stored. The `interp` parameter is a `ppf.math.interpolation` class name: one of `linear`, `loglinear`, `linear_on_zero`, `linear_on_variance` or `cubic_spline`. The assignment

```
interp = eval("ppf.math.interpolation."+interp)
```

attempts to retrieve the `ppf.math.interpolation` module class object corresponding to the given string.

The statement,

```
times, factors = [x[1] for x in curve[1:]],[x[2] for x in
                  curve[1:]]
```

might at first seem a little cryptic. From the COM client's perspective, the `curve` is provided as a two-column array. As we will see later, VBA code to construct the curve would read something like:

```
Dim V As Variant
Dim N As Integer: N = Curve.Rows.Count
ReDim V(N, 2)
Dim I As Integer
For I = 1 To N
  V(I, 1) = Curve(I, 1).Value
  V(I, 2) = Curve(I, 2).Value
Next I
```

On the server side, however, what arrives in Python from the PythonCOM framework will actually be a 3-column array, something similar to the following example:

```
((None, None, None),
 (None, 0.0, 1.0),
 (None, 0.5, 0.97530991202833262),
 (None, 1.0, 0.95122942450071402),
 (None, 1.5, 0.92774348632855286),
 (None, 2.0, 0.90483741803595952),
 (None, 3.0, 0.86070797642505781),
 (None, 4.0, 0.81873075307798182),
 (None, 5.0, 0.77880078307140488),
 (None, 6.0, 0.74081822068171788),
 (None, 7.0, 0.70468808971871344),
 (None, 8.0, 0.67032004603563933),
 (None, 9.0, 0.63762815162177333),
 (None, 10.0, 0.60653065971263342),
 (None, 11.0, 0.57694981038048665))
```

In order to get the required data out of the incoming curve it is necessary to 'skip' the first row, and the first column.

Assuming the preceding operations all succeed,

```
MarketServer.retrieve(tag, 'environments').add_curve(
    str(name), ppf.market.curve(times, factors, interp))
```

retrieves the named environment from the `MarketServer` class object by means of its static `retrieve` function, a new `ppf.market.curve` instance is created and is installed into the environment. One slight but important detail should be mentioned; the presence of invoking the built-in `str` function on the `name` argument in the call to the `class environment` `add_curve` function. The reason for this is that the `name` argument is a *Unicode* string, whereas `ppf` traffics in regular ASCII strings. Invoking `str` handles the necessary 'narrowing' conversion.

AddConstant

The explanation of `AddCurve` above was necessarily lengthy; a great deal of detail was covered. The `AddConstant` function which injects a named constant into a given enviroment,

```
def AddConstant(self, tag, name, value):
  try:
    MarketServer.retrieve(tag, 'environments').add_constant(
      str(name), value)
  except RuntimeError, e: utils.raise_com_exception(e)
```

should now be readily understandable.

AddSurface

The `AddSurface` function uses all the tricks uncovered in the explanation of the `AddCurve` method (see subsection 12.2.2):

```
def AddSurface(self, tag, name, expiries, tenors, values):
  try:
    import numpy
    exp, ten = expiries[1:], tenors[1:]
    surface = [x[1:] for x in values[1:]]
    MarketServer.retrieve(tag,'environments').add_surface(
      str(name),
      ppf.market.surface(exp, ten, numpy.array-(surface)))
  except RuntimeError, e: utils.raise_com_exception(e)
```

In this function, `exp` is an array of M expiries (in years), `tenors` an array of N tenors (in days) and `surface` the surface data as an $M \times N$ array. Figure 12.4 shows how the data for the surface might be arranged in an Excel worksheet.

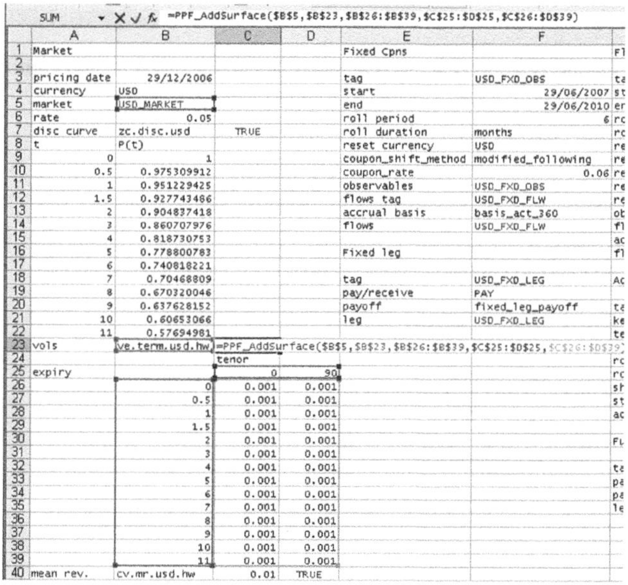

SUM =PPF_AddSurface($B$5,$B$23,$B$26:$B$39,$C$25:$D$25,$C$26:$D$39)

	A	B	C	D	E	F	
1	Market				Fixed Cpns		Fl
2							
3	pricing date	29/12/2006			tag	USD_FXD_OBS	ta
4	currency	USD			start	29/06/2007	st
5	market	USD_MARKET			end	29/06/2010	er
6	rate	0.05			roll period	6	rc
7	disc curve	zc.disc.usd	TRUE		roll duration	months	rc
8	t	P(t)			reset currency	USD	re
9	0	1			coupon_shift_method	modified_following	re
10	0.5	0.975309912			coupon_rate	0.06	re
11	1	0.951229425			observables	USD_FXD_OBS	re
12	1.5	0.927743486			flows tag	USD_FXD_FLW	re
13	2	0.904837418			accrual basis	basis_act_360	ot
14	3	0.860707976			flows	USD_FXD_FLW	fl
15	4	0.818730753					ac
16	5	0.778800783			Fixed leg		fl
17	6	0.740818221					
18	7	0.70468809			tag	USD_FXD_LEG	Ac
19	8	0.670320046			pay/receive	PAY	
20	9	0.637628152			payoff	fixed_leg_payoff	ta
21	10	0.60653066			leg	USD_FXD_LEG	ke
22	11	0.57694981					te
23	vols	ve.term.usd.hw	=PPF_AddSurface($B$5,$B$23,$B$26:$B$39,$C$25:$D$25,$C$26:$D$39)				
24			tenor				rc
25	expiry		0	90			rc
26		0	0.001	0.001			sh
27		0.5	0.001	0.001			st
28		1	0.001	0.001			ac
29		1.5	0.001	0.001			
30		2	0.001	0.001			FL
31		3	0.001	0.001			
32		4	0.001	0.001			ta
33		5	0.001	0.001			pa
34		6	0.001	0.001			pa
35		7	0.001	0.001			le
36		8	0.001	0.001			
37		9	0.001	0.001			
38		10	0.001	0.001			
39		11	0.001	0.001			
40	mean rev.	cv.mr.usd.hw	0.01	TRUE			

Figure 12.4 Adding a surface to a market environment.

Market VBA Client

The foregoing section detailed the workings of the COM object known by the ProgID *'ppf.market'*. What remains is client code on the Excel VBA side to exercise its functionality.

It seems fair to assume that readers with interest in this chapter are familiar with Excel and Excel VBA, so we will make little comment on the example VBA code presented here.

PPF_CreateMarketEnvironment This function calls out to the `class Market-Server CreateEnvironment` method to construct and register an empty `ppf.market.environment.environment` instance.

```
Public Function _
PPF_CreateMarketEnvironment( _
    Tag As String _
  , T As Date) As String
'Create a ppf market data environment
'
On Error Resume Next
  Dim MarketServer As Object
  Set MarketServer = CreateObject("ppf.market")
  PPF_CreateMarketEnvironment =
    MarketServer.CreateEnvironment- (Tag, T)
  If Err.Number <> 0 Then
    PPF_CreateMarketEnvironment = "#err: " & Err.Description
  End If
  Set MarketServer = Nothing
End Function
```

PPF_AddCurve

This function calls out to the `class MarketServer AddCurve` method to register a user-defined curve in a previously constructed environment.

```
Public Function _
PPF_AddCurve( _
    Market As String _
  , Name As String _
  , Curve As Variant _
  , Interp As String) As Variant
  'Add a curve to a ppf market data environment
  '
  On Error Resume Next
  Dim MarketServer As Object
  Dim N As Integer: N = Curve.Rows.Count
  If Curve.Columns.Count <> 2 Then
    PPF_AddCurve = "#err: invalid argument"
    Exit Function
  End If
  Dim V As Variant
  ReDim V(N, 2)
```

```
   Dim I As Integer
   For I = 1 To N
     V(I, 1) = Curve(I, 1).Value
     V(I, 2) = Curve(I, 2).Value
   Next I
   Set MarketServer = CreateObject("ppf.market")
   Call MarketServer.AddCurve(Market, Name, V, Interp)
   If Err.Number <> 0 Then
     PPF_AddCurve = "#err: " & Err.Description
   Else
     PPF_AddCurve = True
   End If
   Set MarketServer = Nothing
End Function
```

PPF_AddConstant

This function calls out to the `class MarketServer AddConstant` method to register a user constant in a previously constructed environment.

```
Public Function _
PPF_AddConstant( _
    Market As String _
  , Name As String _
  , Value As Double) As Variant
   'Add a constant to a ppf market data environment
   '
   On Error Resume Next
   Dim MarketServer As Object
   Set MarketServer = CreateObject("ppf.market")
   Call MarketServer.AddConstant(Market, Name, Value)
   If Err.Number <> 0 Then
     PPF_AddConstant = "#err: " & Err.Description
   Else
     PPF_AddConstant = True
   End If
   Set MarketServer = Nothing
End Function
```

PPF_AddSurface

This function calls out to the `class MarketServer AddSurface` method to register a user-defined surface in a previously constructed environment.

```
Public Function _
PPF_AddSurface( _
    Market As String _
  , Name As String _
  , Expiries As Variant _
  , Tenors As Variant _
  , Surface As Variant)
```

```
'Add a surface to a ppf market data environment
'
On Error Resume Next
Dim NumExp As Integer: NumExp = Expiries.Rows.Count
Dim NumTen As Integer: NumTen = Tenors.Columns.Count
If Surface.Rows.Count <> NumExp Or _
    Surface.Columns.Count <> NumTen Then
  PPF_AddSurface = "#err: invalid argument"
End If
Dim Exp As Variant
ReDim Exp(NumExp)
Dim I, J As Integer
For I = 1 To NumExp
  Exp(I) = Expiries(I).Value
Next I
Dim Ten As Variant
ReDim Ten(NumTen)
For I = 1 To NumTen
  Ten(I) = Tenors(1, I).Value
Next I
Dim Values As Variant
ReDim Values(NumExp, NumTen)
For I = 1 To NumExp
  For J = 1 To NumTen
      Values(I, J) = Surface(I, J).Value
  Next J
Next I
Dim MarketServer As Object
Set MarketServer = CreateObject("ppf.market")
Call MarketServer.AddSurface(Market, Name, Exp, Ten, Values)
If Err.Number <> 0 Then
  PPF_AddSurface = "#err : " & Err.Description
Else
  PPF_AddSurface = True
End If
Set MarketServer = Nothing
End Function
```

12.2.3 Trade Server

Having constructed a market, the next step in numerical pricing is to describe the trade
to be priced. This section outlines the `class TradeServer` COM component. The
code in this section can be found in the `ppf.com.trade_server` module. Instances
of this type wrap the services offered up by the `ppf.core` module, specifically those relating to the `ppf` trade data model (this functionality was explained in Chapter 6). The
code is:

```
import ppf.core
import ppf.pricer.payoffs
import ppf.date_time
import utils
```

```python
class TradeServer(object):
  _reg_progid_ = "ppf.trade"
  _reg_clsid_ = "{E33DA322-B011-4FE9-8AB9-87A964EDD046}"
  _public_methods_ = \
   [
         "GenerateFixedCouponObservables"
             , "GenerateLiborObservables"
                    , "GenerateFlows"
              , "GenerateAdjuvantTable"
            , "GenerateExerciseSchedule"
                         , "CreateLeg"
                         , "CreateTrade"
   ]
  _observables = {}
  _flows       = {}
  _adjuvants   = {}
  _legs        = {}
  _exercises   = {}
  _trades      = {

  retrieve = staticmethod(
       lambda tag, which :
          utils.retrieve('trade_server', 'TradeServer', tag, which))

  def GenerateFixedCouponObservables(
      self
      , tag
      , start
      , end
      , roll_period
      , roll_duration
      , reset_currency
      , coupon_shift_method
      , coupon_rate):
    try:
      observables = \
      ppf.core.generate_fixed_coupon_observables(
            start=utils.to_ppf_date(start)
          , end=utils.to_ppf_date(end)
          , roll_period=roll_period
          , roll_duration=eval("ppf.date_time."+roll_duration)
          , reset_currency=reset_currency
          , coupon_shift_method=
              eval( \
              "ppf.date_time.shift_convention."+coupon_shift_method)
          , coupon_rate=coupon_rate)
      TradeServer._observables[tag] = observables
      return tag
    except RuntimeError, e: utils.raise_com_exception(e)

  def GenerateLiborObservables(
```

```
       self
       , tag
       , start
       , end
       , roll_period
       , roll_duration
       , reset_period
       , reset_duration
       , reset_currency
       , reset_basis
       , reset_shift_method):
     try:
       observables = \
         ppf.core.generate_libor_observables(
             start=utils.to_ppf_date(start)
           , end=utils.to_ppf_date(end)
           , roll_period=roll_period
           , roll_duration = eval("ppf.date_time."+roll_duration)
           , reset_period = reset_period
           , reset_duration = eval("ppf.date_time."+reset_duration)
           , tenor_period = reset_period
           , tenor_duration = eval("ppf.date_time."+reset_duration)
           , reset_currency=reset_currency
           , reset_basis = eval("ppf.date_time."+reset_basis)
           , reset_shift_method=eval( \
               "ppf.date_time.shift_convention."+reset_shift_method)
           , reset_lag = 0)
       TradeServer._observables[tag] = observables
       return tag
     except RuntimeError, e: utils.raise_com_exception(e)

   def GenerateFlows(
       self
       , tag
       , start
       , end
       , period
       , duration
       , pay_currency
       , pay_shift_method
       , accrual_basis
       , observables):
     try:
       flows = ppf.core.generate_flows(
             start=utils.to_ppf_date(start)
           , end=utils.to_ppf_date(end)
           , duration=eval("ppf.date_time."+duration)
           , period=period
           , pay_shift_method=eval(\
               "ppf.date_time.shift_convention."+pay_shift_method)
           , pay_currency=pay_currency
```

```
            , accrual_basis=eval("ppf.date_time."+accrual_basis)
            , observables=TradeServer.retrieve(observables,
                'observables'))
        TradeServer._flows[tag] = flows
        return tag
    except RuntimeError, e: utils.raise_com_exception(e)

    def GenerateAdjuvantTable(
        self
        , tag
        , items
        , tens
        , vals
        , start
        , roll_period
        , roll_duration
        , shift_method):
      try:
        import numpy
        adjuvants = \
            ppf.core.generate_adjuvant_table(
                items[1:]
                , [int(t) for t in tens[1:]]
                , numpy.array([x[1:len(vals[0])] for x in vals[1:]])
                , utils.to_ppf_date(start)
                , rol_period=roll_period
                , roll_duration=eval("ppf.date_time."+roll_duration)
                , shift_method=eval(\
                    "ppf.date_time.shift_convention."
                    +shift_method))
        TradeServer._adjuvants[tag] = adjuvants
        return tag
    except RuntimeError, e: utils.raise_com_exception(e)

    def GenerateExerciseSchedule(
        self
        , tag
        , start
        , end
        , period
        , duration
        , shift_method):
      try:
        sched = \
          ppf.core.generate_exercise_table(
              start = utils.to_ppf_date(start)
              , end = utils.to_ppf_date(end)
              , period = period
              , duration = eval("ppf.date_time."+duration)
              , shift_method = eval("ppf.date_time.shift_convention."
                               +shift_method))
```

```
      TradeServer._exercises[tag] = sched
      return tag
    except RuntimeError, e:
      utils.raise_com_exception(e)

  def CreateLeg(
    self
    , tag
    , flows
    , pay_or_receive
    , adjuvant_table
    , payoff):
    try:
      adjuvants = None
      if adjuvant_table:
        adjuvants = TradeServer.retrieve(adjuvant_table, 'adjuvants')
      leg = \
          ppf.core.leg(
              TradeServer.retrieve(flows, 'flows')
              , eval("ppf.core."+pay_or_receive)
              , adjuvants
              , eval("ppf.pricer.payoffs."+payoff)())
      TradeServer._legs[tag] = leg
      return tag
    except RuntimeError, e: utils.raise_com_exception(e)

  def CreateTrade(
    self
    , tag
    , legs
    , exercise_sched
    , exercise_type):
    try:
      tl = [TradeServer.retrieve(l, 'legs') for l in legs[1:]]
      if exercise_sched:
        exercises = TradeServer.retrieve(exercise_sched, 'exercises')
        if not exercise_type:
          raise RuntimeError, "missing exercise type"
        call_cancel = eval("ppf.core.exercise_type."+exercise_type)
        trade = ppf.core.trade(tl, (exercises, call_cancel))
      else:
        trade = ppf.core.trade(tl, None)
      TradeServer._trades[tag] = trade
      return tag
    except RuntimeError, e: utils.raise_com_exception(e)

if _name_ == "_main_": utils.register_com_class(TradeServer)
```

Subsection 12.2.2 covers the details of what needs to be known to 'technically' understand the above code, so this section need not be as detailed from that perspective.

As is the case for `class MarketServer`, the `class TradeServer` implementation follows a 'mono-state' idiom. Unlike, `class MarketServer`, however, `class TradeServer` maintains multiple dictionaries in its class object state

```
_observables = {} #observable collections
_flows       = {} #flow collections
_adjuvants   = {} #adjuvant tables
_legs        = {} #trade legs
_exercises   = {} #exercise schedules
_trades      = {} #trades
```

As for `class MarketServer`, `class TradeServer` offers a static method for inter-module retrieval of data from these dictionaries.

As for the COM interface, `GenerateFixedCouponObservables` rolls out strips of fixed coupons, whereas `GenerateLiborCouponObservables` rolls out strips of LIBORs (it's left as an exercise to the reader to write the function that rolls out strips of swap rate observables). `GenerateFlows` rolls out flows with observable collections folded in. `GenerateAdjuvantTable` and `GenerateExerciseSchedule` provide the means of constructing adjuvant tables (refer to section 6.3) and exercise schedules respectively. Finally, `CreateLeg` assembles a flow collection, a user-provided payoff string and potentially an adjuvant table into a trade leg (the payoff string needs to map to a class name in the `ppf.pricer.payoffs` module such as, `fixed_leg_payoff`, `float_leg_payoff` for example). Finally, legs and perhaps an associated exercise schedule can be aggregated into trades with the `CreateTrade` method. Figure 12.5 shows how the data for describing a Bermudan swaption might be laid out in an Excel worksheet.

Trade VBA Client

The following shows example client code for interfacing to the *'ppf.trade'* COM object.

E	F	G	H	I	J	K
Fixed Cpns		Float Cpns		Exercise Schedule		
tag	USD_FXD_OBS	tag	USD_FLT_OBS	tag	EX_SCHED	
start	29/06/2007	start	29/06/2007	start		29/06/2007
end	29/06/2010	end	29/06/2010	end		29/06/2009
roll period	6	roll period	6	period		1
roll duration	months	roll duration	months	duration	years	
reset currency	USD	reset period	6	shift method	modified_following	
coupon_shift_method	modified_following	reset duration	months	schedule	EX_SCHED	
coupon_rate	0.06	reset currency	USD			
observables	USD_FXD_OBS	reset basis	basis_act_360	Swap		
flows tag	USD_FXD_FLW	reset shift	modified_following			
accrual basis	basis_act_360	observables	USD_FLT_OBS	tag	SWAP	
flows	USD_FXD_FLW	flows tag	USD_FLT_FLW	trade	SWAP	
		accrual basis	basis_act_360			
Fixed leg		flows	USD_FLT_FLW	Berm		
tag	USD_FXD_LEG	Adjuvant table		tag	BERM	
pay/receive	PAY			ex. type	callable	
payoff	fixed_leg_payoff	tag	USD_FLT_ADJ	trade	=PPF_CreateTrade($J$18,$F$21	
leg	USD_FXD_LEG	keys	spread0		J19)	
		tenors	48			
		values	0			
		roll period	6			
		roll duration	months			
		shift method	modified_following			
		start	29/06/2007			
		adjuvants	USD_FLT_ADJ			
		Funding leg				
		tag	USD_FLT_LEG			
		pay/receive	RECEIVE			
		payoff	float_leg_payoff			
		leg	USD_FLT_LEG			

Figure 12.5   Creating a Bermudan swaption.

PPF_GenerateFixedCouponObservables   This function calls out to the `class Trade-Server GenerateFixedCouponObservables` method to create and register observables to underly a fixed trade leg.

```
Public Function _
PPF_GenerateFixedCouponObservables( _
    Tag As String _
  , Begin As Date _
  , Finish As Date _
  , Period As Integer _
  , Duration As String _
  , Ccy As String _
  , Shift As String _
  , Rate As Double) As String
    'Generate a ppf fixed coupon observable sequence
    '
    On Error Resume Next
    Dim TradeServer As Object
    Set TradeServer = CreateObject("ppf.trade")
    PPF_GenerateFixedCouponObservables = _
      TradeServer.GenerateFixedCouponObservables( _
          Tag _
        , Begin _
        , Finish _
        , Period _
        , Duration _
        , Ccy _
        , Shift _
        , Rate)
    If Err.Number <> 0 Then
      PPF_GenerateFixedCouponObservables = "#err : " & Err.Description
    End If
    Set TradeServer = Nothing
End Function
```

PPF_GenerateLiborObservables   This function calls out to the `class TradeServer GenerateLiborObservables` method to create and register the observables to underly a funding trade leg.

```
Public Function _
PPF_GenerateLiborObservables( _
    Tag As String _
  , Begin As Date _
  , Finish As Date _
  , RollPeriod As Integer _
  , RollDuration As String _
  , ResetPeriod As Integer _
  , ResetDuration As String _
  , ResetCcy As String _
  , ResetBasis As String _
```

```
    , ResetShift As String) As String
    'Generate a ppf libor observable sequence
    '
    On Error Resume Next
    Dim TradeServer As Object
    Set TradeServer = CreateObject("ppf.trade")
    PPF_GenerateLiborObservables = _
        TradeServer.GenerateLiborObservables( _
            Tag _
          , Begin _
          , Finish _
          , RollPeriod _
          , RollDuration _
          , ResetPeriod _
          , ResetDuration _
          , ResetCcy _
          , ResetBasis _
          , ResetShift)
    If Err.Number <> 0 Then
        PPF_GenerateLiborObservables = "#err : " & Err.Description
    End If
    Set TradeServer = Nothing
End Function
```

PPF_GenerateAdjuvantTable   This function calls out to the `class TradeServer`
`GenerateAdjuvantTable` method to build and register an adjuvant table.

```
Public Function _
PPF_GenerateAdjuvantTable( _
    Tag As String _
  , Items As Variant _
  , Tenors As Variant _
  , Values As Variant _
  , Start As Date _
  , RollPeriod As Integer _
  , RollDuration As String _
  , ShiftConv As String) As String
    'Generate a ppf adjuvant table
    '
    On Error Resume Next
    Dim TradeServer As Object
    Set TradeServer = CreateObject("ppf.trade")
    Dim K As Integer
    K = Items.Rows.Count
    If Items.Columns.Count <> 1 Then
     PPF_GenerateAdjuvantTable = "#err : " & "invalid argument"
     Exit Function
    End If
    Dim Keys As Variant
    ReDim Keys(K)
```

```
  Dim I, J As Integer
  For I = 1 To K
    Keys(I) = Items(I).Value
  Next I
  Dim M, N As Integer
  M = Values.Rows.Count
  N = Values.Columns.Count
  If M <> K Then
   PPF_GenerateAdjuvantTable = "#err : " & "invalid argument"
   Exit Function
  End If
  Dim Vals As Variant
  ReDim Vals(M, N)
  For I = 1 To M
    For J = 1 To N
        Vals(I, J) = Values(I, J).Value
    Next J
  Next I
  If Tenors.Rows.Count > 1 Or Tenors.Columns.Count <> N Then
   PPF_GenerateAdjuvantTable = "#err : " & "invalid argument"
   Exit Function
  End If
  Dim Tens As Variant
  ReDim Tens(N)
  For J = 1 To N
    Tens(J) = Tenors(J).Value
  Next J
  PPF_GenerateAdjuvantTable = _
    TradeServer.GenerateAdjuvantTable( _
        Tag _
      , Keys _
      , Tens _
      , Vals _
      , Start _
      , RollPeriod _
      , RollDuration _
      , ShiftConv)
  If Err.Number <> 0 Then
    PPF_GenerateAdjuvantTable = "#err : " & Err.Description
  End If
  Set TradeServer = Nothing
End Function
```

PPF_GenerateFlows   This function calls out to the class TradeServer Generate-Flows method to create and register a flow collection.

```
Public Function _
PPF_GenerateFlows( _
    Tag As String _
```

```
, Begin As Date _
, Finish As Date _
, Period As Integer _
, Duration As String _
, Ccy As String _
, Shift As String _
, Basis As String _
, Observables As String) As String
'Generate a ppf flow sequence
'
On Error Resume Next
Dim TradeServer As Object
Set TradeServer = CreateObject("ppf.trade")
PPF_GenerateFlows = _
  TradeServer.GenerateFlows( _
      Tag _
    , Begin _
    , Finish _
    , Period _
    , Duration _
    , Ccy _
    , Shift _
    , Basis _
    , Observables)
If Err.Number <> 0 Then
  PPF_GenerateFlows = "#err : " & Err.Description
End If
Set TradeServer = Nothing
End Function
```

PPF_GenerateExerciseSchedule   This function calls out to the `class Trade-Server GenerateExerciseSchedule` method to create and register an exercise schedule.

```
Public Function _
PPF_GenerateExerciseSchedule( _
    Tag As String _
  , Begin As Date _
  , Finish As Date _
  , Period As Integer _
  , Duration As String _
  , Shift As String) As String
  'Generate a ppf exercise schedule
  '
  On Error Resume Next
  Dim TradeServer As Object
  Set TradeServer = CreateObject("ppf.trade")
  PPF_GenerateExerciseSchedule = _
    TradeServer.GenerateExerciseSchedule( _
        Tag _
```

```
    , Begin _
    , Finish _
    , Period _
    , Duration _
    , Shift)
  If Err.Number <> 0 Then
    PPF_GenerateExerciseSchedule = "#err : " & Err.Description
  End If
  Set TradeServer = Nothing
End Function
```

PPF_CreateLeg   This function calls out to the class TradeServer CreateLeg function to create and register a trade leg.

```
Public Function _
PPF_CreateLeg( _
    Tag As String _
  , Flows As String _
  , PayOrReceive As String _
  , AdjuvantTable As Variant _
  , Payoff As String) As String
  'Create a ppf trade leg
  '
  On Error Resume Next
  Dim TradeServer As Object
  Set TradeServer = CreateObject("ppf.trade")
  If IsMissing(AdjuvantTable) Then
    PPF_CreateLeg = _
      TradeServer.CreateLeg( _
          Tag _
        , Flows _
        , PayOrReceive _
        , Nothing _
        , Payoff)
  Else
    PPF_CreateLeg = _
      TradeServer.CreateLeg( _
          Tag _
        , Flows _
        , PayOrReceive _
        , CStr(AdjuvantTable) _
        , Payoff)
  End If
  If Err.Number <> 0 Then
    PPF_CreateLeg = "#err : " & Err.Description
  End If
  Set TradeServer = Nothing
End Function
```

PPF_CreateTrade   This function calls out to the `class TradeServer CreateTrade` method to create and register a trade.

```
Public Function _
PPF_CreateTrade( _
    Tag As String _
  , Leg1 As String _
  , Leg2 As String _
  , ExerciseSched As Variant _
  , ExerciseType As Variant) As String
  'Create a ppf trade
  '
  On Error Resume Next
  Dim TradeServer As Object
  Set TradeServer = CreateObject("ppf.trade")
  Dim Legs(2) As String
  Legs(1) = Leg1: Legs(2) = Leg2
  If IsMissing(ExerciseSched) Then
    PPF_CreateTrade = _
      TradeServer.CreateTrade( _
          Tag _
        , Legs _
        , Nothing _
        , Nothing)
  Else
    PPF_CreateTrade = _
      TradeServer.CreateTrade( _
          Tag _
        , Legs _
        , CStr(ExerciseSched) _
        , CStr(ExerciseType))
  End If
  If Err.Number <> 0 Then
    PPF_CreateTrade = "#err : " & Err.Description
  End If
  Set TradeServer = Nothing
End Function
```

12.2.4 Pricer Server

We are very close to achieving the goal as stated in the opening to this section, that is, pricing Bermudans on a Hull–White lattice from Excel.

The last component to consider is the `class PricerServer`, the code for which can be found in the `ppf.com.pricer_server` module:

```
import ppf.model
import ppf.pricer
import utils

class PricerServer(object):
  _reg_progid_ = "ppf.pricer"
```

```
_reg_clsid_ = "{08632905-0B63-45B5-B388-30C73CAE611C}"
_public_methods_ = \
[
    "CreateHullWhiteLatticePricer"
                    , "InvokePricer"
]
_pricers = {}

retrieve = staticmethod(
    lambda tag, which :
        utils.retrieve('pricer_server', 'PricerServer', tag, which))

def CreateHullWhiteLatticePricer(
    self
    , tag
    , trade_id
    , env_id
    , num_states
    , num_std_dev) :
  try:
    from trade_server import TradeServer
    from market_server import MarketServer
    trade = TradeServer.retrieve(trade_id, 'trades')
    env   = MarketServer.retrieve(env_id, 'environments')
    model_args = {"num states": num_states, "num std dev":
    num_std_dev}
    factory = ppf.model.hull_white_lattice_model_factory()
    model = factory(trade, env, model_args)
    pricer = ppf.pricer.lattice_pricer(trade, model, env, None)
    PricerServer._pricers[tag] = pricer
    return tag
  except RuntimeError, e: ppf.com.utils.raise_com_exception(e)

def InvokePricer(self, tag):
  try:
    return PricerServer.retrieve(tag, 'pricers').__call__()
  except RuntimeError, e: utils.raise_com_exception(e)

if __name__ == "__main__": utils.register_com_class(PricerServer)
```

The explanations provided by the earlier sections should make the above code self-explanatory rendering further comment unnecessary. Figure 12.6 shows an example session pricing a Bermudan in an Excel session.

Pricer VBA Client

Here is the example client code for interfacing to the *'ppf.pricer'* COM object.

PPF_HullWhiteLatticePrice   The function for obtaining the price of a trade via the Hull–White model on a lattice.

```
Public Function _
PPF_HullWhiteLatticePrice( _
```

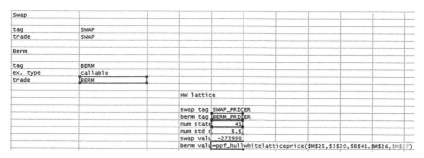

Figure 12.6 Pricing a berm.

```
   Tag As String _
 , trade As String _
 , Env As String _
 , NumStates As Integer _
 , NumStdDevs As Double) As Variant
 'Price trade on a Hull-White lattice
 '

 On Error Resume Next
 Dim PricerServer As Object
 Set PricerServer = CreateObject("ppf.pricer")
 PPF_HullWhiteLatticePrice = _
   PricerServer.InvokePricer( _
     PricerServer.CreateHullWhiteLatticePricer( _
         Tag _
       , trade _
       , Env _
       , NumStates _
       , NumStdDevs))
   If Err.Number <> 0 Then
     PPF_HullWhiteLatticePrice = "#err : " & Err.Description
   End If
   Set PricerServer = Nothing
End Function
```

Appendices

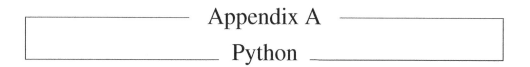

Appendix A
Python

In this appendix, we provide a whirlwind tour of the Python programming language. It will in no way be exhaustive and is not intended to negate the need for learning the language more comprehensively using the many excellent resources available teaching Python.[1] Nonetheless, it should be enough to enable a newcomer to the language to get started.

A.1 PYTHON INTERPRETER MODES

The Python interpreter can be executed in one of two modes: 'interactive' or 'batch'. When run interactively in a shell or on Windows, at a command prompt, the interpreter will wait for input from the user, and when sufficient input has been made for a statement to be executed will execute that statement immediately and go back to waiting for the next. In batch mode, a complete Python script stored in a file is given to the interpreter and executed, all at the same time.

A.1.1 Interactive Mode

To launch an interactive session with the interpreter, from your shell or command prompt, issue the command `python -i`. All being well, the interpreter should then indicate its willingness to begin processing statements by displaying its *primary* prompt, which looks like a sideways chevron '>>>'. On Windows, starting a session might look something like this:

```
c:\Documents and Settings\PythonUser>python -i
python -i
ActivePython 2.5.1.1 (ActiveState Software Inc.) based on
Python 2.5.1 (r251:54863, May 1 2007, 17:47:05) [MSC v.1310 32 bit
(Intel)] on win32
Type "help", "copyright", "credits" or "license" for more
information.
>>>
```

When the interpreter has seen some part of a statement, but not sufficiently enough to execute anything, the Python interpreter will indicate that situation by displaying its *secondary* prompt, which looks like '. . .'.

A.1.2 Batch Mode

To have the interpreter execute a complete Python script stored in a file on disk, simply run the Python executable, passing the name of the script to be executed. For example, assuming

---

[1] A good place to start is the 'Python tutorial' available online at http://docs.python.org/tutorial/

the existence of a file 'hello_world.py' (files containing Python script by convention have a '.py' suffix), we might execute it like so:

```
c:\Documents and Settings\PythonUser>python hello_world.py
```

A.2   BASIC PYTHON

A.2.1   Simple Expressions

The Python interpreter can be used like a calculator to evaluate numerical expressions:

```
>>> 1 + 2 + 3
6
```

Number valued expressions in Python are of integer or floating point type:

```
>>> 22/7
3
>>> 22/7.0
3.1428571428571428
>>>
```

String literal expressions are values too:

```
>>> "Hello world!"
'Hello world!'
>>> "Goodbye cruel" + "world."
'Goodbye cruel world.'
>>>
```

In the last example, we made use of the string concatenation operator '+' to concatenate two string literal expressions into one.

The value of an expression can be associated with a variable using the *assignment operator* denoted '=':

```
>>> x = 1 + 2 + 3
```

Doing so means the evaluation of the named expression can be referred to again later:

```
>>> print x - 6
0
```

Assigning a new expression to an existing variable causes the expression the variable was associated with to be discarded and the variable to become associated with the new expression instead:

```
>>> bar = "baz"
>>> print bar
baz
>>> bar = 42
>>> print bar
42
>>>
```

Comments are indicated by a '#' and are ignored by the interpreter:

```
>>> #this is a comment!
...
>>>
```

A.2.2 Built-in Data Types

We have seen that natively Python supports integers, floating point values and character strings. Python also natively provides incredibly useful heterogeneous container types. The first of these is the *tuple*. A tuple is a fixed collection of values and can be constructed using parentheses like this:

```
>>> t = (1, 2, "foo")
>>> print t
(1, 2, 'foo')
>>>
```

Naturally, tuples can contain values of any type including tuples:

```
>>> s = (t, t, (t,))
>>> print s
((1, 2, 'foo'), (1, 2, 'foo'), ((1, 2, 'foo'),))
>>>
```

The value at the *i*th position of a tuple can be retrieved like this:

```
>>> print t[0]
1
>>> print t[1]
2
>>> print t[2]
foo
>>> print t[3] #uh-oh...
Traceback (most recent call last):
 File "<stdin>", line 1, in <module>
IndexError: tuple index out of range
>>>
```

Tuples can be used to assign to multiple values very concisely:

```
>>> x,y,z=t
>>> print "%d,%d,%s" %(x, y, z)
1,2,foo
```

Tuples are immutable which means a tuple value may not be modified:

```
>>> t[0]=10
Traceback (most recent call last):
 File "<stdin>", line 1, in <module>
TypeError: 'tuple' object does not support item assignment
>>>
```

In fact, integers, floats, strings and tuples are all immutable types.

When a mutable sequence is needed, Python steps in with its *list* type. Lists are created using square brackets like this:

```
>>> l = [1, 1.0, "one"]
>>> print l
[1, 1.0, 'one']
>>>
```

Lists contain values of any type (built-in or user-defined) including of course, tuples and lists.

```
>>> m = [l, t]
>>> print m
[[1, 1.0, 'one'], (1, 2, 'foo')]
>>>
```

Lists as mentioned are a mutable type:

```
>>> l[0], l[1], l[2] = (2, 2.0, 'two')
>>> print l
[2, 2.0, 'two']
>>>
```

Be careful! Because lists are not immutable one needs to be mindful of side-effects resulting from aliasing:

```
>>> ll = l
>>> ll[0] = 3
>>> print l
[3, 2.0, 'two']
>>>
```

Do you see what's happened there? The value referred to by l was modified through an alias ll.

Now, Python has very powerful constructs for creating lists termed *list comprehensions*:

```
>>> u = [i for i in range(10)]
>>> print u
[0, 1, 2, 3, 4, 5, 6, 7, 8, 9]
>>> v = [i*i for i in u]
>>> print v
[0, 1, 4, 9, 16, 25, 36, 49, 64, 81]
>>> print [x for x in v if x > 25]
[36, 49, 64, 81]
```

List comprehensions are very much worth finding out about as early as possible.

Data structures commonly known as *associative arrays* in other programming languages are termed *dictionaries* in Python. They are arrays accessed by *keys* where each key is associated with a value. An empty dictionary is denoted '{}':

```
>>> d = {}
>>> print d
{}
```

A non-empty dictionary can be created by passing a sequence of key-value pairs like this:

```
>>> d = {"1":1, "2":2, "3":3}
>>> print d
{'1': 1, '3': 3, '2': 2}
```

Naturally, dictionary values may be of any type, including lists and tuples:

```
>>> d["list"] = l
>>> d["tuple"] = t
>>> print d
{'1': 1, '3': 3, '2': 2, 'list': [1, 1.0, 'one'],
'tuple': (1, 2, 'foo')}
```

Any immutable type will serve for a dictionary key including tuples (as long as the values of the tuple are themselves all immutable):

```
>>> m = {(1, 2, 3):"a tuple"}
>>> print m
{(1, 2, 3): 'a tuple'}
>>>
```

As previously noted, lists are not immutable:

```
>>> m = {[1, 2, 3]:"a list"}
Traceback (most recent call last):
 File "<stdin>", line 1, in <module>
TypeError: list objects are unhashable
>>>
```

A.2.3   Control Flow Statements

Let's start with simple iteration using the Python for statement:

```
>>> for i in range(10):
...   print i
...
0
1
2
3
4
5
6
7
8
9
>>>
```

Encountered earlier in this piece but not described is the function range. Maybe it's better to delegate explanation to the doc-string for range like this:

```
>>> help(range)
Help on built-in function range in module __builtin__:
```

```
range(...)
    range([start,] stop[, step]) -> list of integers

    Return a list containing an arithmetic progression of integers.
    range(i, j) returns [i, i+1, i+2, ..., j-1]; start (!) defaults
    to 0.
    When step is given, it specifies the increment (or decrement).
    For example, range(4) returns [0, 1, 2, 3]. The end point is
    omitted!
    These are exactly the valid indices for a list of 4 elements.

>>>
```

Now returning to our understanding of the `for` statement example above:

```
>>> for i in range(10):
...     print i
...
```

Note how the `print i` is indented relative to the preceding line (`for i in ...`). This is significant. That is, white space is significant in Python and its use indicates where different parts of statements begin and end much like the use of '{' and '}' in C/C++. To illustrate further, here's a more involved snippet:

```
>>> for i in range(0, 2):
...     print i
... for j in range(0, 10):
...     print " %d" % (j)
... print
...
0
 0
 1
 2
 3
 4
 5
 6
 7
 8
 9
1
 0
 1
 2
 3
 4
 5
 6
 7
 8
 9
>>>
```

Dropping back a level of indentation in line 5 of the above indicated that the `print` statement written there was not part of the inner loop body (the inner `for` statement had reached its conclusion).

`for` statements are more general than just the ability to iterate through a sequence of integers:

```
>>> print 1
[3, 2.0, 'two']
>>> for obj in 1:
...    print obj
...
3
2.0
two
>>>
```

More general iterations can be performed with the `while` statement:

```
>>> i = 0
>>> while i < 10:
...    print i
...    i += 1
...
0
1
2
3
4
5
6
7
8
9
>>>
```

Conditional statements are used to choose one branch of code or another depending on the value of an expression:

```
>>> i = 0
>>> while(i < 10):
...    i += 1
...    if i % 2:
...      print "%d is idd" % i
...    else:
...      print "%d is even" % i
...
1 is odd
2 is even
3 is odd
4 is even
5 is odd
6 is even
```

```
7 is odd
8 is even
9 is odd
10 is even
>>>
```

A.2.4 Functions

The most basic unit of software in Python is the function. A function is a portion of code within a larger program which performs a specific task or computation relatively independently of the rest of the program.

Functions in Python are defined using the `def` statement and, as seen earlier, indentation determines where they begin and end:

```
>>> def square(x):
...     return x*x
...
>>> def cube(x):
...     return x*square(x)
...
>>> print square(4)
16
>>> print cube(4)
64
>>>
```

When a function by its nature has multiple return values, a tuple can be used to aggregate them:

```
>>> def square_and_cube(x):
...     return (square(x), cube(x))
...
>>> print square_and_cube(4)
(16, 64)
>>>
```

Where mutable data-types are involved, beware of the potential for side-effects:

```
>>> def foo(l):
...     l[0] = 12
...
>>> l = [1, 2, 3]
>>> foo(l)
>>> print l
[12, 2, 3]
>>>
```

In general, it's probably good advice to avoid programming in this fashion. Explicit is better than implicit:

```
>>> def foo(l):
...     m = l[:] # use slicing to make a (deep) copy of l
...     m[0] = 12
```

```
...     return m
...
>>> l = [1, 2, 3]
>>> m = foo(l)
>>> print l
[1, 2, 3]
>>> print m
[12, 2, 3]
>>>
```

A.2.5 Classes

There's not much you can't do with the built-in Python types (primitives, tuples, lists and dictionaries). Programs, though, are typically written once and read again many, many times. The programmer should strive hard to convey the meaning of the program to the human reader as much as he/she possibly can. Tuples, lists and dictionaries by themselves do little to aid semantic comprehension of the data elements of a program and that realisation has inspired grouping of related data elements into user-definable aggregate structures from at least as far back in time as Pascal's user-defined `record` data-type. Python permits the programmer to define his/her own types together with operations (in Python terminology – *methods*,) that operate on *instances* of these *class* types.

The most simple `class` in Python can be written like this:

```
>>> class empty(object):
...     pass
...
>>> e=empty()
```

This isn't a very rich type but it is a type nonetheless. Here's another user-defined `class` that is a bit more interesting:

```
>>> class person(object):
...     def __init__(self, age, name):
...         self.age = age
...         self.name = name
...
>>> p = person(25, "John Doe")
>>> print p.age
25
>>> print p.name
John Doe
>>>
>>> print type(p)
< class '__main__.person'>
```

The benefits of improved semantic comprehensibility via the abstraction of the above person p over the representation (25, "John Doe") can be augmented even further with class methods:

```
>>> class person(object):
...     def __init__(self, age, name):
```

```
...        self.age = age
...        self.name = name
...    def birth_year(self, current_year):
...        return current_year - (self.age + 1)
...
>>>    p = person(25, "John Doe")
>>> print p.birth_year(2008)
1982
```

Classes can be used to model IS_A relationships (inheritance):

```
>>> class employee(person):
...    def __init__(self, age, name, salary):
...        person.__init__(self, age, name)
...        self.salary = salary
...    def earns(self):
...        return self.salary
...
>>> e = employee(25, "John Doe", 15000)
>>> print e.birth_year(2008)
1982
>>> print e.earns()
15000
>>>
```

Notice how the methods of the person class are inherited by the employee class. That is, an employee can be substituted for wherever the context calls for a person. Note that any method in a base class can be overriden in a derived class:

```
>>> class manager(employee):
...    def __init__(self, name, age, salary):
...        employee.__init__(self, name, age, salary)
...    def earns(self):
...        raise RuntimeError, "This operation is restricted"
...
>>> m = manager(25, "John Doe", 20000)
>>> print m.age
25
>>> print m.name
John Doe
>>> print m.birth_year(2008)
1982
>>> print m.earns()
Traceback (most recent call last):
  File "<stdin>", line 1, in <module>
  File "<stdin>", line 5, in earns
RuntimeError: This information is restricted
>>>
```

Unlike C++ with its notion of `private`, `protected` and `public` access mechanisms, everything in a class is publicly accessible and due to Python's dynamic nature the definition of a class can even be changed during execution of the script(!):

```
>>> def salary(mgr):
...     return mgr.salary
...
>>> print salary(m)
20000
>>> manager.earns = salary
>>> print m.earns()
20000
>>>
```

Programming with classes is ubiquitous in Python and this section just covers the basics. The newcomer to Python is recommended to take the time to become more familiar with them early on.

A.2.6   Modules and Packages

A module is a lexical unit of Python code stored in a file on disk. Let us suppose the existence of a file 'complex.py' with contents something like the following:

```
class complex(object):
  def __init__(self, re, im):
    self.re, self.im = (re, im)

  def real_part(self):
    return self.re

  def imag_part(self):
    return self.im

  def __str__(self):
    return "%f + %fi" % (self.re, self.im)

  def __add__(self, other):
    return complex(self.re + other.re, self.im + other.im)

  # ...

  def conjugate(x):
    return complex(x.real_part(), -x.imag_part())

# ...
```

We can use the Python `import` directive to bring all of the type declarations and function definitions defined in 'complex.py' into the current scope like this:

```
>>> from complex import *
>>> i = complex(0, 1)
```

```
>>> print i
0.000000 + 1.000000i
>>> print conjugate(i)
0.000000 + -1.000000i
>>> print i + conjugate(i)
0.000000 + 0.000000i
>>>
```

We can `import` symbols into the current scope more selectively using different syntactic forms of the `import` directive:

```
>>> from sys import path # sys is a built-in module
>>> import pprint # so is pprint
>>> pprint.pprint(path)
['',
 'C:\\WINDOWS\\system32\\python25.zip',
 'C:\\Python25\\DLLs',
 'C:\\Python25\\lib',
 'C:\\Python25\\lib\\plat-win',
 'C:\\Python25\\lib\\lib-tk',
 'C:\\Python25',
 'C:\\Python25\\lib\\site-packages',
 'C:\\Python25\\lib\\site-packages\\win32',
 'C:\\Python25\\lib\\site-packages\\win32\\lib',
 'C:\\Python25\\lib\\site-packages\\Pythonwin']
>>>
```

Notice that the last form of the `import` directive required that we prefix our invocation of the `pprint` function with the name of the module in which it resides (i.e module `pprint`).

A more extensive library for complex numbers would offer different representations. Imagine now a directory called 'complex' with two files, 'cartesian.py' and 'polar.py'. The contents of 'cartesian.py' defines the `class complex` as before:

```
class complex(object):
  def __init__(self, re, im):
    self.re, self.im = (re, im)

  def real_part(self):
    return self.re

  def imag_part(self):
    return self.im

  def __str__(self):
    return ""%f + %fi" % (self.re, self.im)

  def __add__(self, other):
    return complex(self.re + other.re, self.im + other.im)

  # ...

def conjugate(x):
```

```
    return complex(x.real_part(), -x.imag_part())

# ...
```

The contents of 'polar.py' defines a different representation for class complex:

```
class complex(object):
    def __init__(self, a, theta):
        self.a = a
        self.theta = theta
    def __str__(self):
        return "%fe ^i (%f)" % (self.a, self.theta)
    # ...
```

We create a third file in the 'complex' directory, '__init__.py':

```
import cartesian
import polar

def polar_to_cartesian(z):
  import math
  x = z.a*math.cos(z.theta)
  y = z.a*math.sin(z.theta)
  return cartesian.complex(x, y)
```

Complex is now a Python *package*. The following snippet exercises the package and demonstrates yet another form of the import directive:

```
C:\Documents and Settings\PythonUser>python -i
>>> import math # math is a built-in module
>>> import complex
>>> from complex import cartesian as rectangular
>>> from complex import polar as polar
>>> i = rectangular.complex(0, 1)
>>> print i
0.000000 + 1.000000i
>>> i = polar.complex(1, math.pi/2)
>>> print i
1.000000e^i(1.570796)
>>> print complex.polar_to_cartesian(i)
0.000000 + 1.000000i
>>>
```

Naturally, packages can contain modules and subpackages which in turn can contain further modules and subpackages.

A.3   CONCLUSION

This has been a whistle-stop tour of the Python language. The basics have been presented and much detail overlooked. It is very much hoped that this has been enough to whet the reader's appetite for Python programming and we strongly encourage the reader to seek out more detailed references for Python programming.

Appendix B
Boost.Python

The Boost.Python library provides a framework for seamlessly wrapping C++ classes, functions and objects to Python, and vice-versa. No special tools are used – just the C++ compiler. The library has been so designed that you should not have to change the C++ code in order to wrap it. Through the use of advanced metaprogramming techniques in Boost.Python, the syntax of the actual wrapping code, has the look of a declarative interface definition language. In this appendix we introduce the core features of Boost.Python. The sections are loosely based on the online Getting Started Tutorial in the Boost.Python distribution. For more exhaustive documentation, the reader is encouraged to consult the online reference manual at http://www.boost.org.

B.1 HELLO WORLD

Let's start with the 'Hello world' C++ function

```
char const* greet()
{
  return ``Hello world'';
}
```

The function can be exposed to Python by writing the following Boost.Python wrapper:

```
#include <boost/python.hpp>

BOOST_PYTHON_MODULE(hello_ext)
{
  using namespace boost::python;
  def(``greet'', greet);
}
```

We can now build this as a shared library and the resulting library is a Python module. An invocation of the function from the Python command line looks like

```
>>> import hello_ext
>>> print hello_ext.greet()
```

B.2 CLASSES, CONSTRUCTORS AND METHODS

Let's consider a C++ class/struct that we want to expose to Python:

```
struct World
{
  World(std::string msg): msg(msg) {}
  void set(std::string other) { msg = other; }
```

```
   std::string greet() { return msg; }
   std::string msg;
};
```

The Boost.Python wrapper for the above class is

```
BOOST_PYTHON_MODULE(hello_ext)
{
  using namespace boost::python;
  class_<World>(``World'', init<std: :string>())
    .def(``greet'', &World::greet)
    .def(``set'', &World::set)
  ;
}
```

The init<std::string>() exposes the constructor. Additional constructors can be exposed by passing more init<...> to the def() member function. For example, suppose World has another constructor taking two doubles, the wrapping code would look like

```
class_<World>(``World'', init<std::string>())
  .def(init<double, double>())
  .def(``greet'', &World::greet)
  .def(``set'', &World::set)
;
```

If our C++ class, world had no explicit constructors, that is if its definition were to read

```
struct World
{
  void set(std::string other) { msg = other; }
  std::string greet() { return msg; }
  std::string msg;
};
```

the compiler would synthesise an implicit default constructor. In such a case, Boost.Python can expose the default constructor by default, implying that the wrapping code could be written,

```
class_<World>(``World'')
  .def(``greet'', &World::greet)
  .def(``set'', &World::set)
;
```

then in the Python interpreter, it could be exercised like this:

```
>>> planet = hello_ext.World()
```

Abstract classes without any constructors can be exposed by using the no_init instead, as seen in the example below:

```
class_<Abstract>(``Abstract'', no_init)
;
```

In C++ we usually avoid public access to data members because it breaks the idea of encapsulation: with access only possible via the accessor methods `set` and `get`. Python, on the other hand, allows class attribute access by default. We replicate this behaviour for wrapped C++ classes by using the `add_property` method of the class `class_` in Boost.Python. To illustrate this, suppose we wish to wrap the following C++ class

```
struct Num
{
  Num();
  float get() const;
  void set(float value);
};
```

then the Boost.Python wrapping code looks like

```
class_<Num>(''Num'')
    .add_property(''rovalue'', &Num::get)
    .add_property(''value'', &Num::get, &Num::set)
  ;
```

and in Python:

```
>>> x = Num()
>>> x.value = 3.14
>>> x.value, x.rovalue
(3.14, 3.14)
>>> x.rovalue = 2.17 # error!
```

Before leaving this section we need to consider constructors with default arguments. To deal with default arguments in constructors, Boost.Python has provides the (tag) type `optional`. A simple example should suffice to explain the semantics. Consider the C++ class:

```
struct X
{
  X(int a, char b = 'D', std::string c = ''constructor'',
                double d = 0.0);
};
```

To add this constructor to Boost.Python, we simply write:

```
.def(init<int, optional<char, std::string, double> >())
```

B.3   INHERITANCE

It is also possible to wrap class hierarchies, related by inheritance, using Boost.Python. Consider the trivial inheritance structure:

```
struct Base { virtual Base(); };
struct Derived : Base {};
```

together with a set of C++ functions operating on instances of `Base` and `Derived`:

```
void b(Base*);
void d(Derived*);
Base* factory { return new Derived; }
```

The wrapping code for both the `Base` and `Derived` is

```
class_<Base>(''Base'')
  /**/
  ;
```

and

```
class_<Derived, bases<Base> >(''Derived'')
  /**/
  ;
```

where we have used `bases<..>` to indicate that `Derived` is derived from `Base`. The corresponding wrapping code for the C++ free functions looks like

```
def(''b'', b);
def(''d'', d);
def(''factory'', factory,
  return_value_policy<manage_new_object>());
```

The `return_value_policy<manage_new_object>` construct informs Python to hold the instance of the new Python `Base` object until the Python object is destroyed.

Both pure virtual and virtual functions with default implementations can be handled by Boost.Python. However, this is one of the rare instances where we have to write some extra C++ code to achieve this. Let's start with pure virtual functions. Suppose we have the following base class:

```
struct Base
{
  virtual Base() {}
  virtual int f() = 0;
};
```

What we need to do is write a little wrapper class that derives from `Base` and unintrusively hooks into the virtual functions so that a Python override can be called. The code for the wrapper class is shown below:

```
struct BaseWrap : Base, wrapper<Base>
{
  int f()
  {
    return this->get_override(''f'')();
  }
};
```

Note that we inherit from both `Base` and `wrapper<Base>`. The `wrapper` template class facilitates the job of wrapping classes that are meant to be overridden in Python. Finally, to expose `Base` we write:

```
class_<BaseWrap, boost::noncopyable>(``Base'')
  .def(``f'', pure_virtual(&Base::f))
;
```

Next we consider virtual functions with default implementations. In this instance, the `Base` class may look like

```
struct Base
{
  virtual_Base() {}
  virtual int f() { return 0; }
};
```

Again we need to introduce a C++ class to help us:

```
struct BaseWrap : Base, wrapper<Base>
{
  int f()
  {
    if (override f = this->get_override(``f''))
      return this->get_override(``f'')();
    return Base::f();
  }
  int default_f() { return this->Base::f(); }
};
```

Just as before, the above class also implements `f`, but now we have to check if `f` has been overriden. The corresponding Boost.Python wrapper code is:

```
class_<BaseWrap, boost::noncopyable>(``Base'')
  .def(``f'', &Base::f, &BaseWrap::default_f)
;
```

Note that we expose both `&Base::f` and `&BaseWrap::default_f` because Boost.Python needs to know about both the dispatch function `f` and its default implementation `default_f`. In Python, we can now do the following:

```
>>> base = Base()
>>> class Derived(Base):
...    def f(self):
...        return 42
...
>>> derived = Derived()
>>> base.f()
0
>>> derived.f()
42
```

B.4   PYTHON OPERATORS

Boost.Python makes it extremely easy to wrap C++ operator-powered classes. A simple example should suffice. Consider the class:

```
class Vector{ /*...*/};
```

```
Vector    operator+(Vector const&, float);
Vector    operator+(float, Vector const&);
Vector    operator-(Vector const&, float);
Vector    operator-(float, Vector const&);
Vector&   operator+=(Vector&, float);
Vector&   operator-=(Vector&, float);
bool      operator<(Vector const&, Vector const&);
```

The class and operators can be mapped to Python by writing:

```
class_<Vector>(''Vector'')
    .def(self + float() )
    .def(float() + self )
    .def(self - float() )
    .def(float() - self )
    .def(self += float())
    .def(self -= float())
    .def(self < self)
;
```

B.5   FUNCTIONS

In C++ it is common to come across functions with arguments and return types that are pointers or references. The problem with such primitive types is that we don't know the owner of the pointer or referenced object. Although most C++ programmers now use smart pointers with clear ownership semantics, nevertheless there exists a lot of older C++ code with raw pointers. So Boost.Python has to be able to deal with them. The main issue to solve is the problem of dangling pointers and references. Let's consider the following simple C++ function:

```
X& f(Y& y, Z* z)
{
  y.z = z;
  return y.x;
}
```

The above function binds the lifetime of the function's return type to the lifetime of y, because f returns a reference to a member of the y object. If we were to naively wrap this using Boost.Python, then deleting y will invalidate the reference to X. In other words we have a dangling reference. To get round these problems, Boost.Python has the concept of call policies. In our example, we can use return_internal_reference and with_custodian_and_ward as follows:

```
def(''f'', f,
      return_internal_reference<1,
        with_custodian_and_ward<1, 2> >());
```

The 1 in `return_internal_reference<1` informs Boost.Python that the first argument of f, in this case `Y& y`, is the owner of the returned reference. Similarly the 1, 2 in `with_custodian_and_ward<1, 2>` informs Boost.Python that the lifetime of the second argument of f, in this case `Z* z`, is tied to the lifetime of the first argument `Y& y`.

It is common in C++ to overload both functions and member functions. Consider the following C++ class:

```
struct X
{
  bool f(int a);
  bool f(int a, double b);
  int f(int a, int b, int c);
};
```

To wrap the overloaded member functions into Python we need to introduce some member function pointer variables:

```
bool (X::*fx1)(int)          = &X::f;
bool (X::*fx2)(int, double)  = &X::f;
int (X::*fx3)(int, int, int) = &X::f;
```

With the member function pointer variables defined, the Boost.Python wrapping code is simply

```
.def(``f'', fx1)
.def(``f'', fx2)
.def(``f'', fx3)
```

We have seen in the above example how Boost.Python wraps function pointers. Many functions in C++ have default arguments, but C++ function pointers hold no information about default arguments. Therefore we have to write thin wrappers so that the default argument information is not lost. Consider the C++ function:

```
int f(int, double = 3.14, char const* = ``hello'');
```

then we have to write the thin wrappers:

```
int f1(int x) { f(x); }
int f2(int x, double y) { f(x, y); }
```

The Boost.Python wrapping code then looks like:

```
def(``f'', f);  // all arguments
def(``f'', f2); // two arguments
def(``f'', f3); // one argument
```

Fortunately Boost.Python has a macro for automatically creating the wrappers for us. For example

```
BOOST_PYTHON_FUNCTION_OVERLOADS(f_overloads, f, 1, 3)
```

The macro creates a class `f_overloads` that can be passed on to `def(...)`. The third and fourth arguments denote the minimum and maximum arguments respectively. The `def(...)` function will automatically add all the variants for us:

```
def(``f'', f, f_overloads());
```

Similarly for member function overloads, we can use the BOOST_PYTHON_MEMBER_FUNCTION_OVERLOADS macro. Suppose we had the C++ class:

```
struct X
{
  bool f(int a, int b = 0, double = 3.14);
};
```

then we would write:

```
BOOST_PYTHON_MEMBER_FUNCTION_OVERLOADS(X_overloads, X, 1, 3)
```

and the generated class X_overloads can be used as an argument to .def(...):

```
.def(''f'', &X::f, X_overloads());
```

B.6 ENUMS

Boost.Python has a clever way of wrapping C++ enums. Python has no enum type, so Boost.Python exposes them as an int. Consider the following example:

```
enum choice { red, blue };
```

the Boost.Python enum_<T> construct can be used to expose to Python:

```
enum_<choice>(''choice'')
    .value(''red'', red)
    .value(''blue'', blue)
    ;
```

The new enum type is created in the current scope, which will usually be the current module. The created Python class is derived from the Python int type and the values can be accessed in Python as follows:

```
>>> my_module.choice.red
m_module.choice.red
```

where my_module is the name of the module in which the enum is declared.

B.7 EMBEDDING

We have seen how to use Boost.Python to call C++ code from Python. In this section we are going to discuss how to call Python code from C++. The first step is to embed the Python interpreter into the C++ code. To do this, we simply #include<boost/python.hpp> and call Py_Initialize() to start the interpreter and create the __main__ module. Note that at the time of writing you must not call Py_Finalize() to stop the interpreter. This may change in future versions of Boost.Python. Although objects in Python are automatically reference-counted, the Python C API requires reference counting to be handled manually. So Boost.Python provides the handle and object class templates to automate the process. The handle template class is beyond the scope of this short primer.

The `object` class template wraps `PyObject*` and Boost.Python comes with a set of derived `object` types corresponding to Python's: `list`, `dict`, `tuple`, `str` and `long_`. Wherever appropriate, the methods of a particular Python type have been duplicated in the corresponding derived `object` type. For example, `dict` has a `keys()` method, `str` has a `upper` method, etc., and `make_tuple` is provided for declaring tuples:

```
tuple t = make_tuple(123, ''Hello, World'', 0.0);
```

Just as for Python's types, the constructors for the corresponding derived `object` types make copies. Consider the following example from the Python command line:

```
>>> l = [1, 2, 3]
>>> m = list(l) # new list
>>> m[0] = 4
>>> print l
[1, 2, 3]
>>> print m
[4, 2, 3]
```

Calling the `list` constructor makes a new `list`. Correspondingly the constructors of the derived `object` types make copies:

```
dict d(x.attr(''__dict__'')); // copies x.__dict__
```

Sometimes we need to get C++ values out of object instances. We can do this by using the `extract<T>` template functions. For example:

```
double l = extract<double>(o.attr(''length''));
dict d = extract<dict>(x.attr(''__dict__''));
```

Note that the dictionary d is in fact a reference to `X.__dict__`, hence writing

```
d[''whatever''] = 3;
```

modifies `x.__dict__`.

To run Python code from C++, Boost.Python provides three related functions:

```
object eval(str expression
        , object globals = object()
        , object locals = object());

 object exec(str       code
        , object globals = object()
        , object locals = object());

object exec_file(str filename
        , object globals = object()
        , object locals = object());
```

`eval` evalulates a given expression, `exec` executes the given code, and `exec_file` executes the code contained in a file. All functions return the results as an `object`. The `globals` and `locals` parameters are Python dictionaries containing the globals and locals of the context in which the code is to be executed. It is almost always sufficient to use the namespace dictionary of the __main__ module for both parameters. To do this we first use the import function of Boost.Python to import the __main__ module:

```
object import(str name);
```

and then get the namespace of __main__ as follows:

```
object main_module = import(''__main__'');
object main_namespace = main_module.attr(''__dict__'');
```

Now that we have the namespace we can execute a Python script, for example:

```
object ignored = exec(''result = 5**2'', main_namespace);
int five_squared = extract<int>(main_namespace[''result'']);
```

B.8   CONCLUSION

The purpose of this primer has been to introduce the reader to some of the tools provided by Boost.Python. The primer is by no means exhaustive. Indeed Boost.Python offers many more features to help the C++ programmer to seamlessly expose C++ classes to Python and embed Python into C++.

Appendix C
Hull–White Model Mathematics

In this appendix we give a brief outline of the Hull–White model. For a more in-depth discussion of the Hull–White model, readers are encouraged to consult [10] and [18]. The Hull–White model belongs to a class of HJM models called extended Vasicek models. This class of one-factor models has, in the risk-neutral measure denoted by $\mathbb{Q}$, the following short rate process

$$dr(t) = (m(t) - \lambda(t)r(t))\,dt + \sigma(t)dW(t) \tag{C.1}$$

with $r(t)$, the short rate at time t, $m(t)$, $\lambda(t)$, $\sigma(t) : \mathbb{R}^+ \mapsto \mathbb{R}^+$ and $W(t)$ is a $\mathbb{Q}$-Brownian motion. The original Hull–White model makes the further simplification that both σ and λ are constant in time. Introducing the auxiliary variables defined below

$$C(t) := \sigma(t)\exp(\lambda t) \tag{C.2}$$

$$\phi(t) := \frac{1 - \exp(-\lambda t)}{\lambda} \tag{C.3}$$

$$M(t) := \exp(-\lambda t)r(0) + \int_0^t \exp(\lambda(s-t))m(s)ds \tag{C.4}$$

it is straightforward to show that

$$R(t, T) := \int_t^T r(s)ds = \int_t^T M(s)ds + \int_t^T (\phi(T) - \phi(s))\,C(s)dW(s). \tag{C.5}$$

The stochastic discount factor and zero coupon bond can be expressed in terms of $R(t, T)$ as follows:

$$B(t)^{-1} := \exp(-R(0, t)) \tag{C.6}$$

$$P(t, T) := \mathbb{E}\left[\exp(-R(t, T))|\mathcal{F}_t\right] \tag{C.7}$$

where $\mathbb{E}$ denotes the expectation in the risk-neutral measure and $\mathcal{F}_t$ the filtration at time t. Before carrying out the above expectations we note that $B(t)$ is called the money-market account and is the numeraire in the risk-neutral measure. Performing the expectations we obtain

$$B(t)^{-1} = P(0, t)\exp\left(-\int_0^t (\phi(t) - \phi(s))\,C(s)dW(s)\right. \tag{C.8}$$

$$\left. -\frac{1}{2}\int_0^t (\phi(t) - \phi(s))^2\,C(s)^2 ds\right) \tag{C.9}$$

and

$$P(t, T) = \frac{P(0, T)}{P(0, t)}\exp\left(-(\phi(T) - \phi(t))\int_0^t C(s)dW(s)\right.$$

$$\left. -\frac{1}{2}\int_0^t (\phi(T) - \phi(t))(\phi(T) + \phi(t) - 2\phi(s))\,C(s)^2 ds\right). \tag{C.10}$$

Note that, as expected, the stochastic discount factor is a $\mathbb{Q}$-martingale, in fact it is an exponential martingale, whereas the zero coupon bond price is not a $\mathbb{Q}$-martingale because, as can be seen below, its SDE has a non-zero drift.

$$dP(t, T) = P(t, T)(r(t)dt + (\phi(t) - \phi(T))C(t)dW(t)).\qquad\text{(C.11)}$$

For non path-dependent pricing problems it is normally convenient to work in the so-called forward $\mathbb{Q}^T$-measure. In this measure the numeraire at time t is simply $P(t, T)$ and Girsanov's theorem implies that $\bar{W}(t)$, as defined below, is a $\mathbb{Q}^T$-Brownian motion

$$d\bar{W}(t) = dW(t) + (\phi(T) - \phi(t))C(t)dt.\qquad\text{(C.12)}$$

Substitution of equation (C.12) into equation (C.10) yields

$$\frac{P(t, T')}{P(t, T)} = \frac{P(0, T')}{P(0, T)}\exp\left(-\left(\phi(T') - \phi(T)\right)\int_0^t C(s)d\bar{W}(s)\right.$$
$$\left. -\frac{1}{2}(\phi(T') - \phi(T))^2 \int_0^t C(s)^2 ds\right),\qquad \forall t \leq T' \leq T.\qquad\text{(C.13)}$$

In other words, the numeraire-rebased zero coupon bond in the forward $\mathbb{Q}^T$-measure is a $\mathbb{Q}^T$-martingale. This to be expected in complete markets, where all numeraire-rebased tradables are martingales. Indeed, let $V(t)$ denote the value at t of any tradable, then by the martingale property we have

$$V(s) = P(s, T)\mathbb{E}^{\mathbb{Q}^T}\left[\frac{V(t)}{P(t, T)}|\mathcal{F}_s\right],\qquad \forall s \leq t.\qquad\text{(C.14)}$$

For an excellent introduction to financial calculus covering everything from measures, filtrations to martingales and arbitrage-free pricing, please consult [2].

Appendix D
Pickup Value Regression

The seminal paper by Longstaff and Schwartz [15], on estimating the early exercise premium, uses regressions of the holding value, i.e. the value of holding on to the option. In this short appendix we develop a simple alternative regression scheme for determining the early exercise premium of a callable structure when pricing using Monte-Carlo.

Consider times $T_1 < T_2 < \ldots < T_N$ and denote B_t as the numeraire at time t. The holding value $HV_{n-1}(T_{n-1})$ at time T_{n-1} is given by the relation below

$$
\begin{aligned}
HV_{n-1}(T_{n-1}) &= B_{T_{n-1}} \mathbb{E}\left[B_{T_n}^{-1} \max(IEV_n(T_n), HV_n(T_n)) | \mathcal{F}_{T_{n-1}}\right] \\
&= B_{T_{n-1}} \mathbb{E}\left[B_{T_n}^{-1}(IEV_n(T_n) - HV_n(T_n))^+ | \mathcal{F}_{T_{n-1}}\right] \\
&\quad + B_{T_{n-1}} \mathbb{E}\left[B_{T_n}^{-1} HV_n(T_n) | \mathcal{F}_{T_{n-1}}\right]
\end{aligned}
\tag{D.1}
$$

where $IEV_n(T_n)$ denotes the immediate exercise values at time T_n. Setting $HV_N(T_N) = 0$ and using the above recursion relation, we obtain

$$
HV_{n-1}(T_{n-1}) = B_{T_{n-1}} \sum_{m=n}^{N} \mathbb{E}\left[B_{T_m}^{-1}(IEV_m(T_m) - HV_m(T_m))^+ | \mathcal{F}_{T_{n-1}}\right]
\tag{D.2}
$$

Let's denote the exercise region at time T_n by $\mathcal{R}_n$,

$$
\mathcal{R}_n = \{\omega \in \Omega : H_n(T_n, \omega) \leq IEV_n(T_n, \omega)\}
\tag{D.3}
$$

$$
= \{\omega \in \Omega : IEV_n(T_n, \omega) - H_n(T_n, \omega) \geq 0\}
\tag{D.4}
$$

The stopping time is then (T_{N+1} denoting no exercise)

$$
\tau(\omega) = min\,\{T_n, n \geq 1 | \omega \in R_n\} \wedge N + 1
\tag{D.5}
$$

The pickup value $PKV_n(T_n)$ at time T_n is defined by

$$
PKV_n(T_n) := IEV_n(T_n) - HV_n(T_n)
\tag{D.6}
$$

At each time T_n we approximate the the pickup value by the following sum:

$$
G_n(T_n, \omega) = \sum_{k=1}^{M} \alpha_k(T_n) X_k\left(\{x_1(T_n, \omega), x_2(T_n, \omega), \ldots, x_p(T_n, \omega)\}\right)
\tag{D.7}
$$

where $\{X_1(\ldots), X_2(\ldots), \ldots, X_m(\ldots)\}$ are the basis functions, the explanatory variable are denoted by $\{x_1(T_n, \omega), x_2(T_n, \omega), \ldots, x_p(T_n, \omega)\}$ and the coefficients $\alpha_1(T_n), \alpha_k(T_n), \ldots, \alpha_M(T_n)$ are found by performing a regression.

In more detail: starting at T_N we perform a regression of $PKV_N(T_N)$ (in this case equal to $IEV_N(T_N)$) giving $\alpha_k(T_N)\ \forall k$. At T_{N-1} we calculate the pickup value using the relation below

$$
PKV_{N-1}(T_{N-1}, \omega) = IEV_{N-1}(T_{N-1}) - B_{T_{N-1}} \mathbb{E}\left[B_{T_N}^{-1}(G_N(T_N, \omega))^+\right]
\tag{D.8}
$$

using $G_N(T_N, \omega)$ found in the previous step. Again we approximate $PKV_{N-1}(T_{N-1}, \omega)$ by $G_{N-1}(T_{N-1}, \omega)$ and perform a regression to obtain $\alpha_k(T_{N-1})\ \forall k$. At T_{N-2} we calculate the pickup value using the relation below:

$$PKV_{N-2}(T_{N-2}, \omega) = IEV_{N-2}(T_{N-2})$$

$$- B_{T_{N-2}} \sum_{m=N-1}^{N} \mathbb{E}\left[B_{T_m}^{-1} (G_m(T_m, \omega))^+ \right] \qquad \text{(D.9)}$$

Again we approximate $PKV_{N-2}(T_{N-2}, \omega)$ by $G_{N-2}(T_{N-2}, \omega)$ and perform a regression to obtain $\alpha_k(T_{N-2}) \; \forall k$. The above steps are then repeated until we have reached T_1.

Bibliography

[1] Andrei Alexandrescu. *Modern C++ design. Generic Programming and Design Patterns Applied.* Addison Wesley, 2001.

[2] Martin Baxter and Andrew Rennic. *Financial Calculus. An Introduction to Derivative Pricing.* Cambridge University Press, 1998.

[3] Don Box. *Essential COM.* Addison Wesley, 1998.

[4] Daniel J Duffy. *Finite Difference Methods in Financial Engineering. A Partial Differential Equation Approach.* John Wiley & Sons, Ltd, 2006.

[5] William H. Press, Brian P. Flannery, Saul A. Teukolsky and William T. Vetterling. *Numerical Recipes in C. The Art of Scientific Computing (Second Edition).* Cambridge University Press, 1999.

[6] Christian P. Fries. Foresight bias and suboptimality correction in Monte-Carlo pricing of options with early exercise: Classification, calculation & removal. *SSRN*, 2005.

[7] Christian P. Fries. Valuing American options by simulation: a simple least-squares approach. *SSRN*. 2007.

[8] Christian P. Fries and Mark S. Joshi. Partial proxy simulation schemes for generic and robust Monte-Carlo greeks. *SSRN*, 2006.

[9] Paul Glasserman. *Monte Carlo Methods in Financial Engineering.* Springer, 2003.

[10] John C. Hull. *Options, Futures, and Other Derivatives (Third Edition).* Prentice Hall, 1997.

[11] Peter Jäckel. *Monte Carlo Methods in Finance.* John Wiley & Sons, Ltd, 1999.

[12] Jaan Kiusalaas. *Numerical Methods in Engineering with Python.* Cambridge University Press, 2005.

[13] Peter Kohl-Landgraf. *PDE Valuation of Interest Rate Derivatives. From Theory to Implementation.* Books on Demand GmbH, 2008.

[14] Hans Peter Langtangen. *Python Scripting for Computational Science (Third Edition).* Springer, Berlin, Heidelberg, 2008.

[15] F.A. Longstaff and E.S. Schwartz. Valuing American options by simulation: a simple least-squares approach. *Review of Financial Studies* 14: 113–147. 2001.

[16] Bernt Øksendal, *Stochastic Differential Equations. An Introduction with Applications (Fifth Edition).* Springer, 1998.

[17] Vladimir V. Piterbarg. A practitioner's guide to pricing and hedging callable libor exotics in forward libor models. *SSRN*, 2003.

[18] Riccardo Rebonato. *Interest-Rate Models (Second Edition).* John Wiley & Sons, Ltd, 1998.

[19] Mark Hammond & Andy Robinson. *Python Programming on Win32.* O'Reilly, 2000.

[20] Francis Scheid. *Schaum's Outlines: Numerical Analysis.* McGraw-Hill, 1988.

Index

Index compiled by Terry Halliday

Printed and bound by CPI Group (UK) Ltd, Croydon, CR0 4YY

12/01/2025

14624501-0002